33 QUESTIONS ABOUT AMERICAN HISTORY YOU'RE NOT SUPPOSED TO ASK

33 QUESTIONS ABOUT AMERICAN HISTORY YOU'RE NOT SUPPOSED TO ASK

★ ★

THOMAS E. WOODS JR.

CROWN
FORUM
NEW YORK

Copyright © 2007 by Thomas E. Woods Jr.

All rights reserved.
Published in the United States by Crown Forum,
an imprint of the Crown Publishing Group,
a division of Random House, Inc., New York.
www.crownpublishing.com

Crown Forum with colophon is a registered trademark of
Random House, Inc.

Library of Congress Cataloging-in-Publication Data
Woods, Thomas E.
   33 questions about American history you're not supposed to ask /
Thomas E. Woods Jr.—1st ed.
      p. cm.
  Includes bibliographical references and index.
   1. United States—History—Miscellanea. 2. United States—
History—Errors, inventions, etc. I. Title. II. Title: Thirty-three
questions about American history you're not supposed to ask.
E179.W828 2007
973—dc22   2007001347

ISBN 978-0-307-34668-1

Printed in the United States of America

Design by Barbara Sturman

10 9 8 7 6 5 4 3 2

First Edition

To Heather

CONTENTS

33 QUESTIONS ABOUT AMERICAN HISTORY YOU'RE NOT SUPPOSED TO ASK

Introduction: Hoaxes and History

★ ★

> The truth, indeed, is something that mankind, for
> some mysterious reason, instinctively dislikes.
> Every man who tries to tell it is unpopular, and
> even when, by the sheer strength of his case, he
> prevails, he is put down as a scoundrel.
>
> —H. L. MENCKEN

Most Americans have forgotten about the great bathtub hoax of early last century.

On December 28, 1917, the great journalist and social critic H. L. Mencken wrote "A Neglected Anniversary" for the *New York Evening Mail.* He regretted that the seventy-fifth anniversary of the invention of the bathtub had passed without any official acknowledgment by any sector of society. Mencken then took it upon himself, on this important occasion, to recall some of the basic history of the bathtub.[1]

The bathtub, Mencken explained, originated in England, where it began as rather a puny thing, little more than "a glorified dishpan." Filling and emptying the water required the work of a servant. Adam Thompson, an American who dealt in cotton and grain, got the idea that the bathing process would be simplified and improved if the water could be transported to the bathtub by means of a system of pipes, and then discarded by the same method.

Thompson pursued the idea, and on December 20, 1842, at his home in Cincinnati, he took the first bath in the first bathtub.

Within days the new invention was the talk of the town. The bathtub became the subject of surprisingly energetic debate. Naturally, a

1

great many Americans delighted in Thompson's invention. But to some critics, the bathtub was a dangerous luxury that would undermine the republican simplicity of American society. The medical profession even denounced it as a health hazard.

Millard Fillmore became the first president to use a bathtub in the White House, where one was installed in 1851. The president's example quieted much of the opposition to the bathtub, which rapidly gained acceptance.

In the wake of Mencken's article, this rudimentary history of the bathtub quickly became the standard account.

But there was a little problem. Mencken had made the whole thing up.

The bathtub had not originated as a "glorified dishpan" and had not been invented in Cincinnati in 1842 by anyone named Adam Thompson. The medical profession had never opposed the bathtub. "What the actual history of the bathtub may be I don't know," Mencken later confessed. "Digging it out would be a dreadful job, and the result, after all that labor, would probably be a string of banalities."[2]

That the article was a hoax—"a burlesque history of the bathtub," Mencken later called it—should have been clear enough from the beginning, he thought; it was filled with "obvious absurdities" from start to finish.[3] But the confident and authoritative tone in which he wrote it, combined with its citation of impressive-sounding (but nonexistent) periodicals, secured the article's triumph over common sense.

Mencken had hoped people might enjoy his clever, but certainly not serious, rendition of the history of the bathtub. But he found that they enjoyed it rather too much, not only accepting his narrative at face value but even, in the case of some readers, writing to him to corroborate facts he had invented! "Pretty soon," Mencken recalled, "I began to encounter my preposterous 'facts' in the writings of other men. . . . They began to be cited by medical men as proof of the progress of public hygiene. They got into learned journals. They were alluded to on the floor of Congress. . . . Finally, I began to find them in standard works of reference."[4]

Mencken recounted his bathtub ordeal "not because it is singular, but because it is typical. It is out of just such frauds, I believe, that most of the so-called knowledge of humanity flows. What begins as a guess—or, perhaps, not infrequently, as a downright and deliberate lie—ends as a fact and is embalmed in the history books." Mencken made particular reference to the propaganda that was permitted to spread during the years of World War I: "How much that was then devoured by the newspaper readers of the world was actually true?" And although much effort was expended in overturning the myths that spread during the Great War, Mencken maintained that "every one of those fictions retains full faith and credit today."[5]

My cynicism doesn't run as deep as Mencken's, which may be why the longevity of certain historical myths, and the slogans and platitudes that support them, still manage to surprise me. This book punctures many of them. It poses 33 questions about American history for which the typical answers are either misleading, grossly unsatisfactory, or clearly and demonstrably wrong. Worse than the standard answers to these questions is that many of them are simply never raised in the first place, since they may give rise to forbidden thoughts that run counter to established opinion.

Nobel laureate F. A. Hayek once observed that our understanding of history decisively influences our interpretation of current events.[6] The less real history we know, the more susceptible we become to manipulation by shysters. No, Adam Thompson didn't invent the bathtub in Cincinnati in 1842. That harmless myth has, at long last, finally perished. Let us begin to emancipate ourselves from other specimens of phony history that, even more widespread than Mencken's bathroom hoax, are no less foolish and far more dangerous.

DID THE FOUNDING FATHERS SUPPORT IMMIGRATION?

★ ★

Though polls consistently find that a majority of Americans believe immigration levels need to be reduced, many people still assume that the right of immigration is a hallowed American principle that no loyal citizen can consistently oppose.

This assumption is false.

Actually, the Founding Fathers were generally wary of immigration. They did not wish to exclude it altogether, but they saw no particular need to encourage it, especially among migrants whose cultural backgrounds were significantly different from their own.[1]

Consider Benjamin Franklin, that well-known cosmopolite and child of the Enlightenment. Franklin, it turns out, said quite a few politically incorrect things about non-British humanity (a category that includes the present writer). On one occasion he asked, "Why should Pennsylvania, founded by the English, become a colony of aliens, who will shortly be so numerous as to Germanize us, instead of our Anglifying them, and will never adopt our language or customs any more than they can acquire our complexion?"[2] Thus immigrants of sufficient number and concentration could radically change the cultural landscape in ways that the native population might not want.

We can already hear the modern liberal laughing at Franklin, pointing triumphantly to German assimilation in America as proof that the Pennsylvanian's concerns were without merit. But the point here is simply this: if unrestricted immigration had really been a traditional American principle, someone must have forgotten to tell Benjamin Franklin. And he was speaking of people who, as fellow heirs and architects of Western civilization, shared a great deal in common with the original settlers of British America. One can only imagine what Franklin would have had to say about current immigration policy.

JEFFERSON AND HAMILTON ON IMMIGRATION

Franklin was not alone. Thomas Jefferson's warning about mass immigration in his *Notes on Virginia* would doubtless come as a surprise to most Americans, since most American history textbooks for some reason choose not to highlight it. Jefferson asked suggestively, "Are there no inconveniences to be thrown into the scale against the advantage expected by a multiplication of numbers by the importation of foreigners?"[3]

"It is for the happiness of those united in society," the sage of Monticello went on to explain, "to harmonize as much as possible, in matters which they must of necessity transact together. Civil government being the sole object of forming societies, its administration must be conducted by common consent." Our government was "a composition of the freest principles of the English Constitution, with others, derived from natural right and reason." Nothing could be more opposed to the principles of our government than those of absolute monarchies, said Jefferson. But it was from such regimes that we could expect the most immigrants.[4]

Such immigrants, Jefferson feared, would "bring with them the principles of the governments they leave, imbibed in their early youth; or, if able to throw them off, it will be in exchange for an unbounded licentiousness, passing, as is usual, from one extreme to another. It would be a miracle were they to stop precisely at the point of temperate liberty." A large influx of immigrants from places without any experience with our kind of government and society could only introduce confusion and discord. "These principles, with their language, they will transmit to their children. In proportion to their numbers, they will share with us the legislation. They will infuse into it their spirit, warp and bias its direction, and render it a heterogeneous, incoherent, distracted mass."[5]

Jefferson concluded that it was "safer" to wait patiently for the natural increase of the American population rather than achieve such increase by mass immigration, and that our government would, as a result, be more peaceable and more durable. He left readers with a useful thought experiment: "Suppose 20 millions of republican Americans [were] thrown all of a sudden into France, what would be the condition of that kingdom? If it would be more turbulent, less happy, less strong, we may believe that the addition of half a million of foreigners to our present numbers would produce a similar effect here."[6]

Jefferson was joined in his wariness by Alexander Hamilton, the nation's first secretary of the treasury. In his draft of a speech for George Washington, Hamilton wrote: "To render the people of this country as homogenous as possible, must tend as much as any other circumstance to the permanence of their union and posterity."[7]

Several years later, when Jefferson called for liberalizing the naturalization laws in his December 1801 message to Congress, Hamilton recalled Jefferson's earlier sentiments from *Notes on Virginia*. (This change of heart appears to have been of partisan origin: Jefferson himself, along with several of his prominent opponents, believed that the foreign vote had won him the election of 1800.) He agreed with Jefferson that it was praiseworthy for the United States to permit the entry of those experiencing genuine hardship and seeking asylum, though even here Hamilton would have reminded his fellow citizens that generosity has its limits if the welfare of the country is to be protected. What he objected to was the suggestion that all such people were necessarily entitled to the privileges of citizenship. He concluded by pointing out that even granting for the sake of argument that American Indians had extended nothing but friendship as the colonists arrived on these shores, it was important to consider the fate of a people whose policy was so magnanimous. "Prudence requires us," Hamilton wrote, "to trace the history further and ask what has become of the nations of savages who exercised this policy, and who now occupies the territory which they then inhabited? Perhaps a lesson is here taught which ought not to be despised."[8] (The American Indians, in short, had a severe immigration problem.)

Hamilton described the safety of a republic as depending "essentially on the energy of a common national sentiment; on a uniformity of principles and habits; on the exemption of the citizens from foreign bias, and prejudice; and on that love of country which will almost invariably be found to be closely connected with birth, education, and family." He then drew out the implications of this point:

> The influx of foreigners must, therefore, tend to produce a heterogeneous compound; to change and corrupt the national spirit; to complicate and confound public opinion; to introduce foreign propensities. In the composition of society, the harmony of the ingredients is all-important, and whatever tends to a discordant intermixture must have an injurious tendency.[9]

For Hamilton, immigration policy was a matter of prudence and good sense, not a moral imperative. He observed at the turn of the nineteenth century that "in the infancy of the country, with a boundless waste to people, it was politic to give a facility to naturalization; but our situation is now changed. It appears from the last census that we have increased about one third in ten years; after allowing for what we have gained from abroad, it will be quite apparent that the natural progress of our own population is sufficiently rapid for strength, security, and settlement."[10]

Still others echoed these sentiments. Writing to John Adams in 1794, George Washington contended that the United States had no real reason to encourage immigration. Washington said that "except of useful mechanics and some particular descriptions of men or professions, there is no need of encouragement [of immigration], while the policy or advantage of its taking place in a body (I mean the settling of them in a body) may be much questioned; for by so doing, they retain the Language, habits, and principles (good or bad) which they bring with them."[11]

Rufus King, who had attended the Constitutional Convention as a delegate from Massachusetts, was concerned about the character of the immigrants whom America might attract. He wrote in a 1798 letter, "It was the practice of the Emigrants from Scotland to bring with them Certificates from the religious Societies to which they belonged, of their honesty, sobriety, and generally of their good Character! Why should we not require some such Document from all Emigrants, and it would be well to add to the Testimonial that the person to whom it was granted was not expelled from his Country and had not been convicted of any crime." King wondered, "If from the emigrations of past time we have suffered inconvenience and our true national character has been disfigured, what are we to expect from the Emigrants of the present Day?"[12]

John Jay, who would become the first chief justice of the United States, in *Federalist* No. 2 positively celebrated the fact that for all its "diversity," the United States consisted essentially of people whose religious and cultural traits were broadly similar and compatible, rather than widely divergent and a potential threat to social comity. "Providence," he wrote, "has been pleased to give this one connected country to one united people—a people descended from the same

> ...*& THE TRUTH*
>
> *The Founding Fathers were generally wary of immigration, and many of them warned about the consequences for the United States if immigration levels were not limited.*

ancestors, speaking the same language, professing the same religion, attached to the same principles of government, very similar in their manners and customs."[13]

According to Thomas G. West, a professor at the University of Dallas, "None of the Founders gave a theoretical account of the right of a political community to exclude would-be immigrants. That is because such a right was obvious to all as an inference from the general principles they all shared. No one in the early debates in Congress on the naturalization laws doubted the government's right to determine exclusionary criteria for citizenship."[14]

At the Constitutional Convention, for example, New York's Gouverneur Morris warned of being "polite at the expense of prudence." He noted that the privileges that immigrants enjoyed in the United States were considerably greater than in the rest of the world, but he concluded by reminding his listeners that "every Society from a great Nation down to a Club had the right of declaring the conditions on which new members should be admitted."[15]

The Founding Fathers' views on immigration do not by themselves settle the modern debate, of course. But they remain one of the best-kept secrets of American history.

QUESTION **2**

DID MARTIN LUTHER KING JR. OPPOSE

AFFIRMATIVE ACTION?

★ ★

Here's a case in which liberals have it right and at least some conservatives have it wrong: the philosophy of Martin Luther King Jr.[1]

The way some conservatives tell it, King believed in an absolutely color-blind approach to racial issues and policy in America. Instead of calling for massive government programs and preferential policies in favor of blacks, King simply demanded of white America that it view individuals on their merits rather than in light of racial prejudice. After all, he envisioned a society in which, as he said so memorably in his "I Have a Dream" speech in Washington in 1963, "my four little children will one day live in a nation where they will not be judged by the color of their skin but by the content of their character."

Thus, this line of reasoning goes, King was demanding only basic libertarian rights of equal treatment before the law. Compensatory programs on behalf of blacks, to say nothing of quota systems and other special privileges, were anathema to him, since they, just as much as segregation, violated his color-blind principles.

For years, the Left has complained that this interpretation of King's thought grossly distorts the man's views, rendering his truly radical message toothless and tame. And in this case the Left is

11

absolutely right. No one interested in the truth and familiar with King's thought could portray it so inaccurately.

A GIGANTIC "BILL OF RIGHTS FOR THE DISADVANTAGED"

The main problem with the conservative claim upon King is that absolutely nothing in King's economic thought supports it. King wanted immediate improvement in the material condition of blacks, and he was prepared to resort to radical measures in order to achieve that goal. He was manifestly not in favor of the free market, which he indicted with the same series of clichés evident throughout the political Left.

King condemned the suggestion that "if the Negro is to rise out of poverty, if the Negro is to rise out of slum conditions, if he is to rise out of discrimination and segregation, he must do it all by himself." Rather, King taught, "the roots of racism are very deep in our country, and there must be something positive and massive in order to get rid of all the effects of racism and the tragedies of injustice."[2] It was not enough that the nation leave behind racial prejudice. The United States "must not only radically readjust its attitude toward the Negro in the compelling present, but must incorporate in its planning some compensatory consideration for the handicaps he has inherited from the past."[3]

Some conservatives have tried to claim that King and the civil rights movement in general sought only equality of basic rights and little, if anything, that would involve real coercion. But in fact King sought an immediate, palpable improvement in blacks' material condition. Especially revealing is his insistence that the black man in his day was "not struggling for some abstract, vague rights, but for a concrete and prompt improvement in his way of life."[4]

How, exactly, did King propose that this "concrete and prompt improvement" be achieved? For one thing, he most certainly believed in preferential policies for blacks, particularly in management positions. And in *Why We Can't Wait,* King spelled out the nature of a compensatory package for blacks that he considered fair:

No amount of gold could provide an adequate compensation for the exploitation and humiliation of the Negro in America down through the centuries. Not all the wealth of this affluent society could meet the bill. Yet a price can be placed on unpaid wages. The ancient common law has always provided a remedy for the appropriation of the labor of one human being by another. This law should be made to apply for American Negroes. The payment should be in the form of a massive program by the government of special, compensatory measures which could be regarded as a settlement in accordance with the accepted practice of common law. Such measures would certainly be less expensive than any computation based on two centuries of unpaid wages and accumulated interest. I am proposing, therefore, that just as we granted a GI Bill of Rights to war veterans, America launch a broad-based and gigantic Bill of Rights for the Disadvantaged, our veterans of the long siege of denial.[5]

RADICALISM

King grew more and more radical toward the end of his life, occasionally repudiating milder positions he had held earlier. "I am sorry to have to say," he remarked in 1967, "that the vast majority of white Americans are racists, either consciously or unconsciously."[6] Reflecting on the state of American society, he said: "For years I labored with the idea of reforming the existing institutions of the society, a little change here, a little change there. I think you've got to have a reconstruction of the entire society, a revolution of values."[7]

In a speech to his staff in 1966 King was more blunt: "We are now making demands that will cost the nation something. You can't talk about solving the economic problem of the Negro without talking about billions of dollars. . . . [W]e are treading in difficult waters, because it really means that we are saying that something is wrong . . . with capitalism. There must be a better distribution of wealth and maybe America must move toward a democratic socialism."[8]

This was rare candor for King. According to one of his aides, King would generally demand that his staff turn off the tape recorder when he offered praise for "what he called democratic socialism, and he said, 'I can't say this publicly, and if you say I said it I'm not gonna admit to it.'" King, the aide went on, "didn't believe that capitalism as it was constructed could meet the needs of poor people" and thought that America "might need to look at what was a kind of socialism, but a democratic form of socialism."[9] By early 1968 King was calling for "a redistribution of economic power."[10]

Speaking before the tenth-anniversary convention of the Southern Christian Leadership Conference, King elaborated further on the path of his economic thinking:

We must honestly face the fact that the Movement itself must address itself to the question of restructuring the whole of American society. There are 40 million poor people here. And one day we must ask the question, "Why are there 40 million poor people in America?" And when you begin to ask that question, you are raising questions about the economic system, about a broader distribution of wealth. When you ask that question, you begin to question the capitalistic economy. And to ask questions about the whole society. We are called upon to help the discouraged beggars in life's marketplace. But one day we must come to see that an edifice which produces beggars needs restructuring. It means that questions must be raised. You see, my friends, when you deal with this, you begin to ask the question, "Who owns the oil?" You begin to ask the question, "Who owns the iron ore?" You begin to ask the question, "Why is it that people have to pay water bills in a world that is two-thirds water?" These are questions that must be asked.[11]

The most significant aspect of this passage is not its failure to note that only a fraction of one percent of all the water in the world is actually drinkable. Its most significant aspect is its economic radicalism. This is not the tame, unthreatening King portrayed by all too many conservatives. A conservative would note that the poor are consistently better off in the least socialist societies, and that capitalism of its very nature leads to improvements in the standard of living of everyone (for reasons we see in Question 21). King called instead for "question[ing] the capitalistic economy." However we want to classify him, King was no conservative.

King, indeed, went well beyond favoring mere affirmative action, calling ultimately for the adoption of some form of socialism in the United States as a means of improving blacks' well-being. But no matter how chic they remain in some quarters even today, socialism and interventionism lead to impoverishment and—as studies of the economic freedom of the countries of the world have shown time and again— worsen the lot of the poor. As we shall see in Question 29, those countries that have managed to lift themselves out of Third World status did so not by embracing socialism but by recognizing private property rights and keeping the predatory instincts of the state relatively limited. On the other hand, the African nationalists who made fools of themselves and slaves of their people by nationalizing industries and implementing socialism in the 1960s and 1970s have nothing but stagnation or even retrogression to show for themselves.

The point can scarcely be debated: people who actually care

... & THE TRUTH

Contrary to the sentiments he expressed in his famous "I Have a Dream" speech, King favored racial quotas. In fact, he called for massive government spending to make up for centuries of discrimination for blacks—"a broad-based and gigantic Bill of Rights for the Disadvantaged." Late in his life he grew more radical, calling for a socialist system in America.

about the welfare of the poor must support free-market capitalism. On the other hand, whatever else we might say about people who—either for demagogic purposes or out of sheer ignorance—call for socialism in order to help the poorest, they are, without a doubt, *not* champions of the poor.

QUESTION **3**

WERE THE AMERICAN INDIANS REALLY

ENVIRONMENTALISTS?

★ ★

In 1991 the Smithsonian Institution published a popular book called *Seeds of Change: A Quincentennial Commemoration*, which informed readers that "pre-Columbian America was still the First Eden, a pristine natural kingdom. The native people were transparent in the landscape, living as natural elements of the ecosphere. Their world, the New World of Columbus, was a world of barely perceptible human disturbance."[1]

Such images have been so consistently and successfully seared into the American consciousness that scarcely anyone would think to question them. But was pre-Columbian America really "a pristine natural kingdom"?

Not at all.

The fact is, the Indians of the New World no more believed in leaving nature untouched than did anyone else in the ancient or modern world. "Like Euro-Americans," writes Fergus Bordewich in *Killing the White Man's Indian,* "not to mention the rest of humanity, Indians used the means at their command to bend nature to their use, and within the limits of their technology, they were no less inherently exploitative of it."[2] Similarly, the University of Wisconsin's William

Denevan concludes that "the Indian impact [on the environment] was neither benign nor localized and ephemeral, nor were resources always used in a sound ecological way. . . . The size of native populations, associated deforestation, and prolonged intensive agriculture led to severe land degradation in some regions."[3]

SLASH AND BURN

The Choctaw and Iroquois, for instance, were known to cut and burn forests in order to make new farmland available. After exhausting that soil, they cut and burned more forests. Wooded areas were also cleared to increase forage for deer, elk, and bison. Though in some cases such burning may have made sense, it contradicts the idea that the Indians left the natural world altogether untouched.

One result of this burning was a depletion of "old growth" forests. In fact, according to some scholars, there may actually have been fewer such forests in America when the white man arrived than there are today.[4] And the Indians' fires caused even more environmental damage. In *The Ecological Indian: Myth and History,* Shepard Krech III reveals that "Indians lit fires that then were allowed to burn destructively and without regard to ecological consequences." Krech cites numerous firsthand accounts of

> fires that Indians ignited inadvertently, became far larger than intended, burned until rains quenched them, and consumed tens and hundreds of thousands of acres in grasslands and forest. . . . Andrew Graham spoke of extensive fires lit "every summer" and "not a track of a living thing" the following winter. In eastern forests and on grasslands, many Indian-lit fires raged until extinguished by rain. . . . These examples could be multiplied. Observers depicted many Indians including the Ojibwa, Cree, Mandan, Arapahoe, Gros Ventres, Shoshone, Blackfeet, Assiniboine, and various Northern Athapaskan people as "careless" burners, by which they meant that Indian fires accidentally blew up into vast conflagrations or burned until rain fell (which may have been what the Indians intended).[5]

Some Indian fires, spreading for weeks at a time over several hundred thousand square miles, utterly destroyed plant and animal life. Grassland fires in the northern plains, for instance, did substantial damage to the buffalo population. "The poor beasts," wrote a contemporary, "have all the hair singed off; even skin in many places is shrivelled up and terribly burned, and their eyes are swollen and closed fast. It was really pitiful to see them staggering about, sometimes running afoul of a large stone, at other times tumbling downhill and falling into creeks not yet frozen over. In one spot we found a whole herd lying dead." Other reports tell us of deer, elk, and wolves perishing by the thousands in these fires.[6]

Sometimes the effects of fire on wildlife were more indirect. Fire-resistant woodlands that grew in the wake of such fires were at times less friendly to wildlife. "In the Southeast," explains economist and environmental expert Terry Anderson, "oak and hickory forests with a higher carrying capacity for deer were displaced by fire-resistant longleaf pine which supported only limited wildlife."[7]

Not only fires but also Indian overhunting damaged wildlife populations. The Cherokees and other Indians helped wipe out the white-tailed deer (which later recovered thanks to restocking programs in the twentieth century). The Cherokees did not reproach themselves for this, since they believed that deer felled in a hunt would be reanimated. As Krech notes, they felt that one killing "begat potentially at least three and as many as six additional lives, and set the stage for three to six future killings."[8] Beaver populations also fared poorly under Indian watch, with the Cree especially wasteful in the numbers they killed and the limited amounts of each animal they used.[9]

A MYTH IS BORN

So if the Indians were practicing slash-and-burn agriculture, destroying forests and grasslands, and wiping out entire animal populations, where in the world did we get the idea that they were the original environmentalists? A major source of this myth is an 1854 speech by Chief Seattle, a Suquamish Indian from the American Northwest.

Former vice president Al Gore included a lengthy quotation from that speech in his book *Earth in the Balance,* portraying Seattle as having said:

> How can you buy or sell the sky? The land? The idea is strange to us. If we do not own the freshness of the air and the sparkle of the water, how can you buy them? Every part of this earth is sacred to my people. Every shining pine needle, every sandy shore, every mist in the dark woods, every meadow, every humming insect. All are holy in the memory and experience of my people. . . .
>
> This we know: the earth does not belong to man, man belongs to the earth. All things are connected like the blood that unites us all. Man did not weave the web of life, he is merely a strand in it. Whatever he does to the web, he does to himself.[10]

The problem is that none of the versions of Chief Seattle's speech that we possess appear reliable, least of all the more modern versions, which in some cases are altogether fabricated. A Dr. Henry Smith originally reproduced the speech from memory in 1887, *thirty-three years* after he claimed to have heard it. According to Rudolf Kaiser, an expert on American Indian history, "The selection of the material and the formulation of the text is possibly as much Dr. Smith's as Seattle's. There is no way of determining the authenticity of this text."[11]

Another of the many problems that Smith's version poses is that Seattle, who spoke no English, first delivered the speech in the Indian language Lushootseed; it was then translated into Chinook Jargon, a regional trading language that included French, English, and Indian words. Chinook Jargon has been described as barely suitable for facilitating barter, let alone conveying complex or abstract ideas, and was certainly incapable of communicating the flights of speech that appear in Smith's text.[12]

The speech has continued to evolve since then. The most recent version, and the one that most Americans familiar with the speech would recognize, comes not from Smith but from Ted Perry, a Texas scriptwriter who freely adapted the address for use in a documentary about the environment. If Smith's version had problems, Perry's is essentially an invention (though, to his credit, Perry has tried without success to let the public know the truth).[13] Perry's version was further adapted in the early 1990s to yield *Brother Eagle, Sister Sky,* a children's book that reached number five on the *New York Times* bestseller list.

Was the purpose of Seattle's speech really to suggest that *everything in nature,* sentient and nonsentient, was "holy" to his people? Certainly not, say scholars. "Seattle's speech was made as part of an argument for the right of the Suquamish and Duwamish peoples to continue to visit their traditional burial grounds following the sale of that land to white settlers," explains Muhlenburg College's William Abruzzi. "This specific land was sacred to Seattle and his people because his ancestors were buried there, not because land as an abstract concept was sacred to all Indians."[14] Writing in the *American Indian Quarterly,* Denise Low likewise explains that "the lavish descriptions of nature are secondary" to the purpose of Chief Seattle's argument, and that he was saying only that "land is sacred because of religious ties to ancestors."[15]

In the most recent version of the speech, Seattle claims to have seen "a thousand rotting buffaloes on the prairie left by the white man who shot them from a passing train." Where to begin? The destruction of the buffalo did not commence until two decades following Seattle's speech—long after his death, in fact. In any case, Chief Seattle lived in what is now Washington State, which is nowhere near the Great Plains, and none of our sources give any evidence that he ever traveled to the prairie. Moreover, the speech refers to "the lovely cry of a whippoorwill," a bird not found in the Northwest and almost certainly unknown to Chief Seattle.[16]

Despite the obvious problems with the ever-changing Chief Seattle speech, environmentalists like Gore have used it to help cultivate the myth of the Indian who left his surroundings in pristine condition out of a deeply spiritual kinship with nature. Such a myth furthers their propaganda, as the environmentalist Indian can be used as a foil against modern America and industrial society in general.

Not especially flattered at being pressed into the service of white men's ideologies, Indian tribes have not always welcomed this putative alliance with environmentalists and other activists. Ontario Indians, for instance, have complained about environmentalists' transformation of "Indian respect for land and communitarianism into a cult-like vision of new-age 'spirituality.'"[17] And the views of animal rights activists on the one hand and Cree hunters on the other are, to put it mildly, radically at odds with one another.[18]

A LESSON WORTH REMEMBERING

What is even more interesting about the real history of the American Indians and the environment is that when the Indians were able to safeguard natural resources, they did so through the use of what we would recognize as property rights, the very institution we are always told they despised or knew nothing about. To be sure, Indian ideas of property rights varied across time and place. But it's notable that when resources became scarce, Indians often shifted away from a communal system to one of established property rights in order to conserve those resources.[19]

We should not be surprised that the Indians adjusted their practices in response to changing conditions. It was easy to maintain communal rights to fishing and hunting when fish and game were plentiful. When such resources became scarce, however, the Indians understood the need to introduce incentives to discourage what has become known as the tragedy of the commons. Without clearly delineated property rights, no hunter has any particular reason not to overhunt; any game he does not kill will simply be taken by others. Any good intention he may have to preserve some quantity of game with an eye to the future will be frustrated by the predatory behavior of others in search of gain. In the absence of clear property rights, therefore, there is no incentive not to exhaust current stocks and every incentive to grab what you can when you can.

> THE MYTH...
>
> ———
>
> *Pre-Columbian America was still the First Eden, a pristine natural kingdom.*

That is why many North American Indian tribes, including the Montagnais-Naskapi of Quebec, the Algonkian, and the Paiute, granted certain family- and clan-based groups the right to hunt in particular areas.[20] These groups thus possessed an incentive both to refrain from overhunting and to exclude those outside the group from hunting in the area. Through this allocation of property rights, the tragedy of the commons was successfully avoided and wildlife effectively preserved.

In the Pacific Northwest the Indians established a comparable system of fishing rights. The Indians' technology for catching salmon was so advanced that they could easily have captured all the salmon, leaving none to spawn in succeeding years, but they instead made express provision for the future. According to a Quileute Indian born around the mid-nineteenth century, "When the Indians had obtained enough fish they would remove the weirs from the river in order that the fish they did not need could go upstream and lay their eggs so that there would be a supply of fish for future years."[21] Unfortunately, the white man's law came to prevail, and it encouraged the very tragedy of the commons that the Indians had taken such care to avoid.[22]

> ... & THE TRUTH
>
> *The American Indians practiced slash-and-burn agriculture, destroyed forests and grasslands, and wiped out entire animal populations.*

The value of the Indians' property-based systems has been lost not only on white society, which is by and large completely unaware of this history, but even on Indian cultures themselves—a fact one can verify with a passing glance at most western reservations, where big game species essentially do not exist today in spite of often excellent habitat. "Over the past 25 years," says outdoor writer Ted Williams, "Shoshones and Arapahoes, equipped with snowmobiles, ATV's and high-powered rifles, have virtually wiped out elk, deer, moose and bighorns on the 2.2-million-acre Wind River Reservation in Wyoming."[23] That is the predictable result when wildlife is said to belong to everyone. So much for the Indians' spiritual kinship with nature. They, like all other human beings, *respond to incentives:* when incentives are in place to discourage overhunting, Indians don't overhunt; when the opposite incentives exist, they do.

Environmentalists have sometimes argued that Americans need to recapture the environmental spirit supposedly possessed by their Indian predecessors on this continent and acquire a quasi-spiritual reverence for the things of nature. It turns out that something like the opposite is true. What Americans can learn from the Indians is not the kind of primitivism with which radical environmentalists would like to fasten us, but rather the Indians' use of property rights as the best way to preserve the environment.

Now there is some lost Indian wisdom that bears repeating.

QUESTION **4**

WERE STATES' RIGHTS JUST CODE
WORDS FOR SLAVERY AND OPPRESSION?

★ ★

F ew ideas in American history are more reviled today than states' rights. The very concept, we are told, is inherently bound up with slavery and racism, such that anyone who so much as raises the idea renders himself morally suspect.

Yet the idea of divided power, with political authority broken up among central and local units, can be found throughout history and in all parts of the world. Medieval Europe, for example, was a radically decentralized society that featured a multiplicity of jurisdictions—a factor to which many historians now attribute the rise of Western liberty. The Catholic Church, giving voice to the rich tradition of Christian social thought, recommends the principle of subsidiarity, according to which each function of society should be carried out by the most local unit possible, since it is both dangerous and dehuman-izing to have major social tasks performed by bureaucratic structures far removed from local communities. The ideas of federalism and states' rights, in short, hold a central and honored place within the Western tradition.[1]

Thomas Jefferson considered states' rights a much more impor-tant and effective safeguard of the people's liberties than the "checks and balances" among the three branches of the federal government.

Those measures prevent the executive, legislative, and judicial branches from encroaching on one another's powers. But what was to prevent the three branches from simply collaborating in an assault on the people's liberties? Or what was to be done if one branch expanded its powers beyond all measure but the other two branches were too timid to do anything about it?

Jefferson believed another institutional safeguard was necessary, which is why he and a great many other early Americans insisted so strongly on the rights of the states. Jefferson once wrote, "When all government, domestic and foreign, in little as in great things, shall be drawn to Washington as the center of all power, it will render powerless the checks provided of one government on another, and will become as venal and oppressive as the government from which we separated."[2] To resist this centralizing trend, the sage of Monticello was convinced, the states needed some kind of corporate defense mechanism.

In the late 1790s Jefferson and James Madison took the doctrine of states' rights to the next level. In 1798 the legislatures of Virginia and Kentucky approved resolutions that affirmed the states' right to resist federal encroachments on their powers. If the federal government had the exclusive right to interpret the Constitution and judge the extent of its own powers vis-à-vis those of the states, warned the resolutions' authors (Madison and Jefferson, respectively), it would continue to grow—regardless of elections, the separation of powers, and other much-touted limits on government power—by simply handing down decisions in its own favor. The Virginia Resolutions spoke of the states' right to "interpose" between the federal government and the people of the state; the Kentucky Resolutions (in a 1799 follow-up to the original resolutions) used the term "nullification"— the states, they said, could nullify federal laws that they believed to be unconstitutional.[3]

The line of thinking that culminates in the right of nullification can be summarized as follows. The federal government was created when delegates from the original thirteen states gathered in Philadelphia in 1787 and drafted the Constitution. The states being the constituent parts of the proposed Union, each state got one vote in the proceedings, regardless of how many delegates it had sent. Then, one by one, each state voted to ratify the Constitution through special sovereign conventions of the people that were called into being for this purpose. The very fact that each state ratified the Constitution separately testified to the federative character of the Union: instead of a single vote of "the American people" in the aggregate, the decision to ratify or not was up to the people *of each state.*

The states delegated to the federal government those powers listed in Article I, Section 8 of the Constitution, and retained to themselves anything they did not delegate. The Tenth Amendment, which Thomas Jefferson described as the cornerstone of the Constitution, makes the point clear: all powers that the states have not delegated to the federal government, and that are not prohibited to them by the Constitution, remain reserved to them and to the people. And then the key: if the federal government should encroach upon the powers reserved to the states, the states have a right to nullify the offending law and refuse to enforce it—after all, a law that violates the Constitution is no law at all.

Taken together, these ideas became known as the "Principles of '98."[4]

A modern objection raised against scholars impertinent enough to mention nullification today is that it violates the supremacy clause of the Constitution. That clause, found in Article VI, reads: "This Constitution, and the Laws of the United States which shall be made in Pursuance thereof; and all Treaties made, or which shall be made, under the Authority of the United States, shall be the supreme Law of the Land; and the Judges in every State shall be bound thereby, any Thing in the Constitution or Laws of any State to the Contrary notwithstanding." A state that nullifies a federal law, the objection runs, is therefore at odds with the supremacy clause and is ipso facto engaged in illegitimate behavior.

But a nullifying state does not deny the principle that the Constitution and laws made in pursuance thereof are the supreme law of the land. On the contrary, it *defends* that principle, as it disputes whether the law in question is itself pursuant to the Constitution in the first place. (Moreover, it's probably safe to assume that Jefferson and his supporters, who knew a little something about the Constitution, were familiar with the supremacy clause.)

To give the federal government the exclusive power to determine such matters is a recipe for federal domination. That was Thomas Jefferson's point. If the federal government is allowed a monopoly on constitutional interpretation—that is, if the states have no real power to contest and resist the federal government's interpretation—then in effect it gets to determine the extent of its own powers. Human nature being what it is, the federal government will tend to expand its own powers vis-à-vis those of the states as it hands down rulings in favor of itself. How could that be in any way unexpected?

STATES' RIGHTS: THE *NORTHERN* TRADITION

The impact of the Principles of '98 on American history, according to the standard narrative, was pretty much confined to South Carolina's nullification of the tariffs of 1828 and 1832. But one of the best-kept secrets of early American history is that the northern states referred to and took refuge in these important principles far more often than did the southern states.

Consider, first, Thomas Jefferson's policy of "peaceable coercion," introduced in 1807 against the British and French. In response to British and French depredations against American neutral rights on the seas, the federal government under Jefferson declared an embargo, according to which no American ship could depart for any foreign port anywhere in the world. (The rationale was that trade with the United States was a key ingredient in British and French prosperity and thus that economic pressure might persuade those countries to change their policies.) The U.S. Navy was granted the power to stop and search any ship within U.S. jurisdiction if its officers had "reason to suspect" the ship was violating the embargo. Likewise, customs officials were "authorized to detain any vessel . . . whenever in their opinions the intention is to violate or evade any provisions of the acts laying an embargo." Such standards fell far short of the "probable cause" requirement that generally governed the issuing of warrants for searches.[5]

33 Questions About American History You're Not Supposed to Ask

New England was especially hard hit by the embargo because so many of its people were employed either directly in foreign commerce or in proximate fields. Opposition did not appear right away, partly since the northern ports were frozen at the time and no one could ship anything anyway. But with the coming of spring came violations of the embargo and anger at the federal government's heavy-handedness.

In 1808 a federal district court, in the case of *United States v. The William,* ruled the embargo constitutional. The Massachusetts legislature begged to differ. The Massachusetts Senate reminded the court that the Union was "a confederation of equal and independent States with limited powers." Had the district court's decision settled the matter of the embargo? Not at all, said the House: "Were it true, that the measures of government once passed into an act, the constitutionality of that act is stamped with the deal of infallibility, and is no longer a subject for the deliberation or remonstrance of the citizen, to what monstrous lengths might not an arbitrary and tyrannical administration carry its power. . . . Were such doctrine sound, what species of oppression might not be inflicted on the prostrate liberties of our country? If such a doctrine were true, our Constitution would be nothing but a name—nay, worse, a fatal instrument to sanctify oppression, and legalize the tyranny which inflicts it."[6]

Both houses declared the embargo acts to be "in many particulars, unjust, oppressive, and unconstitutional." They went on: "While this State maintains its sovereignty and independence, all the citizens can find protection against outrage and injustice in the strong arm of the State government." The embargo, furthermore, was "not legally binding on the citizens of this State." Far from calling upon their people to obey the law, they asked simply that "all parties aggrieved by the operation of this act . . . abstain from forcible resistance."[7]

In the midst of the crisis, a New York congressman, giving his explicit sanction to the Virginia and Kentucky Resolutions, said, "Why should not Massachusetts take the same stand, when she thinks herself about to be destroyed?"[8] A Connecticut congressman asked, "If any State Legislature had believed the Act to be unconstitutional, would it not have been their duty not to comply?" He added that the state legislatures, "whose members are sworn to support the Constitution, may refuse assistance, aid or cooperation" if they regard an act as unconstitutional, and so could state officials.[9]

Connecticut governor Jonathan Trumbull shared these views: "Whenever our national legislature is led to overleap the prescribed bounds of their constitutional powers, on the State Legislatures, in great emergencies, devolves the arduous task—it is their right—it becomes their duty, to interpose their protecting shield between the right and liberty of the people, and the assumed power of the General Government." Connecticut's General Assembly passed a resolution that, among other things, directed all executive officials in the state not to afford "any official aid or co-operation in the execution of the act aforesaid."[10]

The General Assembly furthermore declared: "Resolved, that to preserve the Union, and support the Constitution of the United States, it becomes the duty of the Legislatures of the States, in such a crisis of affairs, vigilantly to watch over, and vigorously to maintain, the powers not delegated to the United States, but reserved to the States respectively, or to the people; and that a due regard to this duty, will not permit this Assembly to assist, or concur in giving effect to the aforesaid unconstitutional act, passed, to enforce the embargo."[11]

Rhode Island, when the embargo was at its end, declared that her legislature possessed the duty "to interpose for the purpose of protecting [the people of Rhode Island] from the ruinous inflictions of usurped and unconstitutional power."[12]

Interposition—the language of the Principles of '98.

"THE CITIZENS OF THIS STATE ARE OPPRESSED BY CRUEL AND UNAUTHORIZED LAWS"

During the War of 1812 Massachusetts and Connecticut were ordered to call out their respective militias for the purpose of defending the coast. The call derived from the federal government's authority to call the state militias into service "to execute the Laws of the Union, suppress Insurrections and repel invasions."

Massachusetts governor Caleb Strong, however, maintained that the states reserved the power to determine whether any of these three conditions held. At Strong's request, the Massachusetts Supreme Court offered its opinion. That court agreed with the governor: "As this power is not delegated to the United States, by the Federal Constitution, nor prohibited by it to the states, it is reserved to the states, respectively; and from the nature of the power, it must be exercised by those with whom the states have respectively entrusted the chief command of the militia."[13]

The Connecticut legislature followed suit:

> It must not be forgotten, that the state of Connecticut is a FREE SOVEREIGN and INDEPENDENT state; that the United States are a *confederacy* of states; that we are a confederated and not a consolidated republic. The governor of this state is under a high and solemn obligation, *"to maintain the lawful rights and privileges thereof, as a sovereign, free and independent state,"* as he is *"to support the constitution of the United States,"* and the obligation to support the latter, imposes an additional obligation to support the former.[14]

Thus if the militia were called out for any purpose but those listed in the Constitution, it "would be not only the height of injustice to the militia . . . but a violation of the constitution and laws of this state, and of the United States." The president had no authority to call upon the militia of Connecticut "to assist in carrying on an offensive war" (some New Englanders were convinced that the war was aimed primarily at the annexation of Canada). Connecticut would not comply with the federal order until New England should be threatened "by an actual invasion of any portion of our territory."[15]

In December 1813 a new and more obnoxious embargo than that of 1807–9 was instituted. The Massachusetts legislature found itself inundated with petitions and statements of grievances. A special committee, headed by William Lloyd, was established to devise a response to the situation. The Massachusetts General Court approved the committee's report early the following year. The report read, in part:

A power to regulate commerce is abused, when employed to destroy it; and a manifest and voluntary abuse of power sanctions the right of resistance, as much as a direct and palpable usurpation. The sovereignty reserved to the states, was reserved to protect the citizens from acts of violence by the United States, as well as for purposes of domestic regulation. We spurn the idea that the free, sovereign and independent State of Massachusetts is reduced to a mere municipal corporation, without power to protect its people, and to defend them from oppression, from whatever quarter it comes. Whenever the national compact is violated, and the citizens of this State are oppressed by cruel and unauthorized laws, this Legislature is bound to interpose its power, and wrest from the oppressor its victim.[16]

Once again, the language of the Principles of '98.

WERE STATES' RIGHTS ABOUT SLAVERY? NOT IN THE WAY YOU THINK

At a time when the federal government was using its police powers to enforce the capture of runaway slaves, it was the state governments, expressly recalling the Principles of '98, that determined to resist.[17] At first glance the Principles of '98, whose purpose is to provide relief from unconstitutional federal laws, seem irrelevant to this case. After all, Article 4, Section 2 of the Constitution expressly called for the return of fugitive slaves: "No person, held to service or labour, in one state, under the laws thereof, escaping into another, shall, in consequence of any law or regulation thereof, be discharged from such service or labour, but shall be delivered up on claim of the party to which such service or labour may be due." Given this constitutional provision, how could a state justify in effect nullifying it?

In fact, some northern states offered a serious and substantial argument against the constitutionality of fugitive-slave legislation—particularly the Fugitive Slave Act of 1850, which was especially obnoxious and repugnant.[18] That act, which placed all fugitive slave cases under federal jurisdiction, denied to fugitives both the right to

33 Questions About American History You're Not Supposed to Ask

testify in their own defense and the right to a jury trial. It also included a right to force bystanders to participate in the capture of a fugitive and stiff penalties for sheltering or obstructing the capture of a fugitive.

The act enabled the owner of a runaway slave to present himself in a court in his home state to try to reclaim his slave. The owner had to state in an affidavit that the slave in question had escaped and that the slave owed labor to the claimant, and he had to provide a physical description of the slave. If the judge believed that the owner had demonstrated his case, he then issued an official transcript that the owner could present in whatever jurisdiction he could find the fugitive. That transcript was presented to one of the federal commissioners empowered by the Fugitive Slave Act to determine the identity of accused fugitives. It was the role of the federal commissioner to determine not that the man in question was in fact a runaway slave—that much was already determined by the judge in the slave's home state—but simply whether the man presented before him was the man described in the judge's transcript. If so, then the accused was in effect remanded to slavery. If not, he was set free. No appeal of this decision was allowed.

A great many constitutional objections were raised against the act. One involved the denial of a jury trial for the accused fugitive. Another was more technical: the federal commissioners were obviously exercising judicial power, and yet the conditions of their employment did not comply with those established for judicial officers by the Constitution—appointment by the president, service during "good behavior," and compensation by a fixed salary. (The commissioners were paid not by a salary but by a fee paid in each case brought before them.) Worse, the commissioners received a ten-dollar fee if they returned the accused to slavery and only five dollars if they freed him. Radical antislavery lawyer Lysander Spooner argued that it was the payment by fees itself (as opposed to fixed salaries) that rendered the whole arrangement unconstitutional. A more recent scholar contends that the fee differential was the problem: "To give a commissioner a pecuniary interest in the outcome of a hearing over which he presides and in which he must make findings of fact . . . is a violation of the due process clause of the Fifth Amendment."[19]

Several northern states enacted "personal liberty laws" designed to frustrate the enforcement of the law. Contrary to popular belief then and now, only rarely did these measures directly oppose the law.[20] What they did do was to make the enforcement of the law more difficult and costly by means of every option at the state's legitimate disposal. For instance, they penalized and even impeached state officials who lent their support to a fugitive-slave claimant, refused to allow federal officials the use of local jails to house accused fugitives, and ensured that claimants could not simply snatch accused fugitives from the free states—they had to go before the federal fugitive-slave tribunals. This last provision often made the reclamation of fugitive slaves prohibitively expensive, what with the legal fees and other expenses that a potential claimant would incur.

Still, these various forms of resistance often opened up the northern states to charges of dereliction of constitutional duty. But consider how Wisconsin, which had gone further than any other state in interfering with the enforcement of the Fugitive Slave Act, answered this charge. Her Supreme Court quoted the Virginia and Kentucky Resolutions—the earliest and most precise statements of the Principles of '98—nearly verbatim in defense of a state's right to refuse to enforce laws that went beyond the federal government's powers as the state understood them:

> Resolved, That the government formed by the Constitution of the United States was not the exclusive or final judge of the extent of the powers delegated to itself; but that, as in all other cases of compact among parties having no common judge, each party has an equal right to judge for itself, as well of infractions as of the mode and measure of redress.

Resolved, that the principle and construction contended for by the party which now rules in the councils of the nation, that the general government is the exclusive judge of the extent of the powers delegated to it, stop nothing short of despotism, since the *discretion* of those who administer the government, and not the *Constitution,* would be the measure of their powers; that the several states which formed that instrument, being sovereign and independent, have the unquestionable right to judge of its infractions; and that a positive defiance of those sovereignties, of all unauthorized acts done or attempted to be done under color of that instrument, is the rightful remedy.[21]

Many more examples of the ongoing relevance of the Principles of '98 could be cited. In the midst of a dispute with the federal government over the Second Bank of the United States in 1820–21, the Ohio legislature voted to affirm the Principles of '98.[22] In 1825 Kentucky's governor, answering the claim that the Supreme Court ought to decide constitutional controversies between the federal government and the states, declared:

> When the general government encroaches upon the rights of the State, is it a safe principle to admit that a portion of the encroaching power shall have the right to determine finally whether an encroachment has been made or not? In fact, most of the encroachments made by the general government flow through the Supreme Court itself, the very tribunal which claims to be the final arbiter of all such disputes. What chance for justice have the States when the usurpers

... *&* THE TRUTH

The idea of states' rights is central to American history and political theory. In antebellum America northern states invoked these important principles at least as often as their southern counterparts. Fearful of an unaccountable federal government, Thomas Jefferson and other important Americans even believed the states could nullify unconstitutional laws.

of their rights are made their judges? Just as much as individuals when judged by their oppressors. It is therefore believed to be the right, as it may hereafter become the duty of the State governments, to protect themselves from encroachments, and their citizens from oppression, by refusing obedience to the unconstitutional mandates of the Federal judges.[23]

THE BURIED FACTS

These are facts. They are facts that constitute a central part of antebellum American history. Yet to say that the standard American history text does not discuss them in terrific depth would be rather an understatement. Other than William J. Watkins Jr.'s excellent book *Reclaiming the American Revolution: The Kentucky and Virginia Resolutions and Their Legacy* (2004), one would be hard pressed to find a single book-length treatment of the Virginia and Kentucky Resolutions of 1798 themselves over the past *hundred years,* though tomes documenting all manner of politically correct minutiae line the shelves.

It is no surprise that the historical profession has essentially ignored the legacy of the Principles of '98, given most historians' support for the use of federal government power on behalf of "progressive" (and constitutionally dubious) policies. It's also unsurprising that national politicians take no interest in the subject; why should they want to encourage forms of resistance to federal domination?

But it is perhaps surprising that a few conservatives join with the Left on this subject and portray the idea of states' rights as the pet theory of a few isolated cranks. They do not dare to mention that the idea in fact came to full maturity in the work of *Thomas Jefferson* and was then referred to again and again during some of the greatest controversies of antebellum American history—by northern states as well as southern.

The Principles of '98 raise timeless questions that deserve to be asked and debated rather than suppressed and ignored. If liberty is our desired end, is it more likely to arise in an order of competing jurisdictions—where the people's right of exit serves as a check on the local government, anxious not to lose its tax base—or in a single gigantic jurisdiction?[24]

Before answering that question, consider the example of Nazi Germany, whose states' rights system Adolf Hitler despised and helped to bury.[25]

WHAT WAS "THE BIGGEST UNKNOWN SCANDAL OF THE CLINTON YEARS"?

★ ★

During the 1990s the Republican Party focused the public's attention on numerous White House scandals, some of which many Americans today recall only faintly, like Whitewater, Travelgate, and Filegate. No one, of course, could forget the Monica Lewinsky scandal, the news item that refused to go away no matter how grotesque it got.

Arguably the greatest scandal of the Clinton years, however, has gone all but unnoticed, save by a few reporters here and there. "Throughout the 1990s," writes correspondent Srdja Trifkovic, "the U.S. government aided and abetted al-Qaeda operations in the Balkans, long after [Osama bin Laden] was recognized as a major security threat to the United States." The Clinton administration, which should have stayed out of the conflict in the first place, consistently supported the cause of the Bosnian Muslims against the Serbs, a policy whose end result was "the strengthening of an already aggressive Islamic base in the heart of Europe that will not go away."[1]

In the course of assisting the Bosnian Muslims, moreover, Clinton aided in transporting thousands of mujahideen—radical Islamic fighters—to the region from the Middle East. When the fighting was over, most of them refused to go home, disappearing into the local population instead. U.S. officials from Clinton's day to the present have identified the mujahideen as a source of instability and terrorism in Europe, and European diplomats of all stripes have complained that Bosnia has become an important terrorist staging ground. Greece has declared that al-Qaeda agents in Bosnia are a threat to its national security.

Isn't that slightly more important than the Lewinsky affair?

BUNGLING THE BALKANS

By the late 1980s Yugoslavia, a multinational state created in the aftermath of World War I, was headed toward disintegration as its various republics began moving toward independence. Slovenia was the first to go, in 1991, and it did so with hardly any violence. Much more violent was the secession of Croatia, since the sizable Serbian population there feared the kind of treatment they would receive in an independent Croatia. As a result, fighting broke out over whether Serbian enclaves in Croatia would be able to join Serbia.

The Yugoslav republic of Bosnia and Herzegovina, usually referred to simply as Bosnia, was a special case. There the population was far less uniform than it was in the other republics: according to the 1991 census, Bosnia was 44 percent Muslim Slavs, 31 percent Serbs, and 17 percent Croats, with smaller groups making up the remainder. Croat and Serb leaders secretly discussed a partition plan for Bosnia that would have annexed the Croat and Serb portions of Bosnia to Croatia and Serbia, respectively. When the Bosnian government declared its independence from Yugoslavia in 1992, the Serb section, not wishing to be subject to what it feared would be an Islamic Bosnian regime, declared itself to be a separate Serb Republic. (Alija Izetbegovic, the Bosnian president, had written in the *Islamic Declaration* of 1970, "The Islamic movement must, and can, take over power as soon as it is morally and numerically so strong that it can not only destroy the existing non-Islamic power, but also build up a new Islamic one."[2] That pamphlet was reprinted in 1990, with Izetbegovic's approval.)

Fighting broke out that week and eventually became a three-way war, with terrible atrocities committed on all sides. But for anyone following reports in the Western media, the conflict was a simple matter of good Muslims and Croats against evil Serbs. Andrew Thompson of BBC's *Newsnight* described the lopsided coverage as "the regular presentation of one side as bad (the Serbs) and one side as good (everyone else)." Misha Glenny, who worked for the BBC World Service during the Bosnian civil war, noted that there was such a campaign to demonize the Serbs and so little interest in finding out their position—or even conceding that they had one—that "the general impression [as to why the Serbs were fighting] is because they are stark, raving, mad, vicious, mean bastards."[3]

What was actually happening was that as Yugoslavia was disintegrating, nobody wanted to wind up as a minority in what remained of that ramshackle country or in any successor state that might emerge.[4] The Bosnian Muslims were no different in this respect. Following the secessions of Slovenia and Croatia, the Bosnian Muslims sought to secede from a rump Yugoslavia, consisting of Serbia and Montenegro, that would be dominated by Serbs.

The U.S. government made little effort to be even-handed in the conflict that followed. Acting undersecretary of state Lawrence Eagleburger explained in early 1992 that he aimed to support the Muslims in Bosnia in order to repair the perception of anti-Muslim bias that had tarnished the United States' image in the Islamic world.[5] The Clinton administration continued down the same path, forgoing any semblance of impartiality by demonizing the Serbs and viewing the Bosnian Muslims as benign multiculturalists and pluralists. The U.S. Army Foreign Military Studies Office, on the other hand, vainly observed that a multiethnic ideal for Bosnia "may appeal to a few members of Bosnia's ruling circles as well as to a generally secular populace, but President Izetbegovic and his cabal appear to harbor much different private intentions and goals."[6]

Supposedly committed to toleration and human rights in the Balkans, the Clinton administration did and said nothing in 1995 when the Croats, who were being counseled by American advisers and the CIA, engaged in the most massive ethnic cleansing of the entire Balkan nightmare when they drove out 150,000 Serbs from Krajina, a heavily Serb portion of Croatia. Wrote General Charles G.

Boyd, deputy commander in chief of the U.S. European Command from 1992 to 1995: "Ethnic cleansing evokes condemnation only when it is committed by Serbs, not against them."[7]

The fighting was certainly not inevitable. The Lisbon peace agreement of early 1992, worked out by Portuguese foreign minister José Cutileiro, would have provided for an independent Bosnia organized into ethnic cantons. Naturally, Bosnian president Alija Izetbegovic wanted a single, centralized Bosnian state. According to the *New York Times,* U.S. ambassador Warren Zimmermann recalled that when Izetbegovic spoke of his unhappiness with the Lisbon agreement, "I told him, if he didn't like it, why sign it?"[8] Zimmermann later denied making the remark, but a high-ranking State Department official told the *Times* that the U.S. government's policy "was to encourage Izetbegovic to break with the partition plan,"[9] and it was shortly after his meeting with Zimmermann that Izetbegovic announced his intention of renouncing the plan.

This was not an isolated incident. As David Binder wrote in the *South Slav Journal,* the "only constant" in the "Clinton approach to the war was the continuing support for the Bosnian Muslims."[10] Michael Mandel of Canada's Osgoode Hall Law School likewise observed that "both the [George H. W.] Bush and Clinton administrations took it upon themselves to sponsor the Bosnian Muslims, and encouraged them to avoid compromises on the promise of support, including military intervention by NATO."[11] (Under NATO auspices the Clinton administration ultimately did bomb Bosnian Serb positions in 1994 and 1995.)

In 1995 General Boyd criticized the Clinton administration's favoritism:

> The United States says that its objective is to end the war through a negotiated settlement, but in reality what it wants is to influence the outcome in favor of the Muslims. The United States, for example, watched approvingly as Muslim offenses began this spring, even though these attacks destroyed a cease-fire Washington has supported. This duplicity, so crude and obvious to all in Europe, has weakened America's moral authority to provide any

kind of effective diplomatic leadership. Worse, because of this, the impact of U.S. action has been to prolong the conflict while bringing it no closer to resolution.[12]

In 1995 the Dayton peace accords finally ended the conflict. The agreement established a Republic of Bosnia and Herzegovina, which consisted of an ill-fated Croatian-Muslim Federation and a Republika Srpska, or Serb Republic. The two entities were technically part of the same country, but the central government that ruled them both had next to no authority. An international implementation force under NATO direction would be deployed to the region in a peacekeeping capacity. And what had it all been for? Columnist A. M. Rosenthal observed, "If the West and the Muslims had agreed four years ago to what the U.S. may do now—let Bosnian Serbs out of the newly created Bosnia or give them their own part of it—the war would never have taken place."[13] But the U.S. government had been too committed to the Bosnian Muslims.

THE GROWTH OF ISLAMIC EXTREMISM

Nearly forgotten in the midst of all this is how Clinton's assistance to the Bosnian Muslims paved the way for the growth of Islamic extremism in the Balkans. "From 1992 to 1995," reported *The Spectator*, "the Pentagon assisted with the movement of thousands of mujahedin and other Islamic elements from Central Asia into Europe, to fight alongside Bosnian Muslims against the Serbs."[14] The Dayton peace accords called for foreign fighters to leave the region, but that provision did not translate well into practice, particularly since so many of them became Bosnian citizens at the conclusion of the fighting and determined to remain there. Chief U.S. negotiator Richard Holbrooke admitted that the Bosnian Muslims "wouldn't have survived" without the assistance of

THE MYTH ...

The Monica Lewinsky affair was the worst scandal of Bill Clinton's presidency.

33 Questions About American History You're Not Supposed to Ask

the mujahideen, though he eventually agreed that the use of extremists amounted to a "pact with the devil" that continues to plague the region.[15]

Izetbegovic, the Bosnian president, called for passports to be made available to anyone who had contributed to the Muslim cause. In practice, writes author Diana Johnstone, this meant that "allies of Osama bin Laden were given boxes of blank passports to distribute as they saw fit." Only bin Laden himself appears to have been missing, though no one knows for sure. According to a Bosnian newspaper editor, "If bin Laden does not have a Bosnia-Herzegovina passport, then he has only himself to blame. He should have asked for it in time."[16]

Since the time of Clinton's interventions, the Balkans have increasingly become a stronghold for Islamic terrorists. August Hanning, a German intelligence chief, has described the situation as a cause for "extreme concern."[17] In December 2003 Clifford Bond, the U.S. ambassador in Sarajevo (the Bosnian capital), spoke of the terrorist threat that existed in the Balkans because foreign fighters had flocked to the area during the war and never left. Yet the ambassador was only repeating what the State Department had been privately warning about since at least the year 2000—namely, that the Muslim government in Sarajevo was sheltering Islamic terrorists who could be found throughout the Muslim-controlled areas of Bosnia. According to Srdja Trifkovic, "Eight years of the Clinton-Albright Administration's covert and overt support for the Islamist camp in the Balkans have been a foreign policy debacle of the first order."[18]

> ... & THE TRUTH
>
> *A far greater scandal is that in his war against the Serbs, Clinton aided and abetted the spread of Islamic radicalism into the Balkans.*

At some level even Clinton himself came to realize this. A former senior State Department official told the press that the Clinton White House put pressure on Izetbegovic to address the problem of terrorism originating from Bosnia, "but nothing happened." Bosnia, the official said, had become "a staging area and safe haven" for terrorists.[19] The situation did not improve after Clinton's departure from office. "Many of the foreign mujaheddin, or holy warriors, were expelled after the war, according to the Bosnian government, but others remained and received passports," reported the *Washington Post* in late 2005. "Today, parts of Bosnia framed by the cities of Zenica, Tuzla, Sarajevo and Travnik are home to these immigrants and compose the core regions for Islamic militancy."[20]

The Bosnian connection left its imprint on numerous high-profile crimes around the world. Following the emergence of a wave of armed robberies in northern France in early 1996, for example, French investigators came upon caches of rocket launchers, grenades, automatic weapons, and the like. The armed robberies, it turns out, had been an effort by radical Islamists to raise funds for their "Muslim brothers in Algeria." This was no scattered group of gangsters, as the French had originally thought. "Five years before the sophisticated terrorist assault on the U.S.," the *Los Angeles Times* reported, "the French were starting to uncover loosely linked violent networks spreading into several countries, all tied together by a common thread: Bosnia."[21]

Little wonder that the president's largely uncritical assistance to the Bosnian Muslims has been called "the biggest unknown scandal of the Clinton years."[22]

QUESTION **6**

WAS THE "WILD WEST" REALLY SO WILD?

★ ★

References to the old West conjure up images of gunfights, violence, and premature death. Western movies and folklore have left the impression that the "wild" West was a place where life and limb were insecure, where property was precarious, and where Thomas Hobbes's description of the prepolitical state of nature seemed to hold: life was "solitary, poor, nasty, brutish, and short."

Recent scholarship has cast serious doubt on this picture. In 2004 Stanford University Press published Terry Anderson and P. J. Hill's *The Not So Wild, Wild West,* which draws a very different lesson from the western experience. Anderson and Hill show that crime was actually quite low, and land and property rights secure, in the old West, despite the lack of government institutions. Even in the unusually challenging conditions that prevailed on the frontier, people devised private mechanisms to allocate rights to land and resources like gold and water, resolve disputes, and enforce the law.[1] The institutions that westerners established were neither perfect nor immune to abuses, of course, but any criticism we may be inclined to make of them could apply just as strongly to the state-run institutions that later supplanted them.[2] What is abundantly clear from the historical record is that in spite of the absence of formal government, civilization did not collapse. It thrived.

Among the most important revisionist studies of the American West was W. Eugene Hollon's *Frontier Violence: Another Look* (1976). Hollon contended that "the Western frontier was a far more civilized, more peaceful, and safer place than American society is today." Hollon's work was followed up on and largely confirmed in Robert Dykstra's *Cattle Towns* (1983) and in a series of essays by various authors collected together as *Lethal Imagination: Violence and Brutality in American History* (1999).[3]

Historian Richard Shenkman attributes popular misconceptions about the West mainly to the legacy of those reliably violent western films. "Many more people have died in Hollywood Westerns than ever died on the real Frontier," he says. "In the real Dodge City, for example, there were just five killings in 1878, the most homicidal year in the little town's Frontier history: scarcely enough to sustain a typical two-hour movie."[4] Dykstra's study of five of the major cattle towns (Abilene, Caldwell, Dodge City, Ellsworth, and Wichita) found only forty-five reported homicides from 1870 through 1885, and that in Abilene, which has earned a reputation as one of the wilder towns, there were no killings at all until "the advent of officers of the law, employed to prevent killings."[5]

In addition, the University of Dayton's Larry Schweikart estimates that fewer than a dozen bank robberies occurred in the entire frontier West from 1859 through 1900. What that means, in case the implications are not clear, is that there are "more bank robberies in modern-day Dayton, Ohio, in a year than there were in the entire Old West in a decade, perhaps in the entire frontier period."[6]

What violence did exist sometimes reflected the fact that it was considered socially acceptable for young bachelors, often drunk, to use violence to settle matters of honor. Other kinds of violence, though, were generally not tolerated. "It was a rather polite and civil society enforced by armed men," says Roger McGrath, author of *Gunfighters, Highwaymen, and Vigilantes*. "The rate of burglary and robbery was lower than in American cities today. Claim-jumping was rare. Rape was extraordinarily rare—you can argue it wasn't being reported, but I've never seen evidence hinting at that."[7] Historian Watson Parker writes, "There wasn't an awful lot of violence in Deadwood except for the crooks and drunks killing each other. When everybody has a gun on his hip, they tend to avoid confrontation."[8]

Unusual episodes have often been cited as if they were the norm, thus skewing our conception of the old West. In other cases, the principal actors themselves exaggerated the truth in order to cultivate the mystique of the old West. Buffalo Bill Cody, for example, admitted that he had been wounded in battle with Indians not 137 times, as he had claimed, but only once. The 137 figure, though, was more effective in selling dime novels.[9]

WAGON-TRAIN GOVERNMENT

The process of getting out West was also by and large peaceful. Between 1840 and 1860, some 300,000 people traveled to California and Oregon, in a journey that took them across the Great Plains and the Rocky and Sierra mountains. And these pioneers "created their own law-making and law-enforcing machinery before they started," Anderson and Hill write.[10] That machinery took the form of what has been called wagon-train governments. Each such voluntary organization existed in order to "develop its own rules necessary to police its members and provide protections from outsiders (mainly Indians), to resolve disputes among group members, and to organize production of public goods that required teamwork, such as crossing streams, hunting, and fighting Indians."[11]

How well did these wagon-train governments work? According to John Phillip Reed, the leading authority on the subject, it was "a tale of sharing more than dividing, a time of accommodation rather than discord. . . . The overland trail was not a place of conflict."[12] Political scientist Ryan McMaken writes:

> Entire industries grew up around getting people to their destinations, and serving them once they got there. Markets for scouts, guides, equipment, guidebooks, and teamsters were all readily supplied by enthusiastic entrepreneurs. While government surveyors

like Charles Fremont promoted and helped map the West, the actual settling was always done by men and women looking to make a better living in a new land. In other words, civilization was brought to the West by private citizens, private entrepreneurs, and private law enforcement.[13]

J. H. Beadle, a newspaperman traveling through Denver in 1860, gives us a revealing glimpse at the legal situation there:

> Appeals were taken from one to the other, papers certified up or down and over, and recognized, criminals delivered and judgments accepted from one court by another, with a happy informality which it is pleasant to read of. And here we are confronted by an awkward fact: there was undoubtedly much less crime in the two years this arrangement lasted than in the two which followed the territorial organization and regular government.[14]

Pioneers who settled in the public domain before it was made officially available to the public, and sometimes even before official surveying had been done, relied upon nongovernmental means of establishing and then protecting property rights. Land clubs or claims associations eventually spread throughout the Midwest. Each such association had its own constitution and its own regulations for the adjudication of disputes and the registration of land claims.[15] Frederick Jackson Turner described these land claims clubs as a perfect example of the "power of the newly arrived pioneers to join together for a common end without the intervention of governmental institutions."[16]

Cattlemen's associations also became a common feature of the West, particularly after the 1860s. They established the branding system, adjudicated disputes, enforced property rights, and devised means to exclude outsiders from the range in order to prevent overgrazing, the cattlemen's version of the tragedy of the commons.[17]

Perhaps the best example of nonstate organizations in the old West involves the institutional mechanisms devised by gold miners on the West Coast. The discovery of gold in California, referred to by President James Polk in his 1848 address to Congress, attracted tens of thousands of fortune seekers in a matter of months, from locales as distant as Europe and even China. The territory had just been transferred to the United States following the conclusion of the war with Mexico that year, and no territorial government had yet been established. The military posts established by Americans were the only governmental authority in the area, and they had neither the interest in nor the manpower for enforcing miners' competing claims.[18] When the unprecedented influx of migrants arrived, therefore, they needed to make nongovernmental arrangements not only to provide for their safety but also to establish rules and procedures to protect their gold claims and their gold.

The common law recognized the people's right to do this very thing in the absence of a functioning lawmaking body. According to historian Otis Young:

> The common law also held that in a land otherwise devoid of appropriate law or a lawgiving body (as California practically was), the free citizenry might legislate for its own needs and that, as long as this legislation was reasonable and equitable, subsequent formal sovereigns must recognize this prior legislation as valid. Being instructed to this effect by the many lawyers among them (each of whom had virtually memorized Blackstone or Coke), the argonauts proceeded to organize folk moots, or "miners' meetings," in which placer law was debated and ratified by vote of all adult males present.[19]

An institution known as the mining district was established in order to address the challenges the miners faced. Each such district erected a legal system that punished crimes against life and property, established a system of property rights in mining claims, and could evolve in the face of changing technology and other fluid factors.[20] That they were by and large successful is one of the great untold stories of nineteenth-century American history. "In three years," writes P. J. Hill, "more than 200,000 people had migrated to California, most of them trying to get rich quick. If there were ever a recipe for chaos, this would seem to be one: people of varied backgrounds and ethnicities, all armed and all seeking a valuable resource. But the mining camps quickly evolved rules for establishing mining claims and for judging disputes."[21]

And they were very effective: John Umbeck's systematic study of mining camp rules found that miners avoided violence and instead took the path of contract and voluntarily acceded to the rules of mining districts "not once but 500 times. And the length of time in which this took place was not centuries, but days."[22] This outcome is all the more remarkable when we recall some of the details of miners' lives. These were men of vastly different backgrounds, who were complete strangers (and thus possessed no preexisting community camaraderie upon which to build) and who intended not to put down roots and stay for years but simply to get rich from their gold finds and return home.[23] "Tens of thousands of strangers thrown together for short periods of time, with virtually no social institutions, facing a choice between participating in customary legal institutions or picking up gold off the ground ought to have been a recipe for disaster," writes Andrew Morriss of Case Western Reserve University. "Yet this amazing polyglot of men seeking rapid wealth, and with virtually no intention of building a lasting society, created a set of customary legal institutions which not only flourished in California but successfully adapted to conditions across the West."[24]

> THE MYTH ...
>
> *The old West was violent and lawless, with life and property insecure and no restraints imposed on gunfighters or other criminals.*

The miners settled disputes either through a district-wide meeting or by an elected jury or alcalde. The alcalde kept his position only so long as the miners accepted his rulings as just. They replaced those whose judgments did not conform to generally accepted standards of justice.[25] Crime was also notably low in the districts, a fact attributed to widespread gun ownership among the miners as well as to the efficient nature of the miners' legal system.[26]

Here is an extraordinary example of the evolution of private, voluntary mechanisms that successfully carried out the very functions of which the private sector is routinely assumed to be incapable: defining and enforcing property rights, adjudicating disputes, and protecting people against all manner of crimes. "In sum," writes Morriss, miners' law "was a success. In the face of what in retrospect appear to be almost insurmountable obstacles, a society of strangers wandering in alien lands built a resilient institution capable of adapting to social and technological changes which occurred with a rapidity which makes our present-day society appear tame."[27]

> ... & THE TRUTH
>
> *Even in the absence of government, the old West was far less violent than most American cities today. Frontiersmen developed private mechanisms to enforce the law and define and enforce property rights.*

"WILD"?

As an avalanche of scholarly work continues to demonstrate, the "wild" West in fact reveals the resilience and adaptability of the private sector, even in the production of so-called public goods like legal services, dispute resolution, and law enforcement. This is exactly the opposite of what we have traditionally been taught about the western experience. We are supposed to conclude that discord and violence must result in the absence of formal government and accept the old West as a cautionary tale of what happens when Hillary Clinton and Bob Dole aren't around to keep everyone in line.

HOW ANTIWAR HAVE AMERICAN LIBERALS ACTUALLY BEEN OVER THE YEARS?

★ ★

Judging from public protests against the Vietnam War, and more recently against the war in Iraq, people have often concluded that American liberals are by nature antiwar. Television news programs only reinforce this perception: someone on the Left is always featured as the war opponent, while someone on the Right is always the war supporter—as if this were the natural and logical outcome of these ideologies.

The truth of the matter, both today and in the past, is rather more interesting. Consistently antiwar Democrats are actually quite difficult to find. Even the flamboyant Howard Dean, who has criticized the Iraq war, was all in favor of the wars waged by Bill Clinton. The major newspapers, from the *New York Times* to the *Washington Post,* all supported the Iraq war, as they had the Persian Gulf War of 1991. Hillary Clinton vigorously supported the Iraq war, while *The American Conservative* magazine and a roster of important conservatives opposed it.

It is equally untrue that the Left has long opposed war, as a casual glance at American history makes clear. Ever since the Spanish-

American War of 1898, liberals have more often than not been at the forefront of calls for American military intervention abroad.

TURNING POINT

The Progressive movement of the late nineteenth and early twentieth centuries, a child of liberalism, was overwhelmingly sympathetic rather than hostile to the tendency toward American territorial expansion and foreign policy assertiveness. Domestic reform and foreign intervention, to many Progressives, were simply two sides of the same coin: just as an invigorated federal government would achieve order and "social justice" at home, an interventionist foreign policy would spread the benefits of Progressivism around the world. "At the outbreak of the Spanish-American War," explains historian William Leuchtenburg, "few men saw any conflict between social reform and democratic striving at home and the new imperialist mission; indeed, the war seemed nothing so much as an extension of democracy to new parts of the world, and few political figures exceeded the enthusiasm of William Jennings Bryan for the Spanish war."[1]

The humanitarian aspect of the war—namely, liberating Cuba from Spanish rule—appealed to Progressives. The response of feminist leader Elizabeth Cady Stanton was typical: "Though I hate war per se," she wrote, "I am glad that it has come in this instance. I would like to see Spain . . . swept from the face of the earth."[2]

The Spanish-American War lasted a mere three months but brought the United States significant territorial acquisitions: Puerto Rico, Guam, and the Philippines. When rebel fighters in the Philippines turned on the Americans in an effort to win independence, the long and costly insurrection inspired an anti-imperialist movement in the United States. Groups like the Anti-Imperialist League, formed in Boston in June 1898, wondered what America, born in a war for independence from its own European mother country, was doing holding colonies of its own.

Was the campaign against American expansion fundamentally left-wing? No. Although a few Progressives were consistently antiwar, they did not dominate the movement. The diverse cast of characters included former presidents Benjamin Harrison and Grover Cleveland, writer Mark Twain, labor leader Samuel Gompers, philosopher William James, and businessmen Edward Atkinson and Andrew Carnegie, among many others. In fact, as historian Robert Beisner points out, most anti-imperialists were not Progressives but "traditionalists who believed imperialism to be in sharp conflict with established ideals and practices." Or as Leuchtenburg observes, "first and last, *it was the conservatives* who bore the burden of the anti-imperialist campaign."[3]

More often than not, those who favored a more activist role for the federal government in international affairs favored a more activist federal government at home as well. Herbert Croly, whose book *The Promise of American Life* (1909) was one of the most influential and revealing Progressive texts, pointed to a connection between an aggressive foreign policy abroad and "social reform at home." He wrote that the war had made Hamiltonianism—that is, the philosophy of a strong central government—once again fashionable at home (and not just among the relatively small circle of Progressives). "Not until the end of the Spanish War," he wrote, "was a condition of public feeling created, which made it possible to revive Hamiltonianism. That war and its resulting policy of extra-territorial expansion, so far from hindering the process of democratic amelioration, availed, from the sheer force of the national aspirations it aroused, to give a tremendous impulse to the work of national reform."[4]

Big government at home, therefore, went philosophically hand in hand with big government abroad. Historians, writes Arthur Ekirch, have "overlooked this intimate relationship between the aggressive foreign policy of the progressives and their emphasis on nationalism in home affairs."[5] As Leuchtenburg explains:

> The Progressives believed in the Hamiltonian concept of positive government, of a national government directing the destinies of the nation at home and abroad. They had little but contempt for the strict construction of the Constitution by conservative judges, who would restrict the power of the national government to act against social evils and to extend the blessings of democracy to

33 Questions About American History You're Not Supposed to Ask

less favored lands. The real enemy was particularism, state rights, limited government.[6]

Half a century later American conservatives like Richard Weaver and journalist Felix Morley (one of the founders of *Human Events*, today the oldest conservative newsweekly in America) could still be found who considered 1898 an unfortunate and portentous departure from the noninterventionist foreign policy recommended by the Founding Fathers. They also perceived a connection between intervention abroad and big government at home. Weaver, described in George Nash's book *The Conservative Intellectual Movement in America Since 1945* as one of the three most influential traditionalist thinkers in the United States during the postwar period, believed the old America had suffered a regrettable blow in that fateful year:

> One cannot feign surprise, therefore, that thirty years after the great struggle to consolidate and unionize American power [i.e., the War Between the States], the nation embarked on its career of imperialism. The new nationalism enabled Theodore Roosevelt, than whom there was no more staunch advocate of union, to strut and bluster and intimidate our weaker neighbors. Ultimately it launched America upon its career of world imperialism, whose results are now being seen in indefinite military conscription, mountainous debt, restriction of dissent, and other abridgments of classical liberty.[7]

THE GREAT WATERSHED

If the Spanish-American War was a turning point, World War I was a great watershed. President Woodrow Wilson's crusade to make "the world safe for democracy" was fundamentally leftist in its very nature. Wilson proposed to fight not for specific and finite objectives like the defense of his country and people but rather on behalf of ideology and abstract principles. To those who feared that his proposed League of Nations (a forerunner of the United Nations) would compromise American sovereignty, Wilson replied that he looked forward to the day "when men would be just as eager partisans of the sovereignty of mankind as they were now of their own national sovereignty."[8] Wilson believed that if the United States became a belligerent, the American president would be assured a seat at the peace table when the fighting was over.

When the disastrous peace settlement of 1919 made perfectly clear that Wilson's grandiose visions for self-determination, "peace without victory," and world order—on behalf of which he had sent nearly 120,000 of his countrymen to their deaths—were as dead as could be, he simply denied the evidence and praised the treaty anyway. It was the "incomparable consummation of the hopes of mankind," he said; at one point he even called it an "enterprise of divine mercy."[9] Sigmund Freud said that as early as March 1919 Wilson "was rapidly nearing that psychic land from which few travelers return, the land in which facts are the products of wishes, in which friends betray and in which an asylum chair may be the throne of God."[10]

Few were more bloodthirsty and savage in their support for total war against Germany and unconditional surrender than leftist clergy. Social Gospel theologians, crudely applying Christian language and concepts that they had found malleable enough to make railroad regulation sound like a direct command of Christ, expressed their conviction that the United States was at least in some sense the savior of the world. To America they assigned the righteousness of Christ, and there could be no compromise between Christ and Satan. In the name of bringing about perpetual peace, Progressive clergy helped to legitimize the twentieth century's first total war. According to historian Richard Gamble, "They transported the war out of the sordid but understandable realm of national ambition, rivalry, and interests—where policies and goals can be debated and defined—into the rarified world of ideals, abstractions, and politicized theology, where dissent and limitations are moral failures or even heresies."[11]

Historians have sometimes suggested that World War I marked the end of Progressivism in America. To the contrary, the war in fact represented the culmination, even the fulfillment, of the Progressive program.[12] With the exception of people like Jane Addams and Randolph Bourne, the political Left in America was delighted with the war, not only because it was being waged for what in their view was a righteous cause but also because wartime conditions would give them the opportunity to manage the American economy and, they hoped, leave the free economy behind forever. Wartime economic planning, they were convinced, would help to erode Americans' conservative beliefs in the limits of government and the inviolability of private property.

Shortly after U.S. entry into the war, philosopher and educational theorist John Dewey exclaimed with delight that "this war may easily be the beginning of the end for business." Matters involving production and sales had passed from private hands into those of the government, Dewey observed, and "there is no reason to believe that the old principle will ever be resumed. . . . Private property had already lost its sanctity."[13] *The New Republic* magazine, perhaps the chief repository of "progressive" thought in America, was pleased to see the massive increase in state control over the economy that the war had brought about in European countries, and it looked for the same result in America. The wartime spirit brought with it "the substitution of national and social and organic forces for the more or less mechanical private forces operative in peace." Although war and social reform obviously had different purposes, "they are both purposes, and luckily for mankind a social organization which is efficient is as useful for the one as for the other."[14] No wonder wartime analogies were so prevalent in Franklin Roosevelt's New Deal ("We planned in war," the rallying cry went), Lyndon Johnson's "War" on Poverty, and Jimmy Carter's energy policy (the "moral equivalent of war"): these domestic crusades involved massive material and ideological mobilizations analogous to those of a foreign war.

"VIETNAM WAS A LIBERAL WAR"

Liberal support for military interventionism persisted into the post–World War II period and the Cold War. It was Harry Truman, after all, whose administration set the stage for the global interventionism of the Cold War, against the budgetary and other concerns of skeptical Republicans like Robert Taft, Kenneth Wherry, and Howard Buffett.[15]

Even the Vietnam War, which engendered left-wing protests and thus is the source of the myth that American leftists have traditionally opposed the use of military power, was in fact the brainchild of establishment liberals. Historian Walter McDougall suggests that Lyndon Johnson's Great Society had its foreign policy analogue in the Vietnam War. In the attempt to protect South Vietnam's anti-Communist government from overthrow by a Communist insurgency tied to the North, the U.S. government sought to defeat the enemy by establishing good liberal government in the South that would win the undisputed allegiance of the South Vietnamese. The National Security Council had declared in 1961 that U.S. policy in South Vietnam would be "to create in that country a viable and increasingly democratic society."[16]

Such war aims went well beyond anything that even Truman had asked for from recipient countries when aiding Greece and Turkey or defending South Korea against Communist aggression. But members of the liberal generation that went to war in the 1960s were exponents of what McDougall calls "global meliorism," an ideological model of global uplift based on American cultural, economic, and political models. He declares that "those who thought the war symptomatic of a fascistic 'Amerika' were wrong: Vietnam was a liberal war."[17] When President Johnson offered to extend the Great Society programs to the people of North Vietnam, even Arthur Schlesinger ridiculed the idea as "a form of imperialism unknown to Lenin: sentimental imperialism."[18]

THE MYTH ...

American liberals, today as yesterday, have opposed American wars, while conservatives have just as naturally supported them.

Novelist Graham Greene, who hated the war, was nevertheless attracted to the social work aspect of the American intervention. The American presence in Vietnam, he said, "had its origins in the same presidential impulses that gave birth to the Great Society and the April 1965 offer to North Vietnam of a billion-dollar economic development program for the Mekong River."[19]

Since the 1990s some on the Right have observed wryly that the polit-ical Left is indeed willing to use military force, just so long as no dis-cernible American interest is at stake. This point carries a certain weight, to be sure; recall Robert Frost's playful description of a liberal as someone who refuses to take his own side in an argument. The American Left by and large supported Bill Clinton's interven-tions in the Balkans—over Bosnia and later Kosovo—whose connection to American security and national interests was essen-tially nonexistent.

But this point can be applied only so far. After all, it was not Clinton but George H. W. Bush, during the waning months of his presidency, who initiated American military action in Somalia, perhaps the most frequently cited example of a purely "humanitarian" intervention. Conversely, Hillary Clinton and the establishment Left, along with the overwhelming majority of the media including the *Washington Post* and the *New York Times,* strongly supported the recent war with Iraq, which was justified primarily in terms of American security.[20]

Sociologist Robert Nisbet, one of the most significant conservative thinkers since World War II, finds the common distinction between left-wing peaceniks and right-wing warmongers to be totally unconvincing. Of all the misapplications of the word *conservative* in recent memory, Nisbet wrote in the 1980s, the "most amusing, in an historical light, is surely the application of 'conservative' to . . . great increases in military expenditures. . . . For in America throughout the twentieth century, and including four substantial wars abroad, con-servatives had been steadfastly the voices of non-inflationary military

> ... & THE TRUTH
>
> *The truth is not so simple. Liberals supported all major American wars, in-cluding (initially) even Vietnam. On the other hand, tra-ditional conserva-tives like Richard Weaver and Sena-tor Robert Taft have been cautious about the use of military power, and skep-tical of utopian claims about what it can accomplish.*

budgets, and of an emphasis on trade in the world instead of American nationalism."[21]

Nisbet recalled that contrary to popular opinion, the political Left for the most part had not opposed war per se, as we have seen. In fact, he showed that hard leftists have found much revolutionary potential in war. "Napoleon was the perfect exemplar of revolution as well as of war, not merely in France but throughout almost all of Europe, and even beyond. Marx and Engels were both keen students of war, profoundly appreciative of its properties with respect to large-scale institutional change. From Trotsky and his Red Army down to Mao and Chou En-lai in China today, the uniform of the soldier has been the uniform of the revolutionist."[22]

The same conservative philosophy that looks with skepticism on what government can accomplish at home has traditionally rejected utopian visions of what that same government can accomplish abroad. Woodrow Wilson, who lacked such ideological restraint, believed he was making the world safe for democracy by waging war against the German government in 1917–18. But many historians have argued that Wilson's entry into the war alongside the Allies made it possible for the victorious powers to impose harsh peace terms on Germany—peace terms that the Nazis and their hyperpatriotic politics happily exploited before a resentful German population on their way to power. Marshal Foch said of the Treaty of Versailles, "This is not peace. It is an armistice for twenty years." He was right.

Shortly after the Second World War, no less an authority than George Kennan—among the most influential American diplomats of all time—wondered aloud: "Today if one were offered the chance of having back again the Germany of 1913—a Germany run by conservative but relatively moderate people, no Nazis and no Communists—a vigorous Germany, full of energy and confidence, able to play a part again in the balancing-off of Russian power in Europe, in many ways it would not sound so bad."[23] Richard Weaver, in his description of the typical American southerner, might have been speaking about the conservative statesman when he said that he "accepts the irremediability of a certain amount of evil and tries to fence it around instead of trying to stamp it out and thereby spreading it. His is a classical acknowledgment of tragedy and of the limits of power."[24]

Ultimately, though, are we not being unfair to the Left? Have some leftists not sincerely opposed war over the years? If you look hard, you can find some. But as they will readily admit, they are vastly outnumbered by spokesmen of the establishment Left, who by and large have supported the use of American military power. One thing the establishment Left is good at, to be sure, is opposing wars once they have become domestically unpopular. But that is mere opportunism, not principle, of which mainstream liberalism is more and more bereft.

QUESTION **8**

DID THE IROQUOIS INDIANS INFLUENCE
THE U.S. CONSTITUTION?

★ ★

According to the U.S. government, they certainly did.
During the 1987 bicentennial of the Constitution, the U.S.
Senate passed a resolution by Senator Daniel Inouye "to acknowledge the contribution of the Iroquois Confederacy of Nations to the
development of the United States Constitution."[1] It affirmed that "the
confederation of the original Thirteen Colonies into one republic
was influenced by the political system developed by the Iroquois
Confederacy as were many of the democratic principles which were
incorporated into the Constitution itself."[2] The U.S. Bicentennial
Commission lent its official sanction to a ceremony on the Mall in
Washington by a group of Iroquois Indians celebrating the U.S. government's acknowledgment of their role in influencing the American
political system.[3] Since then some American schools have incorporated into their curricula the alleged Iroquois role in the development
of American political institutions, as if it were a noncontroversial
thesis.

Some scholars have gone well beyond even the government's
rather bold claim. Cultural anthropologist Jack Weatherford, for
example, maintains that the Iroquois didn't merely *influence* the
American political system but in fact *invented* it, coming up with the

62

model of "several sovereign units united into one government"—what we know as the federal system.[4] In *Exemplar of Liberty* Bruce E. Johansen and Donald A. Grinde Jr. draw broader conclusions. They claim that we can thank the Indians for such ideas as

> life, liberty, and happiness (Declaration of Independence); government by reason and consent rather than coercion (Albany Plan and Articles of Confederation); religious tolerance (and ultimately religious acceptance) instead of a state church; checks and balances; federalism (United States Constitution); and relative equality of property, equal rights before the law, and the thorny problem of creating a government that can rule equitably across a broad geographic expanse (Bill of Rights of the United States Constitution). Native America had a substantial role in shaping all these ideas.[5]

Actually, "Native America" had a negligible role, and more likely no role at all, in shaping any of those ideas, all of which had become common currency over the course of many generations of European thought.

SCANT EVIDENCE

Focusing instead on the lesser but more plausible claims of the influence thesis, we find an argument that essentially boils down to this: the Iroquois influenced the American political tradition, first, in that prominent Indians on various occasions during the eighteenth century urged the colonies to unite, and second, because the Iroquois League (or Confederacy) itself served as a potential model for such a union.

In 1744 a treaty conference in Lancaster, Pennsylvania, brought representatives of Pennsylvania, Virginia, and Maryland into direct contact with leaders of the Iroquois League. One of those leaders, Canasatego, recommended that the colonies form a union among themselves, noting that union had benefited the Iroquois nations. Benjamin Franklin, it is said, was impressed by these words and had the Iroquois League in mind when, ten years later, he submitted his plan for intercolonial union, known as the Albany Plan of Union. The Albany Plan, in turn, served as an important model for the Articles of Confederation.

Johansen and Grinde cite a famous 1751 letter from Benjamin Franklin to New York postmaster James Parker that read, in part:

> It would be a very strange Thing, if *Six Nations* of ignorant Savages should be capable of forming a Scheme for such a Union, and be able to execute it in such a Manner, as that it has subsisted Ages, and appears indissoluble; and yet that a like Union should be impracticable for ten or a Dozen *English* Colonies, to whom it is more necessary, and must be more advantageous; and who cannot be supposed to want [i.e., lack] an equal Understanding of their Interests.[6]

Although Franklin points to the Iroquois example, he does not indicate that this example gave him the idea of a confederation. In fact, Nancy Dieter Egloff of the College of William and Mary undertook an extensive study of the relationship between the Iroquois example and the Albany Plan. Her conclusion: "Franklin *never* stated that the Iroquois League was his model for the Albany Plan of Union."[7] Moreover, Franklin's 1751 reference to the Indians as "ignorant Savages" does not exactly reveal a frame of mind inclined to follow their political example unless he was already in favor of a confederation.

> THE MYTH ...
>
> *"Native America had a substantial role in shaping" everything from the basic principles animating the Declaration of Independence to the political system established by the U.S. Constitution.*

There was no shortage of plans for colonial union from which Franklin could have drawn inspiration. Between 1643 and 1744, when Canasatego supposedly enlightened the colonists with the idea of a confederation-style union, there were no fewer than eleven different plans for uniting the colonies.[8] William Penn, for example, advanced a "Plan for a Union of the Colonies in America" in 1697. Beyond such plans there were plenty of examples of successful confederations with which Americans were familiar, including the Swiss and Dutch confederations in Europe and even the seventeenth-century Confederation of New England. What Canasatego told the colonists about the value of confederations was nothing but a commonplace.

Grinde and Johansen are sometimes forced to rely on strained inferences in defense of their position. Their work contains an unusual number of statements to the effect that so-and-so must have discussed Indian political theory at this or that meeting with one or more prominent Americans, or that it is likely that the subject of governmental systems was raised here or there. Well, these things are *possible* (if not as "likely" or "probable" as our authors assure us), but we usually cannot know for sure. Even at those meetings at which we know Iroquois political ideas were mentioned, such references were exceedingly brief. At the 1744 meeting Canasatego devoted a total of four sentences to recommending a colonial union, out of ten times he rose to speak; at a separate meeting ten years later Hendrick, another important Iroquois leader, uttered a single sentence containing a vague reference to the operation of the Iroquois League.

> ... & THE TRUTH
>
> *American Indians did almost nothing to influence the Declaration or the Constitution. The Iroquois League bears virtually no resemblance to the U.S. system of government for which it supposedly was a model.*

WHAT RESEMBLANCES?

A more pertinent question might be: Does the Iroquois League even resemble the government established by the U.S. Constitution? If it does, the resemblances are cleverly hidden. The League included representatives from the five (and later six) tribes that comprised the Iroquois. The senior members of these tribes were the clan mothers. Under this matriarchal system, the chief statesmen were chosen by the clan mothers to serve on the Grand Council during good behavior—

that is, as long as the clan mothers believed they were carrying out their responsibilities. The consent of all was required in order for a measure to pass; if the various tribes of the League could not agree, then the League itself could not act.[9] Finally, instead of meeting on a regular basis, the council convened only when necessary.[10]

That is not exactly the embodiment of the American political tradition, whether represented by the Constitution, the Articles of Confederation, or any other historical document.

Grinde and Johansen also suggest that the Iroquois League provided a model of the separation of powers that would become fundamental to the U.S. system of government. They argue that John Adams's book *A Defence of the Constitutions of Government of the United States of America* expressed admiration for the Iroquois' separation of powers, and that Adams conveyed this admiration to the rest of the Framers, since it was "the best example of the governmental separation of powers available to Americans for direct observation."[11] But in fact when Adams spoke of "the existence of the three divisions of power" in the Iroquois League, he was not speaking of the executive, legislative, and judicial branches into which America's federal government would be divided. He was referring instead to the division into the one, the few, and the many, which has nothing to do with the American conception of separation of powers. In any event, no references to Adams's mentioning the Indians' system are found in James Madison's notes of the Constitutional Convention's proceedings.

To be fair to Grinde and Johansen, they never contend, as do authors like Jack Weatherford, that the Indians "invented" federalism, or that the Iroquois League was the only or even the major intellectual influence on the Constitution. Their thesis is simply that given the number of references one can find to Indian examples in the discourse of the Framers and given the treaty contacts the two sides had over the years, the Indian example may have constituted at least one of the many strains that came together to form the American political tradition in general and the Constitution in particular. The problem here is that Americans would have had no reason to refer to Indian examples in order to learn the basic principles of federalism, confederation, and the utility of unified action on behalf of sovereign entities. Those principles were already well established.

A USEFUL MYTH

What if the historical record did clearly indicate that the Iroquois League had served as one model among many for America's Framers? What if elaborate inferences were not necessary to make the argument plausible? All we would establish was that the Iroquois' "influence" amounted simply to this: they lived under a successful confederation and thus reminded early Americans of the potential usefulness of a model they already knew. This is not exactly a historiographical revolution.

Naturally, the Iroquois influence thesis serves an important ideological purpose for the multicultural lobby—which may explain why, in spite of all its shortcomings, it has become comfortably entrenched in American classrooms.

DID DESEGREGATION OF SCHOOLS SIGNIFICANTLY NARROW THE BLACK-WHITE EDUCATIONAL ACHIEVEMENT GAP?

★ ★

In the wake of the civil rights movement, Lyndon Johnson's Great Society began pouring billions of dollars into new programs to address the sizable gap in educational achievement between blacks and whites. This gap was very real and indeed troubling. Unfortunately, the solution that politicians and government bureaucrats came up with—and that in many cases federal judges forced on the schools— was deeply flawed.

The problem was that they were working from faulty assumptions. Since well before the *Brown v. Board of Education* school desegregation decision (1954), some social scientists had been arguing that school segregation instilled a sense of inferiority in blacks, thereby harming their academic performance. Desegregation, they claimed, would raise black self-esteem and educational achievement and would have the added benefit of reducing white prejudice against blacks, as it would allow whites to move beyond stereotypes and ignorance.[1]

In a 1967 report called *Racial Isolation in the Public Schools,* the U.S.

Commission on Civil Rights took this thesis to a new level. It was no longer just schools segregated by law that made blacks feel inferior. The Civil Rights Commission now argued that racially segregated schools in and of themselves, regardless of whether the segregation was legally mandated or the natural result of residential demographics, harmed the self-esteem of minority students and contributed to their poor educational performance.

Political activists and government bureaucrats seized on these findings in support of increasingly radical means of bringing about racial integration, including forced busing. They should have given more thought to a study released the previous year by the Department of Health, Education, and Welfare. That study's major conclusions were radically at odds with the typical argument put forward about desegregation and the disparities between black and white schools. Popularly known as the Coleman Report, the study found that black and white schools were in fact roughly similar in expenditures, physical plant, and other resources. Any differences between them were as likely to favor black schools as white. The report also argued that black academic achievement, which was well below that of whites, could not be accounted for by any small differences that might exist in resource allocation between white and black schools, and was much more strongly correlated with the socioeconomic background of a student's family (a factor that had no connection to the degree of racial mixture of the school he attended).

Of course, that was not exactly what academics and political activists wanted to hear. The federal government spent the next few decades working relentlessly to close the educational gap by focusing almost exclusively on the racial mix of schools.

The results have been dismal.

THE UGLY CONSEQUENCES

By the 1990s billions of dollars had been spent on integration programs by all levels of government. The results? Recent data from the National Assessment of Educational Progress (NAEP) show that the average black student about to complete his senior year of high school performs at a slightly lower level than the average white eighth-grader in reading and American history, and far below the average white eighth-grader in mathematics and geography.[2] Only 3 percent of black students could demonstrate more than a "partial mastery" of the fundamental skills necessary for "proficient work" in twelfth-grade mathematics; for whites the figure was seven to ten times higher. While 3.4 percent of white students were ranked as "advanced" in science and 2.2 in mathematics, the corresponding figures for black students were 0.1 and 0.2 percent, respectively.[3] (Given these data, it would be surprising if there *weren't* income disparities between blacks and whites; see Question 18.)

From the 1970s through the late 1990s—the period that the NAEP data illuminate for us—the story has been one of overall stagnation (with the exception of reading scores, which show blacks improving from the tenth to the twenty-third percentile). Although some black progress was evident until around 1990, those gains had been completely erased by 1999, for reasons that are not altogether clear. "During a period in which school class size has dropped and spending has gone up—particularly that directed toward the least advantaged—black performance in math has slid back to its 1978 level," report Abigail Thernstrom and Stephan Thernstrom, two distinguished scholars on racial issues. The numbers in science show blacks averaging in the eighth percentile in 1977 and in the tenth in 1999.[4] On the math SAT only seven hundred black students in America scored above 700 in the year 2001, while more than sixteen thousand Asian American students did so, in spite of being substantially outnumbered by blacks.[5]

The racial disparity in achievement and skill level is evident even in the earliest years. The National Center for Educational Statistics found that blacks entering kindergarten were already disproportionately testing in the bottom quarter of students in reading, math, and general knowledge. Between one-third and one-half of black students tested that low in the various subjects, as compared with about one-sixth of whites. Two years later, when the same students were tested again, the black-white gap was unchanged.[6]

Behavioral differences are also evident that early, and they persist into the future. On average, black students are much less likely than

33 Questions About American History You're Not Supposed to Ask

whites to be described by kindergarten teachers as attentive, eager to learn, and persistent in carrying out assigned tasks, and they are more likely to be described as argumentative, quick-tempered, and violent.[7] These discipline disparities persist over time. Later in life blacks are two and a half times as likely to be suspended or expelled from school as whites. Faced with statistics like these, "civil rights" groups typically accuse white teachers of arbitrarily singling out blacks for punishment. To the contrary, black teachers have been found to be even more critical of black students than white teachers are.[8] Moreover, Asian students are less than half as likely as whites to be suspended or expelled; are we to believe that an antiwhite, pro-Asian bias permeates the American educational system?[9]

Educational disparities between the races persist even when social class is taken into account.[10] To be sure, students from higher socioeconomic backgrounds do better than students from lower ones, but this phenomenon is true for blacks and whites alike. The racial gap becomes only marginally smaller as we compare blacks and whites from similar backgrounds. A good example is Shaker Heights, Ohio, an affluent Cleveland suburb whose high school spends 50 percent more per pupil than the national average. The town's black residents are only slightly below their white counterparts in education and income levels, but the racial gap in achievement persists there.

The Thernstroms run down the dismaying statistics.[11] For one thing, even though the school makes a special effort to urge black students to take advanced placement courses—students may take whatever courses they want, regardless of test scores or past grades—only 30 percent do, compared with 87 percent of whites. Two-thirds of the city's blacks failed at least one of Ohio's state proficiency tests in 1999–2000, whereas the same was true of only one-sixth of whites. And while over half the white students passed the tests with honors, only 4 percent of blacks did. That number, according to the Thernstroms, "was no higher than the statewide average for African Americans, despite the fact that the income and educational levels of black families in Shaker Heights were far above those for blacks in Ohio as a whole, and their children were attending integrated schools that were regarded as among the best in the state."

Various explanations have been advanced to account for these discrepancies, among them the much greater prevalence of single-parent families in the black community than among whites or Asians, as well as cultural differences between racial groups—reflected in parents' expectations of children, emphasis on academic achievement, and similar factors. This latter point is usually ignored, but pretending it does not exist has not done black students any favors or made the problem go away. One study, for instance, asked students of various races what grades they would have to get before they got in trouble with their parents. On average, Asian students responded that anything below an A– was liable to get them a lecture; for whites the threshold was B–, a full letter grade lower. But blacks and Hispanics reported that they got into trouble only for grades below C–.[12]

The occasional renegade black intellectual, like John McWhorter and Shelby Steele (and, more recently, Bill Cosby), has identified this as a problem the black community must address. But so hostile is the black establishment to observations like these that we have actually reached a point at which it is considered newsworthy, even courageous, when a prominent member of the black community simply steps forward and states the obvious.

THE FAULTY ARGUMENT ENDURES

Even in light of the above, some activists have held fast to the idea that desegregation is, in fact, the solution to the problem. They have merely modified the case for desegregation, arguing that its beneficial results can be achieved if it is accompanied by a host of substantial policy changes, including the use of culturally sensitive textbooks, the relaxation of disciplinary measures to take into account "cultural differences" between blacks and whites, and the abolition of hetero-geneous grouping or ability tracking (since grouping students by academic ability tends to segregate the races).[13] The main reason that the desegregation argument has survived is that, as we have seen, some progress was made in narrowing the black-white gap until about 1990, and the twenty-year period from about 1968 through 1988 saw a greater increase in the proportion of desegregated black students than any other two consecutive decades. Thus it has been easy to attribute these happy results to desegregation itself.

... *& THE* TRUTH

The black-white educational gap— which is as big as four grade levels in some subjects— is alive and well despite decades of desegregation efforts and has shown no greater improve- ment in integrated schools than in largely black ones.

The statistics, however, refuse to support that explanation. Between 1975 and 1988, the years of the greatest black improvement, black thirteen-year-olds in predominantly minority schools achieved essentially the same gains in reading scores as their counterparts in majority-white schools. Blacks in predominantly minority schools actually gained 10 points more in math than did blacks in majority-white schools. Other age groups show similar results. Education scholar David Armor reports that during the same period "age-nine blacks in segregated schools gained 12 points in reading and 17 points in math, compared with 11 points and 16 points, respectively, for blacks in desegregated schools. For age-seventeen blacks, those in segregated schools gained 34 points in reading and 22 points in math compared to 21 and 17 points, respectively, for those in desegregated schools." Overall, by 1990 there was a difference of only a few points in the reading and math scores of age-nine blacks in (de facto) segregated schools versus those in desegregated schools, and hardly any measurable difference at all in the scores of black seventeen-year-olds.[14]

With billions of dollars spent, black and white communities alike turned upside down through mandated busing schemes, and racial strife often aggravated rather than alleviated by forced integration, this is the state of things. In racially integrated schools, in charter schools, and in all kinds of presumably ideal conditions, the black-white achievement gap is not getting any smaller, contrary to the assurances of 1960s activists that integration at all costs would solve the problem. More money, more incentives, more racial integration—all of these things have been tried. But countless decent people to this day, terrified of being condemned as "racists"—or in the black community, ridiculed as traitors and Uncle Toms—hesitate to speak honestly about the subject or even to mention the statistics. Small wonder that so little progress gets made, or that historical myths about race become so firmly entrenched.

Given the emotional hypochondria that so often besets the "civil rights" establishment, anyone citing statistics like these can expect to be accused of favoring legal resegregation of the schools. (Such critics might consider looking in the mirror—their own forced busing policies wound up practically doing just that, as white families simply moved far enough away that their children couldn't be bused.) The point, rather, is that social scientists turned schools and neighborhoods upside down on the basis of a theory that had, and continues to have, no evidence to back it up. Someone really ought to call them on that.

WAS THE CIVIL WAR ALL ABOUT SLAVERY, OR WAS SOMETHING ELSE AT STAKE AS WELL?

★ ★

A ny discussion of the Civil War must begin with a point that professional historians will concede but that most Americans do not realize: Abraham Lincoln did not launch his invasion of the southern states in 1861 to abolish slavery. He said so repeatedly. His aim was to keep the Union together through force—a goal that took 1.5 million people dead, wounded, or missing to accomplish. In fact, Lincoln even said in his first inaugural address that he would support a constitutional amendment that would prevent the federal government from ever interfering with slavery in the states where it existed. Ironically, it would have been the Thirteenth Amendment.

The comic-book version of Lincoln to which nearly all schoolchildren are exposed portrays him as a champion of racial equality. But in a debate with Stephen Douglas in 1858, Lincoln argued that a "physical difference" between the white and black races prevented them from ever living together on terms of social and political equality, and that inasmuch as they could not so live, he favored assigning the superior position to the white race. Lincoln did nothing in his entire career in his home state of Illinois to challenge that state's treatment of blacks, who could not vote, testify in court against whites, serve on juries, or attend a public school system funded in part by their own tax dollars.

Neither were southerners uniformly in favor of slavery. Southern generals Stonewall Jackson and Robert E. Lee opposed slavery, the latter describing it as a "moral and political evil." James Henley Thornwell, one of the most influential southern theologians, put forth a plan for gradual emancipation at the time of the war. The letters and diaries of southern soldiers reveal that most of them fought on behalf of the principle of national self-determination and the right of self-government, the same principles they believed the American revolutionaries had fought to defend.[1]

Moreover, every other country in the western hemisphere that abolished slavery in the nineteenth century managed to do so peacefully. The money spent to wage Lincoln's war could have purchased the freedom of every single slave and given them all forty acres and a mule. And as Jeff Hummel observes in *Emancipating Slaves, Enslaving Free Men,* "The fact that emancipation overwhelmed such entrenched plantation economies as Cuba and Brazil suggests that slavery was politically moribund anyway."[2] He continues:

> Slavery was doomed politically even if Lincoln had permitted the small Gulf Coast Confederacy to depart in peace. The Republican-controlled Congress would have been able to work toward emancipation within the border states, where slavery was already declining. In due course the Radicals could have repealed the Fugitive Slave Law of 1850. With chattels fleeing across the border and raising slavery's enforcement costs, the peculiar institution's destruction within an independent cotton South was inevitable.[3]

In short, the matter is not nearly so neat and tidy as the popular caricature would suggest.

THE RISE OF THE MODERN STATE

Lincoln's informed defenders generally acknowledge all this and have the honesty to admit that when he called up those first 75,000

33 Questions About American History You're Not Supposed to Ask

militiamen in 1861 to put down the "rebellion" in the South, he had no intention of waging a war to abolish slavery. What they argue instead is that as the war progressed, the meaning of the northern war effort *evolved* in Lincoln's mind, becoming a war not only for the Union but also for human liberation. The more mystical among them suggest that this had in some sense been the war's purpose all along, but that only gradually did Lincoln himself become aware of the significance of the historical moment into which he had been placed.

Isn't it possible that the South's own self-understanding also evolved over the course of the war? Even if some people did believe they had seceded over slavery—as some certainly did—is it not possible that they, too, may eventually have begun to appreciate larger issues at stake in the conflict just as Lincoln is said to have done?

Emory University's Donald Livingston has identified one of these larger issues.[4] In the modern age, Livingston observes, we have seen what he calls federative polities giving way to modern states. A federative polity is one in which a variety of smaller jurisdictions exist— like families, voluntary organizations, towns and states, and in medieval Europe institutions like guilds, universities, and the Church. Each of these social authorities has powers and rights of its own that the central government cannot overturn. Each of them is also a potential source of resistance to the central government. Prior to the rise of the modern state, political leaders who desired centralization therefore found themselves up against the historic liberties of towns, guilds, universities, the Church, and similar corporate bodies.

It was in the federative polities of medieval Europe that the Western practice of liberty began to take root. Following the dissolution of the Roman Empire, no continent-wide empire took its place. "Instead of experiencing the hegemony of a universal empire," writes historian Ralph Raico, "Europe evolved into a mosaic of kingdoms, principalities, city-states, ecclesiastical domains, and other entities."[5] Historian Jean Baechler has argued that the decentralized nature of European political life, beginning in the Middle Ages, contributed to the development of liberty.[6] This multiplicity of jurisdictions meant that the prince risked losing population (and his tax base) if he engaged in excessive taxation or interference in his people's economic lives—they could simply move to another political unit close by.

The very idea of sovereignty, according to which every political order must possess a single irresistible voice, competent and forceful enough to make its will felt throughout society, was essentially alien to medieval political thought and practice. Institutions other than the central government possessed rights that no "sovereign"—whether a king or a democratic majority—could simply overturn at will.

Thomas Hobbes, on the other hand, set out parameters for the modern state in *Leviathan* (1651) that developed into unexamined premises that later thinkers (even putative opponents like John Locke) took for granted. The modern state about which Hobbes theorized is one in which the central government is absolutely supreme, and in which society is thought of as being composed not of independent social authorities, as in a federative polity, but of a simple aggregate of individuals. There are no truly independent social authorities in the modern state because nothing is thought to be independent of, or to have existed prior to, the central government. All potential for group resistance is gone; mere individuals, by contrast, are typically helpless against a strong central government. Instead of a series of layers, as in a federative polity, society is here conceived of as a single, flat plain.

> THE MYTH ...
>
> ---
>
> *The Civil War was a simple morality play between supporters of slavery on the one hand and opponents on the other.*

In a federative polity, when another social authority blocked the power of the central government—medieval towns, for example, won many of their liberties by confronting the king and making demands of him, particularly when he needed their aid during war—it was a normal event, even a virtue. But the modern state trains its citizens to think otherwise. When another institution attempts to resist the encroachments of the central government of a modern state, it is guilty of *treason*. What was once a virtue now becomes the gravest possible crime. The nation, citizens are taught to believe, is "one and indivis-

33 Questions About American History You're Not Supposed to Ask

ible." This new morality inclines the people to view the central government's suppression of lesser bodies as something natural and normal, and resistance by those bodies as reprehensible and unpatriotic.

Thus in a federative polity autonomous institutions with liberties of their own sometimes had to protect those liberties by resisting the center. Nothing in the modern state, on the other hand, can seriously be described as autonomous except the central government itself. Every other institution is fundamentally subject to and inferior to the central government, and no institution possesses truly inherent and inalienable liberties. Whatever liberties any lesser institution possesses are considered gifts of the central government, to be revoked at will, rather than held *by right*. No longer restrained by these smaller authorities and their potential for resistance, the central governments of modern states became capable of all manner of atrocities, of which the twentieth century afforded one gruesome example after another.

Now what has all this to do with the American Civil War? That war began the transformation of the United States from a federative polity into a modern state. Europeans understood that the war amounted to an attempt to transform the decentralized American system into a unitary modern state; in December 1866 the British *Spectator* was delighted to write: "The American Revolution marches fast towards its goal—the change of a Federal Commonwealth into a Democratic Republic, one and indivisible."[7] What had once been a decentralized system in which the states, the Union's constituent parts, actively resisted the central government on a great many occasions in defense of their liberties would become a unitary modern state in which any such resistance would henceforth be demonized as treasonous. The war to prevent

> ... & THE TRUTH
>
> *For starters, Lincoln aimed to keep the Union together, even if that meant protecting slavery, and many southerners viewed slavery as an evil. But for the South, there was a larger issue at stake: preserving the last check on the power of the federal government.*

southern secession became a war against the very idea of secession and in favor of a consolidated central government. Livingston's conclusion is that we must give the moral benefit of the doubt to people who were fighting to prevent the destruction of America's federative character and who would instead have given the world the moral example of a federal republic that acknowledged the sovereignty of its constituent parts.

"THE STAKE WHICH WAS LOST AT RICHMOND"

The best southern thinkers, though of course they could not have known just how strongly vindicated they would be after the atrocities of the twentieth century and the crimes of the modern state, understood this principle. Consider the lament of Alexander Stephens, vice president of the Confederate States of America:

> If centralism is ultimately to prevail; if our entire system of free Institutions as established by our common ancestors is to be subverted, and an Empire is to be established in their stead; if that is to be the last scene of the great tragic drama now being enacted: then, be assured, that we of the South will be acquitted, not only in our own consciences, but in the judgment of mankind, of all responsibility for so terrible a catastrophe, and from all guilt of so great a crime against humanity.[8]

Likewise, Robert E. Lee wrote to the great British libertarian Lord Acton:

> I yet believe that the maintenance of the rights and authority reserved to the states and to the people, not only are essential to the adjustment and balance of the general system, but the safeguard to the continuance of a free government. I consider it as the chief source of stability to our political system, whereas the consolidation of the states into one vast republic, sure to be aggressive abroad and despotic at home, will be the certain precursor of that ruin which has overwhelmed all those that have preceded it.[9]

"Had the Confederate States of America survived," Livingston argues, "the world would have had the model of a vast-scale federative polity with a strong central authority explicitly checked by the ultimate right of a state to secede." It would have shown the world that an alternative existed to the modern state, its crimes, and its destruction of competing power centers in society. Instead, movements for national unification (as in Germany and Italy) were and are portrayed as indisputably progressive and as fully in line with the forward march of history, when in fact the world would have been spared a good deal of grief had a decentralized political order remained the rule in central and southern Europe.

Given its aggressive and destructive character, how had the idea of the centralized modern state caught on in the first place? An important part of the answer is that people were promised that the modern state could protect them from the oppressions of other social and political authorities. Thus the modern state could end slavery in one fell swoop, as in the American case. But as Livingston points out, those who favored the modern state for such reasons failed to read the fine print. For it could also carry out great atrocities, of a kind the world had never before seen. State slavery would reemerge, not only in the form of the Soviet gulag and the Nazi concentration camps, but also in the form of universal military conscription, a largely modern idea. Nearly three times as many men would be killed in just four years in World War I as there were slaves in the South. (World War II would take more than 50 million lives.) Tens of millions would perish in slave labor camps, dwarfing the 11 million slaves brought to the New World (5 percent of whom went to North America) in four hundred years of the slave trade.[10]

What must be emphasized here, according to Livingston, is that what was primarily responsible for this staggering destruction was neither advanced technology nor the wickedness of leaders like Hitler and Stalin. Even the most powerful monarchs of centuries past could not have engaged in such destruction, since their authority was hemmed in by other social authorities that had the power to thwart them. The very structure of the modern state, which destroyed or co-opted all lesser associations and amassed all power at the center, made these terrible atrocities possible.[11]

It was his forebodings about the modern state, rather than any nostalgia for slavery, that so saddened Lord Acton about the South's defeat, for that defeat would surely bolster the cause of those who pointed to political centralization as the wave of the future. In a November 1866 letter to Lee, Acton wrote:

> I saw in States' rights the only availing check upon the absolutism of the sovereign will, and secession filled me with hope, not as the destruction but as the redemption of Democracy. . . . Therefore I deemed that you were fighting the battles of our liberty, our progress, and our civilization, and I mourn for the stake which was lost at Richmond more deeply than I rejoice over that which was saved at Waterloo.[12]

These are some of the reasons that so many people who abhor slavery have nevertheless rejected the standard morality play about the war that is peddled in the typical classroom and in popular culture. With the destruction of state sovereignty that resulted from the northern victory went both the main institutional restraint on the power of the federal government as well as the important moral example of a polity organized along different lines from those of the centralized states that would come to dominate the political landscape in the nineteenth and twentieth centuries and beyond. That, and not a fondness for slavery, explains why Lord Acton, the great British classical liberal, sympathized with the southern cause. Even radical libertarians like the nineteenth century's Lysander Spooner and the twentieth century's Murray Rothbard—often referred to as "Mr. Libertarian"—have been sharply critical of Abraham Lincoln and the war he waged.[13] It is not difficult to see why.

There are still a good many libertarians and conservatives who, denigrating state sovereignty and political decentralization, seek to secure liberty by means of a strong central government, kept in check by periodic elections, that protects people's individual rights. That this model has not exactly been a smashing success—just compare our present federal government with the limited and modest institution James Madison describes in *Federalist* No. 45—ought to make such thinkers reconsider their enthusiasm for the superficially plausible but dramatically failed project of liberty through centralization whose American founding father was Abraham Lincoln.

CAN THE PRESIDENT, ON HIS OWN AUTHORITY, SEND TROOPS ANYWHERE IN THE WORLD HE WANTS?

★ ★

Ever since the Korean War, Article II, Section 2 of the Constitution—which refers to the president as the "Commander in Chief of the Army and Navy of the United States"—has been interpreted to mean that the president may act with an essentially free hand in foreign affairs, or at the very least that he may send men into battle without consulting Congress. Democrats and Republicans alike have insisted upon this interpretation, which may help to explain the bipartisan silence on the issue. Both parties have a vested interest in making sure it is never raised.

But what the Framers of the Constitution meant by that clause was that *once war has been declared,* it is the president's responsibility as commander in chief to direct the war. The president acting alone was authorized only to repel sudden attacks. (Hence the decision to withhold from him the power to "declare" war, not to "make" war, which was thought to be a necessary emergency power in case of foreign attack.)

The Framers were abundantly clear in assigning to Congress what political scientist David Gray Adler has called "senior status in a partnership with the president for the purpose of conducting foreign policy." Consider what the Constitution has to say about foreign affairs. Congress possesses the power "to regulate Commerce with foreign Nations," "to raise and support Armies," to "grant Letters of Marque and Reprisal," to "provide for the common Defense," and even "to declare War." Congress shares with the president the power to make treaties and to appoint ambassadors. As for the president himself, he is assigned only two powers relating to foreign affairs: he is commander in chief of the armed forces, and he has the power to receive ambassadors.[1]

For the Framers to repose such foreign policy authority in the legislative rather than the executive branch of government, Adler notes, was a clear and deliberate break from the British model of government, in which the executive branch (in effect, the monarch) possessed all such rights, including the exclusive right to declare war.[2] The Framers believed that history amply testified to the executive's penchant for war. As James Madison wrote to Thomas Jefferson, "The constitution supposes, what the History of all Governments demonstrates, that the Executive is the branch of power most interested in war, and most prone to it. It has accordingly with studied care vested the question of war in the Legislature."[3] (Madison elsewhere wrote: "Hence it has grown into an axiom that the executive is the department of power most distinguished by its propensity to war: hence it is the practice of all states, in proportion as they are free, to disarm this propensity of its influence.")[4]

At the Constitutional Convention, Pierce Butler was for "vesting the power in the President, who will have all the requisite qualities, and will not make war but when the nation will support it." Butler's motion did not receive so much as a second.

James Wilson assured the Pennsylvania ratifying convention, "This system will not hurry us into war; it is calculated to guard against it. It will not be in the power of a single man, or a single body of men, to involve us in such distress; for the important power of declaring war is vested in the legislature at large: this declaration must be made with the concurrence of the House of Representatives: from this circumstance we may draw a certain conclusion that nothing but our interest can draw us into war."[5]

In *Federalist* No. 69, Alexander Hamilton explained that the president's authority "would be nominally the same with that of the King of Great Britain, but in substance much inferior to it. It would amount to nothing more than the supreme command and direction of the military and naval forces, as first general and admiral of the confederacy; while that of the British king extends to the declaring of war, and to the raising and regulating of fleets and armies; all which by the constitution under consideration would appertain to the Legislature."[6]

Abraham Lincoln explained the principle this way:

Allow the President to invade a neighboring nation, whenever *he* shall deem it necessary to repel an invasion, and you allow him to do so, *whenever he may choose to say* he deems it necessary for such purpose—and you allow him to make war at pleasure. . . . Study to see if you can fix *any limit* to his power in this respect, after you have given him so much as you propose. If, to-day, he should choose to say he thinks it necessary to invade Canada, to prevent the British from invading us, how could you stop him? You may say to him, "I see no probability of the British invading us" but he will say to you "be silent; I see it, if you don't." . . .

The provision of the Constitution giving the war-making power to Congress, was dictated, as I understand it, by the following reasons. Kings had always been involving and impoverishing their people in wars, pretending generally, if not always, that the good of the people was the object. This, our Convention understood to be the most oppressive of all Kingly oppressions; and they resolved to so frame the Constitution that no one man should hold the power of bringing this oppression upon us. But your view destroys the whole matter, and places our President where kings have always stood.[7]

According to John Bassett Moore, the great authority on international law who (among other credentials) occupied the first professorship of international law at Columbia University, "There can hardly be room for doubt that the framers of the constitution, when they vested in Congress the power to declare war, never imagined that they were leaving it to the executive to use the military and naval forces of the United States all over the world for the purpose of actually coercing other nations, occupying their territory, and killing their soldiers and citizens, all according to his own notions of the fitness of things, as long as he refrained from calling his action war or persisted in calling it peace."[8]

In conformity with this understanding, George Washington's operations on his own authority against the Indians were confined to defensive measures, conscious as he was that the approval of Congress would be necessary for anything further. "The Constitution vests the power of declaring war with Congress," he said, "therefore no offensive expedition of importance can be undertaken until after they have deliberated upon the subject, and authorized such a measure."[9]

Today someone advancing this position can expect to be told by supporters of modern presidential war powers that the president has sent troops into battle hundreds of times without congressional authorization, and that these many examples prove congressional authorization to be unnecessary.

Let's see how well the claim stands up.

A CLOSER LOOK AT THE RECORD

Supporters of broad executive war powers have sometimes appealed to the Quasi War with France, in the closing years of the eighteenth century, as an example of unilateral war-making on the part of the president. But that example is completely invalid. According to Francis Wormuth, an authority on war powers and the Constitution, President John Adams "took absolutely no independent action. Congress passed a series of acts that amounted, so the Supreme Court said, to a declaration of imperfect war; and Adams complied with these statutes."[10] (Wormuth's reference to the Supreme Court recalls a decision rendered in the wake of the Quasi War, in which the Court ruled that Congress could either declare war or approve hostilities by means of statutes that authorized an undeclared war. The Quasi War was an example of the latter case.)

Congress passed a law in April 1798 that increased the size of the navy. When asked by Secretary of War James McHenry whether the legislation gave the president the power to initiate hostilities, Hamilton (who was appointed major general of the army that year) replied:

> Not having seen the law which provides the *naval armament,* I cannot tell whether it gives any new power to the President; that is, any power whatever with regard to the employment of the ships. If not, and he is left at the foot of the Constitution, as I understand to be the case, I am not ready to say that he has any other power than merely to employ the ships as convoys, with authority to *repel* force by *force* (but not to capture) and to repress hostilities within our waters, including a marine league from our coasts. Anything beyond this must fall under the idea of *reprisals,* and requires the sanctions of that department which is to declare *or make war.*[11]

Thus according to Hamilton (normally a proponent of a strong executive), the war-making power was still very much in the hands of Congress, where the Framers had placed it.

Another incident frequently cited on behalf of a general presidential power to deploy American forces and commence hostilities involves Thomas Jefferson's policy toward the Barbary states, North African powers that demanded protection money from governments whose ships sailed the Mediterranean. Immediately prior to Jefferson's inauguration in 1801 Congress passed naval legislation that, among other things, provided for six frigates that "shall be officered and manned as the President of the United States may direct." It was to this instruction and authority that Jefferson appealed when he ordered American ships to the Mediterranean. In the event of a declaration of war on the United States by the Barbary powers, these ships were to "protect our commerce & chastise their insolence—by sinking, burning or destroying their ships & Vessels wherever you shall find them."[12]

In late 1801 the pasha of Tripoli did declare war on the United States. Jefferson sent a small force to the area to protect American ships and citizens against potential aggression, but he insisted that he was "unauthorized by the Constitution, without the sanction of Congress, to go beyond the line of defense"; Congress alone could authorize "measures of offense also." Thus Jefferson told Congress: "I communicate [to you] all material information on this subject, that in the exercise of this important function confided by the Constitution to the Legislature exclusively their judgment may form itself on a knowledge and consideration of every circumstance of weight."[13]

Jefferson consistently deferred to Congress in his dealings with the Barbary pirates. According to Louis Fisher, one of the nation's top authorities on presidential war powers,

> Recent studies by the Justice Department and statements made during congressional debate, imply that Jefferson took military measures against the Barbary powers without seeking the approval or authority of Congress. In fact, in at least ten statutes, Congress explicitly authorized military action by Presidents Jefferson and Madison. Congress passed legislation in 1802 to authorize the President to equip armed vessels to protect commerce and seamen in the Atlantic, the Mediterranean, and adjoining seas. The statute authorized American ships to seize vessels belonging to the Bey of Tripoli, with the captured property distributed to those who brought the vessels into port. Additional legislation in 1804 gave explicit support for "warlike operations against the regency of Tripoli, or any other of the Barbary powers."[14]

Consider also Jefferson's statement to Congress in late 1805 regarding a boundary dispute with Spain over Louisiana and Florida. According to Jefferson, Spain appeared to have an "intention to advance on our possessions until they shall be repressed by an opposing force. Considering that Congress alone is constitutionally invested with the power of changing our condition from peace to war, I have thought it my duty to await their authority for using force. . . . But the course to be pursued will require the command of means which it belongs to Congress exclusively to yield or to deny. To them I communicate every fact material for their information and the documents necessary to enable them to judge for themselves. To their wisdom, then, I look for the course I am to pursue, and will pursue with sincere zeal that which they shall approve."[15]

James Madison, Jefferson's successor, likewise respected the constitutional role of Congress in matters of war. On the eve of the War of 1812, Madison's war message referred to declaring war as "a solemn question which the Constitution wisely confides to the legislative department of the Government."[16] Congress did in fact vote to declare war on Britain.

In 1824 an apprehensive Colombian government, fearful of an attack by France, asked John Quincy Adams, the American secretary of state, whether in light of the Monroe Doctrine (which urged European nations not to consider the Americas as possible subjects for any future colonization) the United States intended to resist such outside intervention. In his diary Adams summed up what a cabinet meeting decided on the subject: "The Colombia republic to maintain its own independence. Hope that France and the Holy Allies will not resort to force against it. If they should, the power to determine our resistance is in Congress. The movements of the Executive will be as heretofore expressed. I am to draft an answer." He then told the Colombian government that "by the Constitution of the United States, the ultimate decision of this question belongs to the Legislative Department of the Government."[17] (As it turned out, France never invaded.)

The Mexican War of 1846–48 is another instructive episode in the history of presidential war powers. On May 11, 1846, President James Polk called for war against Mexico after announcing to Congress that Mexico had shed "American blood upon American soil." Two days later Congress voted overwhelmingly for war, though some people remained suspicious about the war's precise origins.

Abraham Lincoln, then a congressman from Illinois, introduced the "spot resolution" into Congress, demanding to know the exact spot on which hostilities had broken out. It turned out that Mexico had fired upon American troops not in indisputably American territory but in precisely the disputed land—the area between the Rio

Grande and Nueces Rivers—that had provoked diplomatic hostility between the two nations in the first place. Polk had neglected to mention that in his war message.

Senator John Middleton Clayton said, "I do not see on what principle it can be shown that the President, without consulting Congress and obtaining its sanction for the procedure, has a right to send an army to take up a position where, as it must have been foreseen, the inevitable consequence would be war."[18] In 1848 Congress voted 85–81 to censure Polk, arguing that the president had abused his power. The war, the resolution said, had been "unnecessarily and unconstitutionally begun by the President of the United States."[19]

On closer inspection, therefore, the nineteenth century turns out not to provide the precedents for presidential war-making that its proponents would prefer to see. Not until the closing years of that century do we see anything approaching the staggering authority that they would grant the president, and even then we see it only in miniature.

Cornell University's Walter LaFeber pinpoints the origins of modern presidential war powers in an obscure incident from 1900. In 1898 a group of anti-foreign Chinese fighters known to the West as the Boxers rose up in protest against foreign exploitation and extraterritorial privileges in their country. They targeted Christian missionaries and Chinese converts, as well as French and Belgian engineers. After the German minister was killed in 1900, several nations sent troops to restore order amid the growing terror. McKinley contributed five thousand American troops. This apparently minor action, however, was pregnant with consequences, as LaFeber notes:

> McKinley took a historic step in creating a new, twentieth-century presidential power. He dispatched the five thousand troops without consulting Congress, let alone obtaining a declaration of war, to fight the Boxers who were supported by the Chinese government. . . . Presidents had previously used such force against nongovernmental groups that threatened U.S. interests and citizens. It was now used, however, against recognized governments, and without obeying the Constitution's provisions about who was to declare war.[20]

Now what of those "hundreds" of cases of presidential war-making? This argument—surprise—originated with the U.S. government itself. At the time of the Korean War a number of congressmen contended that "history will show that on more than 100 occasions in the life of this Republic the President as Commander in Chief has ordered the fleet or the troops to do certain things which involved the risk of war" without the consent of Congress.[21] In 1966, in defense of the Vietnam War, the State Department adopted a similar line: "Since the Constitution was adopted there have been at least 125 instances in which the President has ordered the armed forces to take action or maintain positions abroad without obtaining prior congressional authorization, starting with the 'undeclared war' with France (1798–1800)."[22]

We have already seen that the war with France in no way lends support to those who favor broad presidential war powers. As for the rest, presidential scholar Edward S. Corwin pointed out that this lengthy list of alleged precedents consisted mainly of "fights with pirates, landings of small naval contingents on barbarous or semi-barbarous coasts, the dispatch of small bodies of troops to chase bandits or cattle rustlers across the Mexican border, and the like."[23]

The claim that the president may act with a free hand in foreign affairs, dispatching troops and committing them to offensive operations at will, is therefore absolutely indefensible. Supporters of this position are counting *chases of cattle rustlers* as examples of presidential war-making and as precedents for sending millions of Americans into war with foreign governments on the other side of the globe.

Senator Robert A. Taft—known in his day as "Mr. Republican"— aptly summed up the matter when in 1951 he said of the Korean War: "My conclusion, therefore, is that in the case of Korea, where a war was already under way, we had no right to send troops to a nation, with whom we had no treaty, to defend it against attack by another nation, no matter how unprincipled that aggression might be, unless the whole matter was submitted to Congress and a declaration of war or some other direct authority obtained."[24]

In the wake of the Vietnam War, perceived by some Americans as an example of presidential war power run amok, Congress passed the War Powers Resolution of 1973. As the history books would have it, Congress thereby restrained presidential war powers and reasserted traditional congressional prerogatives in foreign policy as envisioned by the Constitution. But if anything, the resolution—sympathetic mythology to the contrary notwithstanding—actually emboldened the president and codified executive war-making powers that would have astonished the Framers of the Constitution.

The War Powers Resolution certainly did not restore the proper constitutional balance between president and Congress in matters of war. It permits the president to commit troops to offensive operations anywhere in the world he chooses and for any reason without the consent of Congress (though he should consult them in advance "in every possible instance," a toothless proviso that means nothing), for a period of sixty days, though he must at least inform Congress of his action within forty-eight hours. After the initial sixty days he must secure congressional authorization for the action to continue. He then has another thirty days to withdraw the troops if such authorization is not forthcoming. Until the War Powers Resolution, no constitutional or statutory authority could be cited on behalf of such behavior on the part of the president. Now it became fixed law, despite violating the letter and the spirit of the Constitution.

Furthermore, it so happens that thanks to a loophole in the resolution (in Section 5, part b), the sixty-day clock begins only if and when the president reports to Congress specifically under Section 4(a)(1) of the resolution. Surprise, surprise: presidents have therefore reported to Congress in a more generic manner (e.g., "consistent with the War Powers Resolution") rather than expressly "pursuant to" that specific section.[25]

Even still, in a few cases presidents have acted as if the sixty-day limit were in effect, perhaps out of political considerations (even if from a strictly legal point of view it was not). But Bill Clinton's multiyear military intervention in Bosnia alone, without so much as a nod in the direction of Congress, made perfectly clear that the resolution was effectively a dead letter.[26]

Another problem is that the War Powers Resolution leads opponents of presidential actions to believe they have some recourse when in fact the options offered them are almost completely ineffectual. For example, those opposing a president's military intervention have sometimes appealed to the courts for redress, waving the resolution before federal judges. For a variety of reasons, those judges have hesitated to intervene, which is why Louis Fisher and David Gray Adler, two experts on presidential war powers, call such judicial challenges "futile." Fisher and Adler also point out that Congress gets sidetracked by "fruitless legislative debate over whether presidential 'consultation' had been sufficient, whether presidential reports were timely and complete, and whether the president should have reported under Section 4(a)(1), 4(a)(2), or some other provision." Such diversions prevent Congress from taking concrete steps to stop the president, such as refusing to fund a president's military action.[27]

THE MYTH ...

The Constitution gives the president an essentially free hand in foreign affairs, allowing him to send troops into battle without consulting Congress.

A partial repeal of the resolution was attempted in 1995, but the slimmed-down version would actually have accentuated presidential power and eclipsed Congress even further. House Speaker Newt Gingrich, supposedly the great opponent of Bill Clinton, called on the House "to, at least on paper, increase the power of President Clinton." Gingrich wanted to "strengthen the current Democratic President because he is the President of the United States. And the President of the United States on a bipartisan basis deserves to be strengthened in foreign affairs and strengthened in national security." Some forty-four Republicans abandoned Gingrich—these were still the days when at

33 Questions About American History You're Not Supposed to Ask

least some Republicans thought presidential power was something to restrain—and the effort failed.[28]

It was in the context of the Clinton years that an exasperated Fisher and Adler called for repeal of the War Powers Resolution, a law for which "there is no constitutional warrant," they said.[29] Clinton dispatched the military dozens of times during his two terms.[30] Most noteworthy from a legal point of view was the 1999 Kosovo intervention. Clinton, siding with the Muslims of Kosovo and acting through NATO, orchestrated a bombing campaign against Serbia that extended from March until June 1999. But he didn't just do so without consulting Congress, as had become customary and unremarkable among modern presidents. He carried on with the bombing for months *after* the House voted against legislation to authorize the air war. David Gray Adler called it "one of the most flagrant acts of usurpation of the war power in the history of the Republic," since it was "the first time in our history that a president waged war in the face of a direct congressional refusal to authorize the war."[31]

WHAT WOULD THE FRAMERS SAY?

In 2002, on the eve of war with Iraq, Congressman Ron Paul (R-TX) insisted, as he had throughout the Clinton years, that if the country were to go to war, the Constitution required that Congress approve a declaration of war—not simply a cowardly resolution authorizing the president to use force if and when he chose, thereby

> ... *&* THE TRUTH
>
> *In a deliberate break from the British tradition, the Framers of the Constitution specifically invested the legislative branch,* not *the executive, with war-making powers. Today Republicans and Democrats alike claim that it is outdated to believe the president cannot send troops into battle without congressional approval, but the historical justifications they push to make this case are misleading or just plain wrong.*

abdicating their constitutional authority to the White House. He was told by prominent Republicans that his position was outdated and that things weren't done that way anymore.

A stunned Congressman Paul replied, in effect, that he could find no expiration date on his copy of the Constitution.

IS IT TRUE THAT DURING WORLD WAR II

"AMERICANS NEVER HAD IT SO GOOD"?

★ ★

Whenever an earthquake, a flood, or a tornado strikes, some reporter somewhere claims that on net it will boost the local economy, since the rebuilding effort will create jobs and increase business for local merchants. Similarly, whenever a war breaks out, the same reporter can be counted on to emphasize the economic stimulus it will allegedly confer.

As if on cue, in May 2004 the *Washington Post* published an article headlined "Across America, War Means Jobs." Although it acknowledged that the matter wasn't quite so simple, the article nevertheless quoted a great many people who asserted that war was a boon for the economy. "If it wasn't for [Defense Department] contracting," said Brian Smith of Columbia Sewing Company, "we would not be here, and 200 people would be out of a job." Roanoke mayor Betty Slay Ziglar was thrilled: "These people have grown up sewing in textile plants, and there are so few now. They were desperate to have jobs, and it's going to expand again. I'm so grateful." Appliance salesman Gary Gayer told the *Post,* "The economy is always helped by war. That's just a fact."[1]

War does stimulate *certain sectors* of the economy, of course. But it is illogical to equate stimulus in certain sectors with prosperity for the

American people *as a whole.* And that, after all, is the whole point of economics: to consider every policy or event not simply in terms of its short-run, visible effects on parts of the economy—anyone can make simple observations like that—but also in terms of its *long-run effects on the whole economy.*

It was with this point in mind that Frédéric Bastiat, writing in the mid-nineteenth century, exposed the "broken window" fallacy. A shop window broken by the owner's "careless son" is said to benefit the economy, since the company that fixes the window enjoys a "stimulus," which in turn is passed along to those with whom the window company does business. What this analysis overlooks is that the man would have spent his money on other things if he had not needed to buy new glass to replace his window. The "stimulus" that would have been bestowed on, say, the bookstore, where he could have spent his money, now never occurs because he had to replace his window. Had the window not been broken, the shopkeeper would have had a window and a book. Now he has only a window.

The repair of the window is *what is seen,* and focusing on it leads poor logicians to conclude that the breakage was actually a boon. The lack of a book *is not seen* but is no less a consequence of the unfortunate incident.

The same kind of analysis can be fruitfully applied to war. The jobs created for the production of weapons and other military equipment, as well as the jobs in the armed forces, are what is seen. But they are paid for by taxing the private economy. Financing wartime activities diminishes private incomes and thus the ability of Americans to buy the goods they need. And because people and capital goods are now producing war-related items and services, fewer are available to produce goods for consumer needs. Those consumer goods that are now not produced, because the funds to produce them (and to employ people in producing them) have been siphoned off into war production, are what is not seen. The fact that some high-profile jobs are created is only the beginning of the story; other jobs that had catered to the consumer have now been destroyed. Consumers, now with less disposable income, cannot spend what they used to, and some private production must come to an end.

Wartime economic conditions include other negative effects as well. In extreme cases, the government rations certain crucial goods to ensure adequate supplies for the military. During World War II, for example, supposedly a time of great domestic prosperity, consumers suffered from (among other things) the effects of price controls and the deprivation that accompanies rationing. It was difficult to obtain adequate supplies of quality gasoline, rubber, meat, sugar, and a great many other products, and it was altogether impossible to purchase new homes, cars, or appliances, since the government had banned their production.

Quality deterioration was one way that manufacturers dealt with the controls. "Fat was added to hamburger," notes economic historian Gene Smiley. "The butterfat content of milk was reduced. Cornstarch was added to spices. Coffee was stretched with fillers." Between 1939 and 1943 nineteen of twenty candy bars were reduced in size, thereby concealing what was in effect a 23 percent price increase. Similar effects were felt in clothing. One official, says Smiley, testified that "quality deterioration took forms such as men's shorts made of cheesecloth with enough added sizing to give it form until washed once; women's slips made of coarse, heavily sized muslin; 'water-resistant' baby pants that allowed a third of a glass of water to drain through after being washed once; and cotton sweaters that were so loosely knit they could not hold their shape."[2]

Even when outright rationing is not undertaken, government purchases nevertheless distort the economy. For example, large purchases of steel will lead to price increases, making it more difficult for private businesses that use steel to meet their competition in a global market. If the higher prices attract new steel producers, this new production comes at the cost of abandoning other industries, thus further skewing the economy in favor of the government's preferences over those of the consumer.[3]

WARTIME PROSPERITY?

Consider this approach, which I have used in my own classroom. In a classroom with five equal rows of students, the first four rows represent the working population during the latter 1930s, while the last row represents the roughly one-fifth of the labor force that was officially unemployed. (The average unemployment rate from 1933 to 1940 was 18 percent—nearly one-fifth of the labor force.) That one row does not contribute to production at all. The other four rows are engaged in producing consumer goods—which, for simplicity's sake, we shall limit to food and clothing. A modest portion of the earnings of the first four rows is devoted to relief payments to the unemployed fifth row.

Now think about the working population during the war. During the war some 40 percent of the labor force was either serving in the armed forces, employed by the armed forces on a civilian basis, employed in the defense industry, or unemployed. The last two rows of students, therefore, now represent this bloc of the labor force. Now only the first three rows are producing food and clothing. One full row has been diverted from the production of those things, so there are now fewer of them for everyone, and they will tend to be more expensive than they would otherwise have been. To top it off, it is out of the paychecks of the students in the first three rows that the students in the last two rows receive their salaries. Ask the students in the first three rows, who represent the productive economy, how prosperous they feel now. Is the class as a whole more prosperous? Of course not: we have simply redistributed resources, and in ways that produce enormous deadweight losses for society in general.[4]

Fewer, dearer goods and less money with which to buy them: there is your wartime prosperity. And that is not to mention all the wealth that could have been produced if the requisite labor and material inputs had not been diverted into war production.

It is no answer to say that the armed forces and the munitions are necessary in order to win whatever war it is. True as that may be, it is not the issue here. The question is, *Does war make Americans more prosperous?*

THE BIZARRE AND DANGEROUS CONVENTIONAL WISDOM

The view that war brings prosperity had until recently become entrenched as the conventional wisdom, particularly in historians' treatments of World War II. The war, we are told, lifted the country out of the Great Depression. Scholars on the Left and the Right alike can be found predictably repeating this claim. Seymour Melman sums up the conventional view: "The economy was producing more guns and more butter. . . . Americans never had it so good."[5]

As late as 2004 I actually thought recent scholarship had at last corrected this bizarre and dangerous misunderstanding of a central episode of our country's economic history, finally proving that the alleged "wartime prosperity" had been, and logically *had* to be, only an illusion. Then, in an appearance on a major radio program that pitted me against a distinguished professor several decades my senior, the myth resurfaced all over again. I explained why the idea of wartime prosperity was, on the face of it, obviously a fantasy no different from the fallacies we hear all the time from the mainstream media about the jobs that earthquakes and floods will bring to their devastated areas. My opponent, on the other hand, simply pointed to the national income statistics of the early 1940s, which reveal a tremendous economic boom.

> ... & THE TRUTH
>
> *The "wartime prosperity" that historians frequently describe was nothing but an illusion. World War II was in fact a period of deprivation. Thanks to government rationing and the diversion of so much of the private sector's efforts to war-related work, consumer goods were less readily available and more expensive, and people had less money with which to buy those goods.*

A more egregious lack of acquaintance with modern scholarship can hardly be imagined. Since the 1990s important scholarly work has completely undercut the fable of economic prosperity during World War II. This scholarship has directly confronted the typical arguments: the wonderful GDP figures for the war, the incredible 20 percent annual growth rates from 1941 to 1943, and so on. Simply put, *these statistics are completely meaningless.*

Robert Higgs, one of the finest living American economic historians, has been producing scholarly work for years that forces historians who might be inclined to accept the idea of wartime prosperity during the early 1940s to rethink their assumptions and take a good, hard look at the statistics on which they have relied. That something was seriously wrong with official GDP data during the war years should be obvious, says Higgs:

> Consider that between 1940 and 1944, real GDP increased at an average annual rate of 13 percent—a growth spurt wholly out of line with any experienced before or since. Moreover, that extraordinary growth took place notwithstanding the movement of some 16 million men (equivalent to 28.6 percent of the total labor force of 1940) into the armed forces at some time during the war and the replacement of those prime workers mainly by teenagers, women with little or no previous experience in the labor market, and elderly men. Is it plausible that an economy subject to such severe and abruptly imposed human-resource constraints could generate a growth spurt far greater than any other in its entire history? Further, is it plausible that when the great majority of the servicemen returned to the civilian labor force—some 9 million of them in the year following V-J Day—while millions of their relatively unproductive wartime replacements left the labor force, the economy's real output would fall by 22 percent from 1945 to 1947?[6]

Gene Smiley, with Higgs one of a small but growing number of dissenters, likewise concludes in his *The American Economy in the Twentieth*

Century, "The national income data showing such amazing prosperity during the war is simply not believable."[7] Similarly, Ohio University economists Richard Vedder and Lowell Gallaway warn that "aggregate economic statistics need to be viewed with a skeptical eye, particularly in periods such as this where there are pronounced governmental interventions in markets."[8]

A central problem is that no meaningful national-product accounting is possible without market prices. And the U.S. economy during World War II did not generate real market prices. It was a command economy full of distorted prices. "In a command economy," Higgs explains, "the fundamental accounting difficulty is that the authorities suppress and replace the only genuinely meaningful manifestation of people's valuations, namely, free market prices."[9] The prices the U.S. government paid for the goods and services it bought were essentially arbitrary in that they had no foundation in consumer choice, as all other prices do. When the government places more of the economy into the command system (with spillover effects on the nominally private economy that remains outside the government's immediate control), the resulting output figures become more and more tainted by arbitrariness.

GDP figures are especially arbitrary during economic conditions like those of World War II, a time when at least two-fifths of national output was part of the war economy, and large classes of the remainder were controlled in one way or another (and thus arbitrarily priced).[10] Adding up a whole bunch of arbitrary, nonsense numbers yields nothing but a gigantic, arbitrary, nonsense number.[11] And yet it is nonsense numbers like these—that is, the GDP figures for the war years—on which even professional economic historians have relied in painting a picture of wartime prosperity.

One way economists estimate a country's capacity to produce is to draw a constant rate-of-growth line connecting the output produced in two benchmark years. Higgs did exactly that for the years 1929 and 1948, drawing a line depicting the rate at which the U.S. economy would have grown in the absence of the unusual conditions prevailing during the Depression on the one hand and the war on the other. Not surprisingly, he found that the United States produced well below capacity during the 1930s, the decade of the Depression. But during the war years he found that the American economy produced *far above* its production capacity—a contradiction in terms, which is why Higgs contends that "the apparent super-trend wartime boom in output was nothing but an artifact of an unjustifiable accounting system."[12]

Another problem with taking these GDP statistics at their face value is that we are also forced to accept what they tell us about the extremely prosperous year of 1946. As the official statistics would have it, the U.S. suffered a terrible depression in that year. Real GNP fell by more than 20 percent in 1946 alone, the worst single-year downturn in American history. Real output fell by 22.7 percent from 1944 to 1947.[13] But the Great Depression of 1946 is every bit as much a phantom as the "wartime prosperity" to which the very same faulty statistics also point: Americans were fantastically prosperous and enjoyed low unemployment in 1946. If you accept one, though, you must accept the other. Since there was no Great Depression of 1946, we should feel all the more vindicated in rejecting the equally misleading GDP data from the war years.

What GDP figures obscure is that the *private economy* performed extraordinarily well in 1946. Private output increased by 30 percent that year alone—by far the most extraordinary single-year jump in private output in American history. *That* is a measure of prosperity: not how much the government is spending, but how much the civilian economy is producing. That is where wealth is created and living standards are raised. On the other hand, the private economy shrank dramatically during the war.

THE VALUE OF COMMON SENSE

As the official statistics would have it, World War II was a time of great prosperity, and 1946 was a time of depression. The truth is just the opposite. What these statistics really show is just how substantially government activity can distort the true economic picture. And they also show that common sense must always prevail: diverting wealth away from private use, and taxing consumers to pay for the diversion, is not how prosperity is created. Are we asking too much to expect our historians to grasp that point?

QUESTION **13**

HOW DOES SOCIAL SECURITY

REALLY WORK?

★ ★

Most people probably think they understand how the Social Security program works. They are taxed a certain amount over the course of their working lives, and in return they gain a right to receive old-age benefits on the basis of what they have paid into the program. The money they pay in Social Security taxes goes into a trust fund, from which they will draw in their old age. The program is analogous to a private insurance program, with Social Security taxes akin to a traditional insurance premium.

This description, repeatedly sold to the American people for more than seventy years, is false in virtually every particular.

IN THE BEGINNING

When Social Security legislation was initially presented in 1935, it was replete with references to insurance, and its supporters explained the program in terms of an insurance policy. That insurance language was later suppressed when lawmakers feared the Supreme Court might invalidate the legislation on the grounds that the Constitution gave the federal government no authority to establish an insurance

106

program. Instead of portraying the program as one in which taxes are collected in order to fund benefits, the taxing and benefit portions of the bill were separated, with no express link between them. Thomas Eliot, the legislative draftsman of the first Social Security bill, later confessed that he had deliberately made the bill confusing.[1] According to Andrew Achenbaum, author of *Social Security: Visions and Revisions,* "Lest the court take judicial notice of the way officials were trying to sell the program, administrators believed it was imperative to keep the language sufficiently opaque."[2]

Following the legislation's passage, supporters of the program— President Franklin Roosevelt, congressional leaders, and spokesmen for the Social Security Administration, as well as journalists and popular writers—once again reverted to the insurance language in order to market the program to the public. Americans were told hundreds upon hundreds of times that they were participating in an insurance program, in which their Social Security tax constituted a premium that guaranteed them an absolute right to receive benefits in their old age. None of this was true, as the government would later admit under pressure, but it was necessary in order to get a self-reliant population to accept what otherwise would have been disdained as a mere welfare program.

Naturally, people accepted this explanation of the program. The president himself told them:

> Get these facts straight.
>
> The Act provides for two kinds of insurance for the worker.
>
> For that insurance both the employer and the worker pay premiums, just as you pay premiums for any other insurance policy. Those premiums are collected in the form of the taxes you hear so much about.
>
> The first kind of insurance covers old age. Here the employer contributes one dollar for every dollar of premium contributed by the worker; but both dollars are held by the government solely for the benefit of the worker in his old age.
>
> In effect, we have set up a savings account for the old age of

the worker. Because the employer is called upon to contribute on a fifty-fifty basis, that savings account gives exactly two dollars of security for every dollar put up by the worker.[3]

"We put those payroll contributions there so as to give contributors a legal, moral and political right to collect their pensions," FDR privately remarked. "With those taxes, no damn politician can ever scrap my social security program."[4] What FDR meant was that Americans, having put their money into the program with the expectation of receiving payments in their old age, would ensure that the program kept going. In practice, that means the program would go on even if current workers decided they no longer wanted it, since the money paid to current recipients comes from current workers, and current recipients expect their money as a matter of right; most of them even believe that they have paid into a fund with their names on it.[5]

Insurance was well regarded in the 1930s; insurance companies, by and large, had not failed during the Great Depression and continued to pay out claims even in those difficult years. By using the insurance analogy, therefore, FDR not only made the program all but untouchable politically; he also linked Social Security in people's minds with an institution that seemed stable and reliable.[6]

THE TRUTH COMES OUT—BRIEFLY

Whether people really had a legal claim on their Social Security payments was tested by the 1960 Supreme Court case of *Flemming v. Nestor.* It involved Bulgarian-born Ephram Nestor, who was deported in 1956, having been involved in Communist activity in the 1930s. The federal government denied him his Social Security benefits, citing 1954 amendments to the Social Security Act that denied payments to anyone deported for criminal activity after August of that year. Nestor sued on the grounds that "throughout the history of the Social Security Act, old-age insurance benefits have been referred to as a right of the recipient which he has earned and paid for."[7]

The federal government prepared a legal brief in defense of its position that Nestor was not entitled to his benefits. The brief explained that Social Security was

> in no sense a federally administered "insurance program" under which each worker pays premiums over the years and acquires at retirement an indefeasible right to receive for life a fixed monthly benefit, irrespective of the conditions which Congress has chosen to impose from time to time. . . . The "contribution" exacted under the social security plan from an employee . . . is a true *tax*. It is not comparable to a premium under a policy of insurance promising the payment of an annuity commencing at a designated age.[8]

Oh, and "no contractual obligation on the part of the Government and no contractual right of a beneficiary could coexist with this reservation of power"—a reference to the vastly underreported Section 1104 of the Social Security Act, which reads: "The right to alter, amend, or repeal any provision of this Act is hereby reserved to Congress."[9]

So let's see: Social Security is *not* an insurance program in which workers pay premiums and possess a right to receive benefits in the future, and the Social Security "contribution" is merely a tax, and *not* comparable to an insurance premium *entitling* the payer to receive an annuity beginning at a certain age. Where did people ever get these ideas? Could it be from the federal government's consistent, relentless propaganda for over two decades that promised the very things it now denied in *Flemming v. Nestor*?[10]

And even after *Flemming* the government shamelessly continued to peddle the old propaganda, repeatedly advancing claims it had now expressly denied in court. By 1975 one Social Security expert had already counted sixty-one references in Social Security Administration literature to its taxes as "contributions" and "premiums."[11]

ALL THINGS TO ALL PEOPLE

The incoherence of the government's position became especially clear in 1954, when Social Security coverage was extended to self-employed farmers. This change set up a confrontation with the Amish, whose religious beliefs forbid the use of insurance: Amish communities are to care for themselves.[12] When Social Security officials asked if they would pay the tax and simply decline the benefits or whether they wished to opt out of both the tax and the benefits, Amish representatives explained that they would pay the tax if it was just a tax but that they could not participate in any form of insurance. An IRS official met with Amish leaders in 1956 to settle the dispute and explained that the Social Security "contribution" was simply a tax and not an insurance premium. (Thus Social Security is whatever it has to be in order to secure compliance: to get people to accept the program in the first place, the payment is an insurance premium, but when religious scruples prevent some people from taking part in it, it is a tax.)

Some Amish felt unable even to pay the tax, in spite of the government's official denials that it represented an insurance premium. Those denials did not seem credible to Amish critics: the program itself, they said, was expressly billed as an insurance program. Valentine Byler, an Amish farmer in New Wilmington, Pennsylvania, responded to the government's claim that the Social Security levy was a tax rather than an insurance premium by asking simply, "Doesn't the title say 'Old Age, Survivors and Disability *Insurance*'?" The federal government used various means to secure payment from these Amish objectors, drawing from their bank accounts and taking a portion of their sale of farm goods. In Byler's case, the federal government responded to his $308.96 delinquency by dispatching IRS agents, while he was out plowing, to unhitch his horses and send them away to be auctioned off—all to fund a retirement program he didn't even want.

In 1965 the federal government finally exempted the Amish from the Social Security program.

THE POWER OF MYTHOLOGY

Every time Social Security has experienced a crisis, the mythology of the program has dominated the debate. In the early 1980s, for example, the mere suggestion of reform provoked massive letter-writing campaigns from people who had bought the entire propaganda package. A letter to the editor of the *Detroit Free Press* was sadly

33 Questions About American History You're Not Supposed to Ask

typical: "Where do you get the nerve to insinuate that Social Security recipients are 'supported' by workers? Social Security is an insurance program, generously contributed to by workers and by employers."[13] Another wrote to the *Chicago Tribune:* "Columnists should stop writing about Social Security as if it were social welfare for senior citizens. Where this notion got started we don't know, but it should be laid to rest once and for all."[14] Even the American Association of Retired Persons (AARP), which obviously knows better, speaks of an "insurance program" giving rise to an "earned right" to benefits.[15]

THE REALITY: "A PAPER IOU"

Now what about that "trust fund" that is supposed to contain everyone's Social Security money?

This is what actually happens. When Social Security receipts exceed the amount needed to pay benefits, the surplus goes into the so-called trust fund. That money is then *instantly spent* by the federal government on whatever current expenditures the government chooses to use it for. It is not earmarked for a specific individual; it is not even earmarked for retirement payments in general. It is devoted to expenditures that are totally unrelated to the Social Security program. The money people contribute to Social Security, therefore, is not sitting there waiting to be paid back to them in their retirement; much less is it productively invested and earning interest. Some of it goes from their pockets directly to current Social Security recipients, and some goes to the federal government's general expenditures.

After raiding the trust fund, the government then replaces the money with special nonmarketable Treasury bonds. Those bonds preserve the fiction that the government hasn't really raided the Social Security fund, since the fund now contains assets in the form of Treasury bonds in the exact amount of the money that the government took.

The problem here goes well beyond the fact that these are rather dubious assets, since they are special-issue bonds that cannot be sold on the open market. To understand the bigger problem, consider two scenarios. In the first situation, the alleged trust fund is altogether empty, containing no bonds at all, and the Social Security Administration experiences a shortfall, with Social Security tax receipts coming up $50 billion short of the amount necessary to honor existing benefits.[16] The federal government will have to come up with that money either by raising taxes by $50 billion, cutting spending by $50 billion, or borrowing $50 billion. One way or another, the American people will have to make up the shortfall.

Now imagine the second scenario, in which Social Security is $50 billion short, but this time the trust fund contains $50 billion in bonds that the federal government has placed there. The bonds are thus sufficient to cover the shortfall. But when the Social Security Administration cashes in the bonds, how does the government pay them? Either by raising taxes by $50 billion, cutting spending by $50 billion, or borrowing $50 billion—just as in the previous example. From the American people's point of view the "bonds" are, for all intents and purposes, nothing more than an accounting fiction. They, along with the trust fund itself, may as well not exist.

> THE MYTH ...
>
> ---
>
> *Social Security operates like an insurance program: individuals pay a premium into a fund and are thereby entitled to receive benefits in the future. This is just as President Franklin Roosevelt sold the program to the American people.*

Thus when the time comes that Social Security receipts are not sufficient to cover the benefits owed to recipients, the bonds in the trust fund will have to be redeemed. And again, since the federal government has no money that it hasn't first taxed away from Americans, the money to cover those bonds will come from the taxpayers.

General Hugh Johnson, who had once headed FDR's National Recovery Administration, was critical of the Social Security program on essentially these grounds, describing the so-called reserve as nothing but "a paper IOU": "When the time comes to pay, there won't be any more value there than if the workers had paid nothing in taxes all over these years." Instead of a trust fund waiting for them upon retirement, what did people really get? A promise "to tax your children to take care of you in your old age."[17]

FRAUD

The late John Attarian, author of *Social Security: False Consciousness and Crisis,* argued that the misconceptions about Social Security— misconceptions deliberately fostered by the government itself— make serious and obviously necessary changes to the program (much less its total abolition) practically impossible. The insurance metaphor has cultivated exactly what FDR hoped it would: a politically impregnable sense of entitlement among the program's beneficiaries. It has created a senior lobby so powerful that all changes to the program are inevitably charged to current taxpayers and future recipients. The program's unfunded liabilities amount to trillions of dollars, which baby boomers expect to receive at retirement, but which will require a crushing tax burden on their children to provide.

The government's attitude, on the other hand, was summed up well by a Social Security official: "Continued general support for the Social Security Administration hinges on continued public ignorance of how the system works. I believe that we have nothing to worry about because it is so enormously complex that nobody is going to figure it out."[18]

> ... & THE TRUTH
>
> *As the U.S. government has conceded only when forced to before the Supreme Court, the Social Security payments an individual makes are not an "insurance premium" but a tax, which does not give the individual the right to any benefit or earmark funds for him. The individual receives nothing but a promise "to tax your children to take care of you in your old age."*

WAS GEORGE WASHINGTON CARVER

REALLY ONE OF AMERICA'S GREATEST

SCIENTIFIC GENIUSES?

★ ★

A 2006 episode of the television program *7th Heaven* portrayed a high school class whose students had been required to write reports on great black Americans. One student, who complained that he was accustomed to writing all his papers on George Washington, was contemptuously told by another that he'd now have to write about George Washington Carver.

At the end of the episode we hear excerpts from some of the students' reports, some of which feature indisputably admirable and accomplished black Americans, of whom everyone can be proud. But no sooner has the student writing about George Washington Carver opened his mouth than the episode ends.

That's a shame, since it would have been interesting to hear the state of the Carver myth as of 2006.

Most educated Americans are familiar with the work of George Washington Carver, who is said to have made significant contributions to the diversification of southern agriculture and, more famously, to have developed some three hundred distinct products out of the ordinary peanut. In light of a more careful and rational examination of the evidence, though, encyclopedias and other reference works have begun to scale back the Carver record in recent years, although not as much as the facts seem to demand.

WORLD'S GREATEST SCIENTIST?

At its height, praise for Carver's work reached a point of almost ridiculous excess. Henry Ford said Carver had replaced Thomas Edison as "the world's greatest living scientist." Major awards, honorary degrees, and prestigious scientific honors followed him everywhere, particularly toward the end of his life. Following Carver's death in 1943, President Franklin Roosevelt signed legislation making Carver's Missouri birthplace a national monument. In all of American history only George Washington and Abraham Lincoln had received such an honor. He was later elected to the Hall of Fame for Great Americans and the National Inventors Hall of Fame.

To be sure, George Carver led an eventful and in some ways quite inspiring life. He was born a slave in Diamond Grove, Missouri, in 1864 or 1865.[1] Transferring from Iowa's Simpson College, where he was accepted in 1887, he went on to become the first black student, and the first black professor, at Iowa State University (which was then Iowa State Agricultural College). In 1897 Booker T. Washington persuaded him to come to Alabama and serve as the Tuskegee Institute's director of agriculture.

Carver, who earned the praise of the ebullient Theodore Roosevelt, was one of only a few Americans at the time to be invited to join England's prestigious Royal Society. His reputation and fame grew still more dramatically following his testimony before the House Ways and Means Committee in January 1921. Carver's presentation, which included discussion of the many uses he had found for the peanut, earned him a tremendous ovation.

But there are problems with some of the more extravagant—yet quite common—claims made on behalf of Carver's work. For example, what about those three hundred products he developed from the peanut? Scientists seeking information from Carver about his work and how he made his products received distinctly unsatisfactory replies. Several professors complained about Carver's evasive answers. Carver told one scientist that he had the formulas for all his peanut products, but had "not written them down yet." Speaking at a New York church in 1924, Carver said that divine revelation, rather than books, was the source of his unique ideas and methods.[2]

Where did the magic number three hundred come from? In part, it came from Carver himself; when asked for a list of his peanut products, he replied, "There are more than 300 of them. I do not attempt to keep a list, as a list today would not be the same tomorrow, if I am allowed to work on that particular product. To keep a list would also give the Institute a great deal of trouble, as people would write wanting to know why one list differs from another. For this reason we have stopped sending out lists."

> THE MYTH ...
>
> *George Washington Carver was one of the greatest scientists in American history, revolutionizing southern agriculture with his discoveries and developing some three hundred distinct products out of the peanut alone.*

Shortly after Carver's death the George Washington Carver Museum released a figure of 287 products, high enough to make the legendary figure of three hundred seem plausible. But the museum's list was filled with duplications, including thirty separate cloth dyes and nineteen leather dyes. Even "salted peanuts" made the list. And as historian Barry Mackintosh pointed out, since "most of the nonstandard products created by Carver could be made more easily from other substances, they were essentially curiosities."[3]

Even if some will admit that the number or merit of Carver's alleged peanut products is questionable, we still hear the argument that his emphasis on the peanut and its benefits contributed substantially to the diversification of southern agriculture. But this claim is untrue too. Southern peanut farming was already undergoing a dramatic increase by the time Carver published *How to Grow the Peanut* in 1916, and it actually declined somewhat in the 1920s, the decade in which Carver attained fame by his association with the peanut.[4]

Given how modest George Washington Carver's achievements were, how did he come to be listed among the greatest scientists of all time and described as a man whose "formulas in agricultural chemistry . . . enriched the entire Southland, indeed the whole of America and the world"?[5]

For one thing, Tuskegee began featuring Carver's name more and more prominently as it realized that his modest renown among scientists could attract more contributions to the Institute. In addition, peanut growers and processors suffering through a postwar slump thought Carver and his work might rekindle interest in and consumer demand for their product.

But there were cultural factors at work as well. Mackintosh, who has done groundbreaking scholarly work on Carver, concludes that a convergence of factors contributed to the appearance and success of the myth. Carver, an unassuming, apolitical man who made few if any overt objections to segregated America, was an appealing figure to many whites. Deferential and nonthreatening, he was a model of desirable black behavior. Black Americans, understandably eager to point to accomplished fellow blacks, also contributed to the inflation of Carver's reputation.[6]

Carver himself must share responsibility for the myth since he never really challenged even the most effusive praise of his work, except perhaps in the form of disclaimers that sounded more like perfunctory modesty. Even Linda McMurry, a sympathetic biographer, concedes that "Carver contributed to the erroneous interpretation of his work because of his deep need for recognition."[7] Carver "was guilty of prostituting his creative genius and of resorting to gimmickry, either consciously or unconsciously—not for monetary gain, but for

> ... & THE TRUTH
>
> *Carver's scientific achievements were quite modest, but many people, including Carver himself, inflated the myth of his scientific genius. The U.S. government even tried to suppress the truth.*

recognition." But, we are then told, "the materialism and racism of the society that required such actions to win its favor must share the guilt."[8] McMurry continues:

> His label as one of America's greatest chemists was erroneous. However, myths often serve useful purposes. The recognition of any black scientist by a white society that believed Afro-Americans could excel only in athletics and the arts was significant. Undoubtedly the Carver myth caused many whites to reconsider their prejudices and many blacks to enter scientific careers.[9]

No comment seems necessary.

SUPPRESSING THE TRUTH

The Carver myth proved very difficult for skeptics to overturn. "Because the Carver myth was of such broad utility and because of the racial sensitivities involved," writes Mackintosh, "those who doubted Carver's advertised achievements generally kept quiet." Thus a spokesman for the Agriculture Department, in response to an inquiry that ensued from a *Reader's Digest* article on Carver, indicated his own awareness of (and unease with) the Carver myth: "Dr. Carver has without doubt done some very interesting things—things that were new to some of the people with whom he was associated, but a great many of them, if I am correctly informed, were not new to other people. . . . I am unable to determine just what profitable application has been made of any of his so-called discoveries. I am writing this to you confidentially and without an opportunity to make further investigation and would not wish to be quoted on the subject."[10]

Years later the National Park Service commissioned a scientific study of Carver's work for its George Washington Carver National Monument. What the scientists produced was so unfavorable to Carver that the Park Service's regional director urged the government to suppress the study. The report's "realistic appraisal of [Carver's] 'scientific contributions,' which loom so large in the Carver legend, is information which must be handled very carefully as far as outsiders are concerned. . . . Our present thinking is that the report should not be published, at least in its present form, simply to avoid any possible misunderstandings."[11]

George Washington Carver did much valuable work in his day and benefited a great many rural blacks who, thanks to him, learned for the first time about modern agricultural practices. But there is no need to make him into the greatest scientific genius who ever lived. His was an honorable and productive life. That should be enough.

WAS THE U.S. CONSTITUTION MEANT TO BE A "LIVING, BREATHING" DOCUMENT THAT CHANGES WITH THE TIMES?

★ ★

While early Americans fought bitterly over constitutional interpretation, hardly any presidential candidate today bothers to show where the Constitution authorizes the countless federal programs with which he promises to lavish us. In fact, anyone who even asks to be shown where the Constitution authorizes some major federal initiative is liable to be dismissed as a crank.

Sometimes, though, the federal government will do something so clearly and obviously at odds with an honest understanding of the Constitution that the question will, for a change, actually be heard: where does the Constitution authorize this? And the answer is rarely edifying.

JUDICIAL ACTIVISM

Yale University's Bruce Ackerman concedes that time after time the federal government has dramatically departed from an interpretation of the Constitution that the Framers would recognize. But he denies that these newer interpretations, which consistently grant the federal government far more power than the states dreamed they were delegating at the time of ratification, are at all illegitimate. According to Ackerman, over the course of time the United States has passed through several "constitutional moments"—particular periods in history during which the American population has spontaneously and overwhelmingly come to support expansions in the power of the federal government. These constitutional moments are *so* spontaneous and overwhelming that they make recourse to the amendment process unnecessary.[1]

In other words, although the Constitution lays out a specific means by which it may be amended over time, Ackerman argues that that cumbersome process may be bypassed altogether during a "constitutional moment." From that moment on the Constitution is to be understood in a new way, and government action taken in light of that new understanding—even though it has not been lawfully inserted into the Constitution by means of the amendment process, and even though it would have baffled those who drafted the Constitution as well as those who voted to ratify it—is no longer unconstitutional. (Alexander Hamilton's words in *Federalist* No. 78 may as well have been directed at judges who are inclined to adopt Ackerman's approach: "Until the people have, by some solemn and authoritative act, annulled or changed the established form, it is binding upon themselves collectively, as well as individually; and no presumption, or even knowledge, of their sentiments, can warrant their representatives in a departure from it, prior to such an act.")

Conservatives and libertarians have long argued against judicial activism, a phenomenon that is at work whenever the courts go beyond their assigned task of interpreting the law as written and instead render decisions that reflect their own political preferences, even in the face of long-established traditions of constitutional interpretation to the contrary. Ackerman will have none of this. According to him, in the wake of a "constitutional moment" it becomes the role of the Supreme Court to protect and to rule in light of the new understanding of the Constitution that has arisen. Judicial activism, therefore, is not opposed to democracy. It in fact protects democracy, since it is the mechanism by which the people's evolving Constitution is safeguarded against those who read the document too literally and refuse to accept the new consensus about its meaning.

WHAT THE FRAMERS MEANT

Ackerman's influential thesis is merely a highbrow version of the common argument that the Constitution is a "living, breathing" document that changes with the times. The idea seems superficially plausible. After all, could a document written in the late eighteenth century anticipate the challenges of the twenty-first? Did not Thomas Jefferson say that no generation had the right to bind succeeding ones?

Plausible or not, the idea of the "living, breathing" Constitution is an invention in direct conflict with the intentions of the Framers. The British had a "living, breathing" constitution, and the oppressions for which it was responsible were precisely what Americans went to war to resist. Having seen such a constitution firsthand, the Founding Fathers were just about the last people on earth who would want to establish one for themselves.

In the Middle Ages the king possessed certain customary rights, but he could not define his own powers at will or overturn the traditional rights of the people or of the subsidiary bodies that comprised his realm. He was expected to cover his expenses out of the revenues he earned from his own estates, and anything beyond that required the consent of the various orders of society. "Almost everywhere in Latin Christendom," writes historian A. R. Myers, "the principle was, at one time or another, accepted by the rulers that, apart from the normal revenues of the prince, no taxes could be imposed without the consent of parliament."[2] This point reflects the broader principle that the king could not arbitrarily step beyond the bounds of his customary rights.

Whether they realized it or not, in their criticisms of the British government the American colonists were giving voice to the medieval principle that the governing authority was not unlimited but rather *was circumscribed by custom and tradition.* The British constitution was not a single document, like our own, but rather a collection of documents, traditions, and customs. To describe some government action as "unconstitutional," therefore, meant something rather different from what it means in the United States today, when simple reference can be made to a single document. It meant to the colonists that the act in question constituted a break with immemorial custom and should be resisted on those grounds.

The British dismissed the American claim as nonsensical, having adopted a new conception of British constitutionalism. According to this view, a measure was ipso facto constitutional if Parliament approved it. This is *legal positivism,* according to which a human law possesses its force not from its conformity to natural law but simply because it has been approved by the pertinent authority. A legal positivist rejects the idea that there can be any appeal to some higher authority or standard—e.g., long-standing tradition—when objecting to a duly promulgated legislative act. The law does not have to justify itself with reference to anything beyond the will of the legislator.

In effect, "because I said so" is sufficient—just as it is when a mother sends her son to bed at seven-thirty on the grounds that she is the authority figure and he is the child. Acts of Parliament were constitutional *because Parliament said so;* no appeal to British history or tradition could be brought against them.

The colonial lawyer James Otis countered the British position in "The Rights of the British Colonies Asserted and Proved" (1763), in which he developed the idea that there was in fact something external to Parliament that limited its power:

> To say the parliament is absolute and arbitrary, is a contradiction. The parliament cannot make 2 and 2, 5; Omnipotency cannot do it. The supreme power in a state, is *jus dicere* [to state the law] only—*jus dare* [to give the law], strictly speaking, belongs alone to God. Parliaments are in all cases to declare what is for the good of the whole; but it is not the declaration of parliament that makes it so: There must be in every instance, a higher authority, viz. GOD.

Should an act of parliament be against any of *his* natural laws, which are *immutably* true, their declaration would be contrary to eternal truth, equity and justice, and consequently void.[3]

In 1761 Otis had famously argued in Massachusetts on behalf of colonial merchants who objected to the issuance of general writs of assistance, which gave British officials sweeping rights to search businesses and even private homes in search of contraband (goods smuggled in from countries other than Britain and for which the applicable tariff had not been paid). Otis argued that such writs were unconstitutional and therefore void, since this kind of offense against the right of privacy and against the people's right to be secure in their homes *had not been one of the British government's traditional powers*. It was an *innovation,* and a dangerous one. (Otis lost, but the British stopped issuing the writs anyway.)

Americans, therefore, attempted to defend this view of British constitutionalism against the legal positivist variant with which they were increasingly confronted after the French and Indian War (1754–63).[4] During that war the British had accumulated a significant debt, which they sought to pay off with the help of revenue to be raised in the colonies. In the course of gathering that revenue, however, the British encroached upon traditional rights and liberties that the colonists believed they enjoyed by virtue of being Englishmen and that interfered with the colonies' traditional practice of self-government. In case after case, the colonists insisted that novel British practices amounted to violations of the British constitution.

The mother country considered this American view of British constitutionalism as outdated at a time when, in the wake of the Glorious Revolution, parliamentary supremacy was becoming the acknowledged norm in Britain.[5] These competing views of the British constitution made the conflict between the two sides perhaps inevitable. This philosophical division also sheds light on the lesser controversies of the 1760s and 1770s that led to the break with Britain, since in many cases the issue could be reduced to a question of constitutionalism: is this measure, which breaks with long-standing tradition, for that reason unconstitutional and void, or is it necessarily constitutional by virtue of having been lawfully passed by the British Parliament?

The developing constitutional conflict between Britain and the colonies, evident in the writs of assistance dispute and colonial opposition to the American Revenue Act (or Sugar Act) of 1764, exploded in the controversy over the Stamp Act of 1765. The act taxed a wide variety of paper products like deeds, wills, newspapers, and books, as well as other items like dice and playing cards.

The colonial response was swift and effective. Boycotts of British goods were quickly organized. The Sons of Liberty intimidated stamp agents. Official remonstrances, in the form of Patrick Henry's Virginia Resolves and the protests of the Stamp Act Congress, proclaimed and justified the colonial intention to resist.

The colonists argued that their right not to be taxed without their consent was an ancient one that could not be denied without doing violence to the British constitution. John Adams spoke of the "grand and fundamental principle of the constitution, that no freeman should be subject to any tax to which he has not given his own consent, in person or by proxy."[6] The only bodies that could legitimately tax them were their own colonial legislatures; attempts by Parliament to extend its jurisdiction over them in domestic matters like taxation had to be resisted.

SELF-GOVERNMENT

Other events in the years leading up to the break with Britain reveal a similar attention to law and history. Consider John Dickinson, the Philadelphia lawyer who played such a critical role in the events of the 1760s and 1770s. In 1767 Dickinson wrote his *Letters from a Farmer in Pennsylvania* in response to the Townshend Acts the British had passed that year. Among other things, those acts imposed a series of new tariffs, on lead, paper, paint, glass, and tea. The British had argued, perhaps disingenuously, that the colonists could have no objection to these tariffs, since Americans had accepted British tariffs in the past more or less without protest (even if they were often evaded in practice).

Now consider the legal precision of Dickinson's argument. It was true, he said, that Americans had accepted the legitimacy of British tariffs in the past, but those had been *protective tariffs designed to regulate trade within the British empire.* That is, they had not been tariffs for revenue—in fact, the British government spent far more enforcing their collection than it actually earned in revenue—but tariffs intended to protect British products from foreign competition. These tariffs on foreign goods— 100 percent taxes on French and Dutch molasses, for example—had been so high that practically no one had ever actually paid them, preferring to buy British goods instead. They had been intended, in short, to channel America's foreign commerce toward Britain and away from her competitors. Since this had been a traditional British prerogative since time immemorial— again, note the emphasis on tradition and custom—Dickinson contended that it legitimately possessed the force of law.[7]

THE MYTH ...

The Constitution is a "living, breathing" document that changes with the times.

But the Townshend duties were qualitatively different from those earlier tariffs, Dickinson explained. These were *revenue tariffs*—tariffs whose rates were low enough that Americans would not necessarily be discouraged from purchasing the taxed goods altogether. Unlike the case of protective tariffs, Americans *would* pay these tariffs, and the British government would earn revenue from them. This, he argued, was an intolerable innovation on the part of the British government:

> What but the indisputable, the acknowledged exclusive right of the colonies to tax themselves, could be the reason, that in this long period of more than one hundred and fifty years, no statute was ever passed for the sole purpose of raising a revenue on the colonies? And how clear, how cogent must that reason be, to which every parliament, and every minister, for so long a time submitted, without a single attempt to innovate?[8]

The British claimed to have concluded from the uproar over the Stamp Act that Americans objected to internal taxes (levied within the interior of the country) but accepted external ones (tariffs, collected at customs houses). Dickinson contended that this artificial distinction missed the point entirely, that it was not the question of *internal* or *external* taxation that agitated the colonists but whether the tax in question *was designed to bring in revenue or not*. If it was, then all the historic restrictions upon taxation without consent came into effect. The liberties of the people, enjoyed for many centuries, thus had to be protected in the face of a British constitution that always seemed to evolve to suit the interests and convenience of the British government.

> ... & THE TRUTH
>
> *It was precisely Britain's own "living, breathing" constitution— and the oppressions it produced— that the Founding Fathers rebelled against.*

It wasn't just particular British measures that the colonists opposed on these grounds. It was British interference in colonial self-government in general. Because the colonists had enjoyed the practice of self-government for so long (with only a few interruptions, like the Dominion of New England in the 1680s), they believed it had become part of the British constitution. By the 1760s and 1770s colonial self-government had become a long-standing tradition in its own right, and interference with it therefore amounted to an unconstitutional act.[9]

"BLANK PAPER"

It is with this background in mind that we should understand Thomas Jefferson's warning in the 1790s that "our peculiar security is in possession of a written constitution" and that Americans must not "make it a blank paper by construction." The amendment process could be used if some defect were found in the Constitution. But simply to approve the exercise of federal powers that were never delegated to the federal government on the grounds that some strained interpretation of the Constitution allowed them, or simply that the amendment process was too cumbersome and time-consuming, was hardly different from having no written constitution at all. Justice Joseph Story, the great nineteenth-century jurist (who interpreted the Constitution more broadly than did Jefferson), agreed that the Constitution must "have a fixed, uniform, permanent, construction . . . not dependent upon the passions or parties of particular times, but the same yesterday, to-day and forever."[10]

The evolution of the unwritten British constitution, the colonists had learned, always seemed to move in the direction of more power for the British government and fewer liberties for the colonies and the people. The written American Constitution was intended to say what it meant and not to allow for the kind of insidious evolution that the colonists had found so dangerous in the British constitution, whose authentic meaning had proven so hard to pin down. Americans, in short, gave their lives fighting *against* a "living, breathing" constitution—a fact worth bearing in mind the next time such a thing is invoked.

DID THE PILGRIMS FLOURISH IN AMERICA THANKS TO INDIAN AGRICULTURAL WISDOM?

★ ★

E very schoolboy has learned the story of Squanto. In March 1621, just months after their arrival in Plymouth, the Pilgrims met a friendly Indian named Tisquantum, whom they came to know as Squanto. Squanto, the traditional tale goes, taught the Pilgrims the Indian practice of using fish as fertilizer in order to make local strains of corn grow in greater abundance. This Indian knowledge helped make it possible for the struggling Puritans to flourish and prosper.

But the central aspect of this story is, in fact, untrue.

First off, it should be noted that the Indians did give the Pilgrims much useful advice, and that Squanto was indeed a fascinating and remarkable figure. He spoke three languages, and he greeted the Pilgrims in clear English. (He had spent time in England, Newfoundland, and Spain.) Squanto helped the new settlers negotiate a treaty with the Massachusett Indians to the north and a truce with the Nauset of Cape Cod. His language skills alone made him indispensable to the colonists.[1]

But as twentieth-century research has revealed, American Indians simply did not use fish as fertilizer—or *any* kind of fertilizer, for that matter. Anthropologist Lynn Ceci first documented this case in *Science* magazine in 1975.[2] Ceci's research demonstrated that no documentary or anthropological evidence existed to show that the Indians of North America used fish as fertilizer. Scattered references to the use of fish fertilizer as an Indian practice can be found here and there among New Englanders of that era, but these observers had no firsthand knowledge of Indian agricultural methods and simply assumed that Squanto was imparting to them a widespread native custom. No reliable ethnohistoric source contains so much as one line written by someone who actually observed an Indian using fish as fertilizer.[3]

THE MYTH ...

A friendly Indian named Squanto taught the Pilgrims a special Indian fertilization practice that enabled the new settlers to grow corn in greater abundance, thus allowing the fledgling colony to flourish.

What worked much better for the Indians was the practice of allowing land to lie fallow for extended periods, or even abandoning land whose soil was exhausted. "Having no easy way to transport large quantities of fish from river to field," writes historian William Cronon, "and preferring quite sensibly to avoid such back-breaking work, Indians simply abandoned their fields when the soil lost its fertility."[4] When Squanto introduced the fish fertilizing technique to the Pilgrims, Ceci therefore concluded, he was actually conveying to them a technique he had learned by observing *Europeans,* probably at settlements in Newfoundland.

So how did the Squanto myth get started in the first place? A December 1621 letter, possibly written by Edward Winslow, a founder of the Plymouth colony, undoubtedly contributed to what later became the historical orthodoxy. "We set the last Spring some twentie Acres of *Indian* Corne," the letter read, "and sowed some six Acres of

Barly & Pease, and according to the manner of the *Indians,* we manured our ground with Herings or rather Shadds, which we have in great abundance, and rake with great ease at our doores."

The trouble with this statement is that neither its author nor any other Pilgrim had at that time observed the Indians engaging in any kind of planting. Its author appears to have taken for granted that Squanto's knowledge represented Indian knowledge more generally. When in the ensuing years the Pilgrims were able to view Indian planting practices for themselves, they seemed surprised to discover that the Indians did not in fact use fish—or indeed, anything else—as a fertilizer.[5]

THE IDIOM OF GRIEVANCE

Despite the thoroughness of Ceci's case, her article in *Science* was greeted by the idiom of grievance to which Americans have by now grown accustomed. Wrote one breathless critic: "After the harm we have done physically and culturally to the American Indian we are still relentlessly pursuing them but now . . . on an intellectual level. Trying . . . to remove the American Indians from even our folklore is incredible."[6] Another, Mashpee Wampanoag spokeswoman A. G. Bringham, accused Ceci of assuming that the Indians were unable to survive without Europeans and even declared that Ceci, as a non-Indian, could not understand Indian knowledge.[7]

These stimulating intellectual responses showed that Ceci's critics, so quick to jump on a perceived grievance, hadn't even bothered to follow her argument. American Indians had no reason to be insulted by Ceci's study; she revealed, in fact, that the Indians hadn't used fish as fertilizer *because to do so would have been foolish.*

Ceci had shown that even if fish increased crop yields to some extent (this is

> ... & THE TRUTH
>
> *American Indians simply didn't use fertilizer. Squanto showed the Pilgrims a technique he had probably learned from Europeans.*

uncertain on the basis of the evidence), it also dramatically accelerated the exhaustion of the soil. (English farmers had switched to other forms of fertilizer by 1640.) Given the limited potential advantages, the significant drawbacks, and the added effort that fertilization would have involved, fertilization with fish simply made no sense for the Indians, especially because they could use the alternative of fallowing. This fertilization practice made sense only for Europeans, who had less land per person and less mobility than did the Indians.[8]

But Ceci's critics ignored all that. Even a relatively restrained opponent argued that Ceci "did not prove conclusively that the Indians of New England were ignorant or incapable of using fish for fertilizer." To which Ceci replied:

> To construe that a cultural analysis of native cultivation was an attempt to slur the capabilities of early Native North Americans reveals a basic misunderstanding of how or why anthropologists study cultural adaptiveness. It also unfairly introduces a notion of ethnic bias and nonscientific motivation into my research. My conclusion that fallowing was the more adaptive cultivation practice for Northeastern Indians implies no value judgment on my part regarding the capabilities of Indians, nor should any scholar interpret it as such.[9]

ENTRENCHED MYTHS

Although critics attacked Ceci when her study came out, scholars today are inclined to accept her thesis. Neal Salisbury, for example, makes respectful reference to Ceci's work in *Manitou and Providence* (1982),[10] and Charles Mann is inclined to accept it as well in *1491: New Revelations of the Americas Before Columbus* (2005).[11] A good deal of the initial response to Ceci consisted of politically motivated objections that had little to do with the facts. Instead of evaluating Ceci's findings on their merits, these critics actually claimed to take offense at her amply documented conclusions. For such critics, history involved not an impartial search for the truth wherever it led but the vigilant custodianship of entrenched myths—and hostility toward contrary evidence.

This certainly wasn't the first time history was used this way, and, as we have seen, it wasn't the last.

QUESTION **17**

WHO IS MOST RESPONSIBLE FOR THE "IMPERIAL PRESIDENCY"?

★ ★

I t does not require especially sensitive historical acumen to observe that the American presidency has grown consistently more powerful over the course of the twentieth century and into the twenty-first. It is a trend to be cheered or deplored but hardly denied.

From time to time we encounter people who oppose the expansion of presidential power as a matter of principle, regardless of whether the presidency happens to be held by a Democrat or a Republican, a liberal or a conservative. They are very much the exception. Liberals who excoriate President George W. Bush for his exercise of executive power were often silent or positively enthusiastic when Bill Clinton acted similarly. The reverse has often been true for conservatives.

To the Left, therefore, the principal villain in this scenario is George W. Bush. To the Right it was Bill Clinton. To Arthur Schlesinger it was Richard Nixon. In general, it's whoever happens to be in office at the time the critic in question is writing.

Above all, both sides typically portray their opponent in the White House as uniquely deviant in terms of the history of the U.S. presidency. The system in general, we are assured, is just fine; it's just that the present occupant of the White House—whoever he happens to be—constitutes a mysterious and unfortunate aberration.

Robert Nisbet, the influential conservative sociologist, has been one of those rare critics of the growth of presidential power regardless of who occupies the White House. Writing in the wake of Watergate, Nisbet took note of "a good deal of resentment against royalism in the White House." He knew it would not be permanent:

> There are too many powerful voices among intellectuals—in press, foundation, and elsewhere—that want a royal President provided only that he is the right kind of individual. . . . I am afraid that the only lessons that have been truly learned in the whole Watergate business are to avoid such idiocies as tapes and illegal, unwarranted break-ins. . . . I would be astonished if the real lesson of Watergate—the Actonian principle that all power tends to corrupt, absolute power absolutely—were other than forgotten utterly once a crowd-pleasing President with the kind of luster a John F. Kennedy had for academy, press, and the world of intellectuals generally comes back into the White House.[1]

Nisbet wrote of the eerie and almost grotesque mystique that has come to surround the American president: "Not only what the President thinks on a given public issue, but what he wears, whom he dines with, what major ball or banquet he may choose to give, and what his views are on the most trivial or cosmic of questions—all of this has grown exponentially in the regard lavished by press and lesser political figures upon the presidency during the past four decades." There were monarchical pretensions in all this, he said, for the first care of royalty "is that of being constantly visible, and naturally in the best and most contrived possible light for the people."[2] Nisbet likewise spoke of "a regard for the monarch that makes him virtually sacred in presence, that thereby gives his person a privileged status in all communications and that creates inevitably the psychology of constant, unremitting protection of the President not merely from physical harm but from unwelcome news, advice, counsel, and even contact with officers of government."[3]

In case comparing the president to the kings of yore seems overwrought, Nisbet invites us to consider the nature of the official iconography, ceremony, and architecture that have come to surround the

American presidency. He quotes the *New York Times*'s Russell Baker describing the massive government buildings that crowd Washington, D.C., and how our leaders in recent decades "have chosen to abandon the human scale for the Stalinesque. Man is out of place in these ponderosities. They are designed to make man feel negligible, to intimidate him, to overwhelm him with the evidence that he is a cipher, a trivial nuisance in the great institutional scheme of things."[4]

The conservative Nisbet replied to Baker's observations with sympathy. "It has always been thus," he wrote. "Merely compare the public architecture of Greece before and after the rise of Alexander; of Rome, before and after Augustus, and before and after the eruption of, first, Renaissance despots in Italy and then divine right monarchs. The change in American government that has taken place during the past several decades is almost perfectly evidenced by the change in the style and character of its buildings in Washington."[5]

Was there a turning point that brought us down this road? Abraham Lincoln certainly exercised extraordinary executive powers during the Civil War, as his supporters and critics alike acknowledge, but the very fact that the sixteenth president acted during wartime limits his usefulness as a source of precedents for peacetime American chief executives (although to this day the "even Lincoln did thus-and-so" argument is still to be heard during episodes of government mischief).

If we had to pinpoint a single individual as being responsible for the modern presidency, it would be a man who in word and deed, in theory and practice, brought unprecedented vigor and visibility to the presidential office. It would be a figure loved and admired to this day by mainstream Left and Right alike.

It would be Theodore Roosevelt.[6]

CULT OF PERSONALITY

Presidential scholar Edward Corwin has spoken of the "personalization of the presidency," by which he means that the accident of personality has played a considerable role in shaping the office. And it is hard to think of a stronger personality than TR who ever served as president. One presidential scholar observed that Roosevelt gave the office "the absorbing drama of a Western movie."[7] And no wonder. Mark Twain, who met with the president twice, declared him "clearly insane." In a way, Roosevelt set the tone for his public life to come at age twenty when, after an argument with his girlfriend, he went home and shot and killed his neighbor's dog.[8] He told a friend in 1884 that when he donned his special cowboy suit, which featured revolver and rifle, "I feel able to face anything."[9] When he killed his first buffalo, he "abandoned himself to complete hysteria," as historian Edmund Morris put it, "whooping and shrieking while his guide watched in stolid amazement." His reaction was similar in 1898 when he killed his first Spaniard.[10]

Roosevelt loathed inactivity. At one point during the 1880s he wrote to a friend that he had been working so hard lately that for the next month he was going to do nothing but relax—and write a life of Oliver Cromwell. One of his sons is said to have remarked, "Father always wanted to be the bride at every wedding and the corpse at every funeral."[11]

Bringing such a personality to the presidency, Roosevelt increased very significantly the visibility of the office and the popular fascination with the person of the president. One presidential historian explained it this way:

> As no president in memory and probably none up to that time, TR became a "personality"—a politician whose every action seemed newsworthy and exciting. His family, his friends, his guests, his large teeth, his thick glasses, his big game hunting, and his horseback riding—all were sources of media attention and delight. In a way that Washington and Lincoln had not done, and even Jackson avoided, TR became a very visible tribune of the people, a popular advocate whose personality seemed immediate, direct, and committed to their personal service.[12]

TR did not merely extend executive prerogative here or there; he put forth a full-fledged philosophy of the presidency that attempted to justify his dramatic expansion of that office. He contended that the president, by virtue of his election by the nation as a whole, possessed a unique claim to be the representative of the entire American people (a position for which Andrew Jackson was sharply rebuked by John C. Calhoun in the 1830s). Each member of the executive branch, but especially the president, "was a steward of the people bound actively and affirmatively to do all he could for the people." He could, therefore, "do anything that the needs of the nation demanded" unless expressly prohibited in the Constitution. "Under this interpretation of executive power," TR later reflected, "I did and caused to be done many things not previously done. . . . I did not usurp power, but I did greatly broaden the use of executive power."[13]

Since TR believed himself to be doing the people's will, and since he believed his own rhetoric that portrayed the president as the people's unique representative in American government, his need to fulfill this special mission overrode concerns about the separation of powers. He remarked privately that in the United States, "as in any nation which amounts to anything, those in the end must govern who are willing actually to do the work of governing; and in so far as the Senate becomes a merely obstructionist body it will run the risk of seeing its power pass into other hands."[14]

To take just one domestic example, TR intervened in the United Mine Workers strike in 1902, ordering the mine owners to agree to arbitration. Should they instead remain obstinate, he threatened to order the army to take over and operate the coal mines. Well known is TR's outburst, when told that the Constitution did not permit the confiscation of private property: "To hell with the Constitution when the people want coal!" Less well known is that at one point TR summoned General John M. Schofield, instructing him: "I bid you pay no heed to any other authority, no heed to a writ from a judge, or anything else excepting my commands." He was to stand ready, at TR's command, to seize the mines from the operators and run them for the government.[16]

When House Republican Whip James E. Watson heard the plan, he objected to the Republican president's face: "What about the Constitution of the United States? What about seizing private property without due process of law?" Roosevelt shot back, "The Constitution was made for the people and not the people for the Constitution."[17]

It was TR who pioneered rule by executive order as a governing style among American chief executives. Many Americans rightly howled during the 1990s when Clinton aide Paul Begala famously said of executive orders, "Stroke of the pen, law of the land. Kinda cool." But Clinton, who once called Theodore Roosevelt his favorite Republican president, was only exercising a power that TR had made a major feature of the presidential office early in the century.

Some uses of executive orders are unobjectionable from any standpoint.[15] It was by means of an executive order that George Washington, upon taking office as the first U.S. president, asked the outgoing government to prepare for him a report on the state of the country, and Andrew Johnson pardoned ex-Confederates following the War Between the States.

But examples of the abuse of executive orders are plentiful as well. As early as 1793 the subject led to a confrontation between Congress and the president. George Washington declared the United States neutral in the wars of the French Revolution, a move some viewed as an abuse of power, given the lack of statutory authority or constitutional prerogative. Ultimately Congress ratified the president's decision.

To appreciate the transformation that occurred in American government under TR, consider the number of executive orders issued by the presidents of the late nineteenth century. Presidents Hayes and Garfield issued none. Arthur issued 3, Grover Cleveland (first term) 6, Benjamin Harrison 4, Cleveland (second term) 71, and McKinley 51. TR issued 1,006.

In foreign affairs, an excellent if consistently overlooked example concerns the details of Roosevelt's decision to take over the customs houses in the Dominican Republic. In what became known as the Roosevelt Corollary to the Monroe Doctrine, TR had declared in 1904 that although the United States had no territorial ambitions in this hemisphere, cases of "chronic wrongdoing" on the part of a Latin American country that might invite occupation by a European power would force America's hand. To forestall European occupation, the United States would intervene to restore order and to see that all just claims were satisfied.

When it looked in early 1905 as though one or more European countries might intervene in the Dominican Republic to recover outstanding debt, Roosevelt put the corollary into effect for the first time by declaring that the United States would administer the Dominican Republic's customs collections to prevent any such foreign intervention.

Here's the part that nearly all historians leave out. From the beginning TR apparently hoped to avoid consulting the Senate at all, even though Senate approval is required to ratify a treaty. The agreement reached with the Dominican Republic was set to take effect February 1, 1905, a mere eleven days after it was signed—obviously too short an interval to allow for Senate discussion or approval.

The president relented and decided to submit the treaty to the Senate after all when he found himself faced with overwhelming opposition, even among his own supporters. Senator Augustus Bacon objected: "I do not think there can be any more important question than that which involves the consideration of the powers of the President to make a treaty which shall virtually take over the affairs of another government and seek to administer them by this Government, without submitting that question to the consideration and judgment of the Senate."[18] For his part, Senator Henry Teller added: "I deny the right of the executive department of the Government to make any contract, any treaty, any protocol, or anything of that character which will bind the United States. . . . The President has no more right and no more authority to bind the people of the United States by such an agreement than I have as a member of this body."[19]

> THE MYTH . . .
>
> *The modern presidency is a wonderful institution that has been mysteriously abused by recent occupants of the White House.*

After the treaty was finally submitted to the Senate, a special session closed without taking a vote on it. Exasperated, Roosevelt simply defied the Senate, drawing up what we would today call an executive agreement, the foreign policy equivalent of an executive order. Roosevelt later recalled in his autobiography: "I went ahead and administered the proposed treaty anyhow, considering it as a simple agreement on the part of the Executive which could be converted into a treaty whenever the Senate acted." Two years later the Senate did finally approve a modified version of the treaty. It hardly mattered to TR. "I would have continued it until the end of my term, if necessary," he wrote, "without any action by Congress."[20]

Before TR's accession to power, the last time a matter of real significance had been carried out by means of an executive agreement was the Rush-Bagot Agreement of 1817, by which Britain and the United States limited naval armaments on the Great Lakes. But even here President James Monroe eventually sought the Senate's opinion as to whether it required ratification; and while that body gave no answer, it did approve the agreement by a two-thirds vote. It fell to TR to convert the executive agreement into a major instrument of American foreign policy.[21]

> ... & THE TRUTH
>
> *Presidential lawlessness goes back a long way— at least to Theodore Roosevelt, whom everyone is taught to love and revere.*

WHAT TR WROUGHT

In 1909 Roosevelt told his son: "I have been a full President right up to the end."[22] He told retired British statesman George Otto Trevelyan: "Whenever I could establish a precedent for strength in the executive, as I did for instance as regards external affairs in the case of sending the fleet around the world, taking Panama, settling affairs of Santo Domingo and Cuba; or as I did in internal affairs in settling the anthracite coal strike, in keeping order in Nevada this year when the Federation of Miners threatened anarchy, or as I have done in bringing the big corporations to book—why, in all these cases I have felt not merely that my action was right in itself, but that in showing the strength of, or in giving strength to, the executive, I was establishing a precedent of value."[23]

Woodrow Wilson, TR's Democratic opponent in the four-way 1912 presidential race, largely shared TR's view of the presidency, belying claims then and now that that election represented a titanic struggle of conflicting ideologies. (Wilson himself admitted his inability to discern any major differences between the Democrats and the Progressive Republicans, apart from the latter's greater allegiance to the protective tariff.)[24] In *Constitutional Government in the United States* (1908), Wilson described the president in terms that TR could only have cheered:

> The nation as a whole has chosen him, and is conscious that it has no other political spokesman. His is the only national voice in affairs. Let him once win the admiration and confidence of the country, and no other single force can withstand him, no combination of forces will easily overpower him. His position takes the imagination of the country. He is the representative of no constituency, but of the whole people. When he speaks in his true character, he speaks for no special interest. If he rightly interpret the national thought and boldly insist upon it, he is irresistible; and the country never feels the zest of action so much as when its President is of such insight and calibre. Its instinct is for unified action, and it craves a single leader.[25]

The president, said Wilson, is "at liberty, both in law and conscience, to be as big a man as he can."[26]

"Conservatives," reports historian Arthur Ekirch, "complained of the usurpation of authority by the government and its executive branch" during the Progressive Era.[27] Even one of the presidents during the Progressive Era voiced misgivings: William Howard Taft, a man of sober disposition who was much more at home on the Supreme Court than he ever was as president, vainly warned of this growth in presidential power and of the great difficulty in keeping that power restrained once unleashed.[28] Nobody was listening.

IS DISCRIMINATION TO BLAME FOR RACIAL DIFFERENCES IN INCOME AND JOB PLACEMENT?

★ ★

When statistics reveal blacks and whites to have different average income levels, or that the races are disproportionately represented or underrepresented in particular occupations, the stock explanation offered by present-day "civil rights" organizations is *discrimination*. Were it not for discrimination, blacks and whites would have equal incomes and be distributed equally across the professions. This diagnosis leads, as night follows day, to calls for additional compensatory programs to transfer resources, wealth, and opportunities from whites to blacks.

The factors that actually account for income and other differences between various racial and ethnic groups in the United States (and elsewhere) are in fact many and varied. Consider this: fully half of Mexican-American women marry in their teens, while only 10 percent of Japanese-American women marry that young. This cultural factor alone would account for considerable differences in incomes between the two groups, since a young married woman will tend to have less mobility and fewer educational opportunities than a young single woman.[1] Likewise, ethnic groups in America often differ considerably

143

in average age, sometimes by as much as a quarter century. That factor alone would be enough to account for a considerable portion of income differences between groups, since an older group will tend to have more education, more job experience, and more accumulated wealth. The various ethnic groups are also distributed very differently across the country, some concentrated in largely low-paying areas and others in high-paying areas. The difference in incomes between Asian Americans and whites (with Asian Americans earning more), and between whites and American Indians or Hispanics, essentially disappears when we control for geographical distribution, education level, and proficiency in the English language.[2]

Differences between blacks and whites that are routinely offered as evidence of racial discrimination also exist between whites and Asians, where that explanation seems rather less convincing. For instance, although whites are approved for mortgages more often than blacks, Asians are approved more often than whites. The explanation we are supposed to accept for the higher infant mortality rates that exist among black women as opposed to white women is that society unfairly deprives blacks of adequate prenatal care; left unmentioned is that Chinese-American women have lower infant mortality rates than whites, in spite of *less* frequent prenatal care. Similar black-white-Asian comparisons have been drawn in the case of the mathematics SAT—whose alleged cultural bias in favor of whites seems rather implausible when Asians outscore whites—and in other areas in which blacks and whites (but hardly ever Asians) are routinely compared.[3] In fact, the performance of Chinese and Japanese Americans has become so embarrassing to supporters of affirmative action that these groups have now been subsumed into the larger category of "Asian and Pacific Islanders" in order to understate their performance by averaging it with that of less successful Samoans, Hawaiians, and Vietnamese.[4]

THE STATISTICAL SPIN

The casual assumption that discrimination necessarily leads to poverty cannot withstand scrutiny either. The Chinese have never enjoyed an equal playing field in Indonesia, Malaysia, the Philippines, Thailand, or Vietnam, yet the Chinese minority in these countries—a mere 5 percent of the population—owns most of these nations' total investments in a variety of key industries. In Malaysia, the Chinese minority suffers official discrimination at the hands of the Malaysian constitution, and yet their incomes are still twice the national average. Italians in Argentina were subject to discrimination but ultimately outperformed native Argentines. Similar stories could be told about Jews, Armenians, East Indians, and many other groups.[5]

In the United States the Japanese were so badly discriminated against that 120,000 of them were confined in detention camps for much of World War II. Yet by 1959 Japanese households had equaled those of whites in income, and by 1969 they were earning one-third more.[6] Most blacks themselves escaped poverty before the civil rights movement moved into high gear and well before affirmative action was introduced. Unfortunately, as Thomas Sowell of the Hoover Institution notes, the "political misrepresentation of what happened— by leaders and friends of blacks—has been so pervasive that this achievement has been completely submerged in the public con-sciousness. Instead of gaining the respect that other groups have gained by lifting themselves out of poverty, blacks are widely seen, by friends and critics alike, as owing their advancement to govern-ment beneficence."[7]

A 2003 study by the National Bureau for Economic Research (NBER) offered statistics suggesting that job applicants with white-sounding names were more likely to be called in for job interviews than applicants with black-sounding names, and it cited this as evi-dence that blacks are not being given a fair chance.[8] The authors of the best-selling *Freakonomics* suggest just a few of the difficulties with the study, apart from the obvious one that it focuses only on interviews rather than on actual job offers. "Was [DeShawn] rejected because his employer is a racist and is convinced that DeShawn Williams is black? Or did he reject him because 'DeShawn' sounds like someone from a low-income, low-education family? A résumé is a fairly undependable set of clues—a recent study showed that more than 50 percent of them contain lies—so 'DeShawn' may simply signal a disadvantaged background to an employer who believes that workers from such backgrounds are undependable."[9]

Of course, the government study also excluded the job programs for which *whites* are never called in. Minority job fairs are held all over America that are entirely closed to whites. Walt Disney Studios, Warner Bros., and 20th Century Fox all sponsor special programs to attract black and minority screenwriters for movies and television. Scores of newspapers offer special scholarship and internship programs for minorities. The major American automakers offer special programs to help blacks become car dealers, up to and including massive financing that is unavailable to whites. The Mead Corporation, Xerox, and Corning all calculate executive bonuses partly on the basis of how many blacks have been hired or received promotions. In its own executive searches Kentucky Fried Chicken keeps separate lists of white and black candidates and then hires from each list; blacks do not compete against whites at all.[10] It would take an entire book just to catalog the endless examples—not to mention affirmative action in *government* employment, which is even more extensive.

As the NBER study suggests, statistics purporting to show how discrimination harms blacks can be thoroughly misleading (as statistics often are). For example, we may possess a statistic on salaries earned by blacks holding doctoral degrees versus the salaries earned by Asians with doctoral degrees. The Asians may well be found to have higher incomes. But is this really evidence of discrimination? Look closer at the data, and it turns out that Asians and blacks tend to have doctoral degrees in different fields, with vastly differing levels of remuneration. Asians, for instance, are many times more likely than blacks to hold doctorates in chemistry, engineering, and mathematics, whereas blacks are much more likely to hold doctorates in education, and indeed fully half of all black doctorates are in that relatively low-paying field.[11]

The issue of members of minority groups holding terminal degrees recalls one of the most potent sources of campus activism in the 1980s and 1990s: student campaigns for more "diversity" among college faculty. Everyone knew perfectly well that these calls for "diversity" referred only to those groups that had a place in the Left's victimological pantheon. Few campaigns were to be found on behalf of more Scandinavians, evangelical Christians, or traditional Catholics among the faculty, even though these groups were, if anything, even less represented in higher education than were members of racial minorities.

Student activists routinely accused college administrations of bad faith or even "racism" for failing to hire enough minority faculty. In the early 1990s, for example, an organization called Students at Harvard Against Racism and Ethnocentrism (SHARE) challenged students to consider the following statement: "The scarcity of minority faculty indicates a racism that pervades the university." More aggressive recruitment of minority candidates, such groups implied, could rectify such manifestly unjust imbalances.

Completely overlooked amid the hysteria for "faculty diversity" was the exceedingly small number of black doctorates graduating every year, and therefore the tiny applicant pool from which the thousands of American colleges were expected to draw all the minority candidates the activists wanted. In my own reply to SHARE years ago, I pointed out that a National Academy of Sciences report had found in 1988 that of the 608 Ph.D. degrees awarded that year in mathematics and computer sciences, 2 were earned by black students. Nearly 500 students earned doctorates that year in earth, atmospheric, and marine sciences. Again, 2 were black. Five blacks earned doctorates in American history, even counting African-American history. Eleven earned doctorates in economics, 5 in anthropology, 7 in political science, and 14 in sociology. Not a single doctorate was awarded to a black student in astronomy, astrophysics, botany, classics, comparative literature, demography, ecology, European history, geography, immunology, and Arabic, Chinese, German, Italian, and Russian languages and literature.[12]

THE ELEPHANT AT THE TEA PARTY

Whatever the explanation for poor educational performance among blacks, household income alone is not it. At an academic symposium at a college where I once taught, I heard a colleague advance the familiar claim that lower standardized test scores among blacks were attributable to their disadvantaged backgrounds and in particular to their inability to pay for the kind of test preparation programs that were available to wealthier students. In response, a student in the audience innocently observed that it cost nothing to go to the local library and check out a book on SAT preparation. No one quite knew what to say to that.

In any event, the fact is that on standardized tests Asians in the lowest income bracket regularly outperform blacks in the highest income bracket.[13] The poverty explanation fails. (See Question 9 for more on this.)

Likewise for the alleged dearth of opportunities for blacks. "At the university where I currently teach," writes San Jose State University's Shelby Steele,

> the dropout rate for blacks is 72 percent, despite the presence of several academic support programs, a counseling center with black counselors, an Afro-American studies department, black faculty, administrators, and staff, a general education curriculum that emphasizes "cultural pluralism," an Educational Opportunities Program, a mentor program, a black faculty and staff association, and an administration and faculty that often announce the need to do more for black students.[14]

Meanwhile the black establishment is not interested in hearing from blacks like the Manhattan Institute's John McWhorter, who argues that the problem has a cultural dimension and that academic achievement is simply not emphasized in the black community to the extent that it is among whites and Asians. "Black America," he wrote, "is caught in certain ideological holding patterns that are today much more serious barriers to black well-being than white racism, and constitute nothing less than a continuous, self-sustaining act of self-sabotage. . . . It has become a keystone of cultural blackness to treat victimhood not as a problem to be solved but as an identity to be nurtured. . . . [B]lack Americans too often teach one another to conceive of racism not as a scourge on the wane but as an eternal pathology changing only in form and visibility, and always on the verge of getting not better but worse."[15]

Leaving aside the immorality of depriving a white student who never harmed anyone of the university admission that his grades and test scores justify, the effect of affirmative action in higher education has been to place countless blacks into educational environments for which they are not academically prepared. At the Massachusetts Institute of Technology, for example, the SAT math scores of the black students enrolled place them on average in the bottom 10 percent of the MIT student body. A private memo circulated at the University of California at Berkeley years before a state referendum abolished affirmative action in California university admissions revealed that candidates admitted under affirmative action had twice the dropout rate of minority students who were accepted on merit alone.[16] (It is extremely rare to come across such numbers; normally, blacks accepted under affirmative action are lumped in with blacks accepted purely on merit, and the results are dishonestly trumpeted as evidence of affirmative action's success.)[17] These are students who might have flourished at a second-tier school but who have now wasted time and money, and suffered terrible blows to their self-esteem, thanks to misguided efforts to help them.

In the early 1990s Timothy Maguire, a student at Georgetown Law School who worked part time in the admissions office, got into trouble when, without naming any names, he publicized the fact that Georgetown had been admitting blacks with dramatically lower test scores than whites. The usual hatred and vindictiveness followed: the Black Law Students Association called for his degree to be withheld, and the law school initiated legal action against him.[18]

But the fact is, Maguire was simply stating what everyone knew who bothered to look. It was public knowledge that the average student at Georgetown at the time had a grade-point average of 3.55 and a Law School Admission Test (LSAT) score of 42 (out of 48). (The LSAT was scored out of a possible 48 until mid-1991, when it began to be scored out of a possible 180.) Information readily available from the Law School Admissions Service revealed that the number of blacks in the entire country who had at least this average score that year was seventeen. Given that Georgetown was admitting seventy blacks per year, the vast majority of them must have been admitted with scores lower than the white average.[19] But this is the elephant at the tea party that everyone must pretend not to notice.

SHAKEDOWNS

Another fashionable cause, particularly during the 1990s and thereafter, involved accusations of discrimination in lending. Since blacks were less likely to receive loans than whites, "civil rights" activists cried discrimination—to them, the only possible explanation for any difference in anything. But disparities in lending are clearly not caused by "racism."

For one thing, although whites are more likely than blacks to get a loan, Asians are more likely than whites to get a loan. Are we to conclude that systematic pro-Asian, antiwhite bias is at work throughout American society? When net worth and other qualifying factors are figured in to the equation, the lending disparity all but disappears. Moreover, if blacks were really being discriminated against and held to a higher standard than whites, they should have a lower default rate—that is, they should default on their loans less frequently than whites. But their default rate is exactly that of whites, which indicates that blacks are indeed being awarded loans on the basis of merit and are not victims of discrimination.

> THE MYTH ...
>
> *Blacks on average lag behind whites in income and educational achievement because of ongoing racial discrimination, plain and simple.*

None of this evidence has prevented the "civil rights" establishment from engaging in massive shakedowns of banks that they believe have not granted enough black loans. Threatening to ruin such banks through endless litigation, activists have managed to extort tens and even hundreds of millions of dollars in coerced loans from bank after bank. Bruce Marks, the self-described "urban terrorist" in Boston who headed something called the Union

Neighborhood Assistance Corporation, provoked a media circus for two years when Fleet Financial Group planned to purchase the failed Bank of New England. Marks accused Fleet of not making cheap enough credit available to borrowers in some of the worst areas of Boston. Fleet ended up having to fork over $140 million to Marks's Union, set aside another $7.2 billion in loans for "low-income" borrowers, and earmark another $800 million in various programs for "inner-city borrowers." Shortly thereafter Fleet was forced to lay off three thousand workers and reduce its operating expenditures by $300 million.[20]

> *... & THE TRUTH*
>
> *The casual assumption that discrimination is the source of all these problems is simply false. In many cases there is a wide range of factors at work, none of which has to do with discrimination. Sometimes, too, black Americans benefit from discrimination* in their favor.

This is what all businesses have come to endure thanks to "antidiscrimination" law. According to libertarian commentator Lew Rockwell:

> Small companies routinely do anything within the law to avoid advertising for new positions. Why? Government at all levels now sends out testers to entrap businesses in the crime of hiring the most qualified person for a job. Pity the poor real estate agent and the owner of rental units, who walk the civil rights minefield every day. If any of these people demonstrate more loyalty to the customer than to the government, they risk bringing their businesses to financial ruin.[21]

One of the best-known recent cases, because of the enormous payout it provoked (an amazing $54 million), involved Denny's restaurant. Two class-action suits alleging discrimination were filed in the 1990s against Flagship, Denny's parent company. People were encouraged to sign up as plaintiffs in hopes of getting a share of the loot; thousands did. The media focused on what were thought to be the two worst cases of Denny's misbehavior. In one case, a federal judge said he had to wait for a table and that other restaurant guests chanted racial slurs in his direction. In another case, six Secret Service agents, who were in Annapolis to provide security for a speech by President Bill Clinton, claimed that they received their food late, and that the waitress rolled her eyes at one of them after he yelled at her. (In the "civil rights" universe nothing—including having your food brought out late at a restaurant—*just happens;* it is always caused by "racism.")

Terrified of the kangaroo proceeding that is all too typical in discrimination cases, Denny's settled. "As part of the settlement," writes Rockwell, "Denny's had to hire a full-time civil rights monitor, introduce a system of private spies to ferret out any internal 'discrimination,' run re-education programs for all nonminority employees, turn over a set number of franchises to minorities for free, and put a hostile person on its board of directors. As part of the same suit, the NAACP pressured Denny's to spend at least $1 billion to find and hire minority managers and turn over restaurants to them."[22]

Oh, and the Oakland law firm that handled the larger of the two suits walked away with a cool $8.7 million. But remember: lawyers support antidiscrimination law out of a pure and pristine passion for justice.

WHERE DID THOMAS JEFFERSON'S RADICAL STATES' RIGHTS IDEAS COME FROM?

★ ★

Historians often suggest that nullification (discussed in Question 4) was an idea that Thomas Jefferson, desperate to do something about the terrible Alien and Sedition Acts, simply developed on the spot as an impromptu response to an emergency situation rather than as a general principle to be regularly observed.[1] Given the political inclinations of most historians, who aren't exactly known as the states' best friends, it's hardly surprising that American history textbooks should want to downplay the significance of this most Jeffersonian of ideas. Oddly enough, though, even some conservative groups and individuals who otherwise pay substantial homage to the sage of Monticello seem almost embarrassed by nullification, all too eager to dismiss it as a bizarre aberration in Jefferson's thinking—or better still, not to mention it at all.

Unfortunately for these folks, they're completely out of luck. As we now know, not only was nullification *not* merely a hasty expedient devised by an anxious Jefferson, but it was also a logical development of *mainstream* political thought in Virginia at the time. The theory of nullification and the political philosophy that supports it predated

Jefferson's great 1798 protests by a full decade. Jefferson's doctrine can be traced all the way to the ratifying convention in Virginia that voted to approve the U.S. Constitution and indeed to the *moderates* at that convention.

THE ORIGINS

At the Virginia ratifying convention, Patrick Henry, the hero of the Stamp Act crisis, expressed his fear that the Constitution's "necessary and proper" clause (discussed in Question 27) would inevitably be interpreted by the federal government as a boundless grant of power, transforming the limited government that supporters of the Constitution promised into an unlimited government that would menace the people's liberties. He was likewise concerned about the "general welfare" clause (discussed in Question 26), since government could justify practically any action it might take by some strained reference to the general welfare of the people.

Edmund Randolph, the leading Federalist speaker at the convention, argued that Henry's fears were unfounded. Those phrases could not have the expansive meaning that Henry attached to them because, Randolph explained, the only powers possessed by the federal government would be those *expressly* conceded to it by the states. Those powers were listed in Article I, Section 8 of the Constitution, which Randolph described as an exhaustive list and which he then proceeded to read aloud. "All rights are therein declared to be completely vested in the people, unless expressly given away," he concluded. "Can there be a more pointed or positive reservation?"[2]

Randolph's views were of particular significance, since he had spent the past decade as Virginia's first attorney general. More to the point, Randolph belonged to a committee of five men whose task it was to draft the ratification instrument—that is, the statement by which Virginia would officially ratify the Constitution. To say the least, his opinion meant something.

George Nicholas, another member of that committee, echoed Randolph's views, assuring the convention that if Virginia assented to the Constitution, it would do so on the basis of the clear and manifest meaning of that document:

> If thirteen individuals are about to make a contract, and one agrees to it, but at the same time declares that he understands its meaning, signification and intent, to be, what the words of the contract plainly and obviously denote; that it is not to be construed so as to impose any supplementary condition upon him, and that he is to be exonerated from it, whensoever any such imposition shall be attempted—I ask whether in this case, these conditions on which he assented to it, would not be binding on the other twelve? In like manner these conditions will be binding on Congress. They can exercise no power that is not expressly granted them.[3]

Randolph also insisted to the convention that what he called "the stile of ratification" would protect Virginia against the federal government's usurpation of its powers. That "stile" consisted of a binding ratification instrument that would clarify Virginia's limited conception of the Union beyond all doubt:

> If in the ratification we put words to this purpose,—that all authority not given, is retained by the people, and may be resumed when perverted to their oppression; and that no right can be cancelled, abridged, or restrained, by the Congress, or any officer of the United States; I say, if we do this, I conceive that, as this stile of ratification would manifest the principles on which Virginia adopted it, we should be at liberty to consider as a violation of the Constitution, every exercise of a power not expressly delegated therein.—I see no objection to this. It is demonstrably clear to me, that rights not given are retained, and that liberty of religion, and other rights are secure.[4]

By the slimmest of margins the Virginia convention went on to ratify the Constitution, but on the terms of their instrument of ratification, whose exegesis they had heard from Randolph and Nicholas. They had announced to the people of the other states how they understood the document, and that Virginia should be exonerated from it should the new government stray from this understanding. They had acceded to a compact establishing a federal government that possessed only those powers expressly granted to it and no more. That government was in effect a league among the states, one whose powers Virginia retained the right to interpret for itself. They had certainly not joined a single, consolidated union whose government had the exclusive right to judge the extent of its own powers. That much is abundantly clear from the records.

A FINE PEDIGREE

Already in 1790 Virginia was expressing its displeasure with the direction of the federal government. Alexander Hamilton had proposed federal assumption of the state debts, in order to bind the wealthy more closely to the success of the new federal government. (In other words, the wealthy would have a vested interest in the success of the new government, since if it failed, their bonds would be worthless.) Patrick Henry introduced into the Virginia state legislature a resolution, approved by both houses, calling Hamilton's plan "repugnant to the Constitution . . . as it goes to the exercise of a power not expressly granted to the General Government." Not for nothing was the language of Henry's resolution "borrowed directly from the assurances that Edmund Randolph had made in the Richmond Ratification Convention," as historian Kevin Gutzman has shown.[5] Henry's resolution passed both houses of the Virginia legislature.

> THE MYTH . . .
>
> *Thomas Jefferson concocted his radical theory of nullification on the spot to address the terrible Alien and Sedition Acts. This notion was a radical departure from the American political tradition.*

In 1793 political thinker and pamphleteer John Taylor of Caroline argued that the state legislatures had the authority and indeed the duty to enforce the original understanding of the Constitution and to prevent the federal government from usurping the reserved powers

33 Questions About American History You're Not Supposed to Ask

of the states. Taylor's work and Henry's resolution of 1790 reflect the legacy of Virginia's ratifying convention and especially of Randolph's assurances there. For this reason Gutzman concludes that the doctrine of nullification, "which has seemed controversial to historians who have considered the Kentucky Resolutions in the past sixty years, was not controversial among Virginia Republicans at the time."[6]

It is to Gutzman's scholarly work that we are indebted for our present understanding—which still needs to trickle down to most historians—of the origins of the great Principles of '98. Gutzman summarizes his argument thus:

> The pedigree of the "Principles of '98" can be traced through James Madison and Thomas Jefferson to Patrick Henry and, ultimately, Edmund Randolph. It was he who paved the road to Virginia ratification by assuring his fellow members of the Virginia political elite that the Constitution they were being asked to ratify in the summer of 1788 would have very limited significance, that it was more another league of sovereign states than a consolidated union they would be entering. What have been portrayed as extremist and Anti-Federalist principles, then, were not extremist or Anti-Federalist in their origins at all. They were the products of the most moderate of Federalists.[7]

Gutzman's important revisions to the received view are essential to a proper understanding of American history. They prove that the Principles of '98, so long reviled by friends of government power, at the very least possess an honorable and important intellectual lineage and constitute an entirely defensible way of thinking about the American Union.

... & THE TRUTH

Jefferson's theory grew directly out of the mainstream political tradition, as it had been articulated by such esteemed Founders as James Madison, Patrick Henry, and Edmund Randolph.

Incidentally, you might think, in light of the federal government's staggering growth over the past two centuries, that opponents of the

Principles of '98 might at least be able to treat them and their modern-day sympathizers with the respect that prophetic utterances normally merit, particularly given the illustrious thinkers who gave them birth. You'd think so, but try speaking about them respectfully in a book, article, or speech, and watch the guardians of respectable opinion on Left and Right alike leap into action. A once-honorable position has become an unthinkable heresy.

WHAT REALLY HAPPENED IN THE WHISKEY REBELLION, AND WHY WILL NEITHER YOUR TEXTBOOK NOR GEORGE WASHINGTON TELL YOU?

★ ★

The standard version of the Whiskey Rebellion runs like this. In 1791 the federal government imposed a 25 percent tax on whiskey, to be paid by the producer at the point of production rather than by the consumer at the moment of purchase. Three years later unruly frontiersmen in western Pennsylvania not only refused to pay the tax but also, in some cases, physically assaulted tax collectors. President George Washington, at the urging of Treasury Secretary Alexander Hamilton, restored order with the help of nearly fifteen thousand militiamen. The antitax rebellion was suppressed, and federal government power had won an important early victory.

This version of events, while not altogether wrong, leaves out the most interesting and important parts of the story, then draws the wrong conclusion.[1]

What really happened is only gradually beginning to emerge from the documentary record, in large part from obscure sources long neglected by historians.[2] Resistance to the tax was not an isolated incident, confined to western Pennsylvania. To the contrary, such resistance swept the frontier regions of the country, where essentially no one ever paid the tax on whiskey. Far from a victory for the federal government against an isolated pocket of violent resistance to federal taxation, the Whiskey Rebellion was a largely peaceful—and in the long run successful—campaign of popular resistance to an oppressive tax.

OPPOSITION

Students of American history should not carelessly infer that the federal government used force to bring about compliance with the whiskey tax in western Pennsylvania simply because that was where resistance to the tax was to be found. In fact, from the federal government's point of view, noncompliance had reached epidemic proportions throughout the frontier regions of the United States. The Whiskey Rebellion, writes historian Thomas Slaughter, "was not confined to western Pennsylvania, but was a frontier-wide movement that tells us much about our national history."[3] Evasion of the tax was evident not only in western Pennsylvania but also in Kentucky and the frontier regions of Virginia, Maryland, and North and South Carolina.[4]

Discontent with the whiskey tax did not emerge in a vacuum. For decades the frontier regions had seethed with frustration and resentment. The eastern portions of their states were unfamiliar with and unconcerned about their peculiar difficulties, frontiersmen alleged, and the states' systems of representation gave the east disproportionate influence in state government. People on the frontier also believed that the unique sacrifices they had to make and the particular dangers to which they were exposed—and against which they received little to no assistance from state government—ought in all fairness to entitle them to exemption from at least some portion of the regular tax burden (particularly when, as in the case of the whiskey tax, it did proportionately far greater damage to the frontier than to more heavily settled regions). By the end of the eighteenth century serious secession movements had developed throughout the frontier, a trend only

33 Questions About American History You're Not Supposed to Ask

partially diminished by the admission of Kentucky and Vermont, formerly frontier regions themselves, to statehood.

For westerners, writes historian Leland Baldwin, whiskey was "an article that lay at the bottom of their social and economic life and was regarded as an indispensable necessity to life, health, and happiness." It was central to the economy of a place like Kentucky, which had no effective way to transport goods to the east, much less to foreign markets.[5] The most valuable good per unit weight that they could produce, whiskey was the only product Kentuckians could sell at a profit. "A horse could transport four bushels of rye at a time," explains Baldwin, "but turn it into whiskey and he could carry twenty-four—that is two eight-gallon kegs."[6] And in the remote frontier, whiskey usually had to substitute for specie as a medium of exchange. A tax on it would be unusually disruptive and burdensome.

From Kentuckians' point of view, they were being taxed on their most important good while at the same time the federal government was ignoring their most pressing problems. For one thing, nothing was being done to provide defense against the Indians, a constant problem on the frontier. For another, the federal government seemed less than zealous to secure navigation rights on the Mississippi River from Spain, and as a result transportation remained difficult and expensive.

Alongside these immediate and pressing practical grievances could be found some very real ideological objections to internal taxation (that is, taxes on goods inside the United States, as opposed to external taxation, or tariffs imposed on goods coming into the country from elsewhere). Americans had argued against excise taxes on philosophical grounds since the Stamp Act of 1765. The main argument against the British use of such taxes had been that they were unconstitutional, both because the British had never imposed them on Americans in the past and because of the traditional liberty of British subjects not to be taxed without their consent.

Some continued to argue against excise taxes even after independence. In the debates over the Constitution, the "Federal Farmer" explained: "Internal taxes, as poll and land taxes, excises, duties on all written instruments, etc. may fix themselves on every person and species of property in the community; they may be carried to any lengths, and in proportion as they are extended, numerous officers must be employed to assess them, and to enforce the collection of them."[7] External taxes, on the other hand, were both less burdensome and less dangerous to liberty. "External taxes are import duties, which are laid on imported goods; they may usually be collected in a few seaport towns, and of a few individuals, though ultimately paid by the consumer; a few officers can collect them, and they can be carried no higher than trade will bear, or smuggling permit—that in the very nature of commerce, bounds are set to them."

THE MYTH . . .

In one of the earliest tests of the federal system established by the Constitution, frontiersmen in western Pennsylvania rebelled against a tax on whiskey. President George Washington swiftly restored order by leading a militia into Pennsylvania, thus winning an important victory for the federal government.

Only the most local level of government could justly impose an internal tax, some opponents of the tax argued, because only the most local officials could be aware of local conditions.[8] An excise imposed by a distant central government could be little to no burden at all for people in some areas of the country but devastating to those in others. Some contended that even the state governments were too distant from certain constituencies to be able to levy an internal tax.[9]

Not surprisingly, the British government had encountered powerful opposition at home more than a century and a half earlier when trying to impose an excise tax on liquor. In 1643 opposition to the excise led to tax men being attacked in their homes, beaten, horsewhipped, and worse. One had his nose cut off; another, not quite so lucky, was pulled out of his bed and murdered in front of his family.[10]

The combination of these factors, both practical and ideological, yielded the Whiskey Rebellion.

Alexander Hamilton did not anticipate the extent of the opposition that would emerge to the tax when he first proposed it. The federal government hardly knew what to do in the face of the massive civil disobedience that ensued. Substantial evidence suggests that Hamilton and indeed Washington's entire cabinet deliberately concealed from the public the extent of tax evasion outside of western Pennsylvania.[11] There can be no doubt that the cabinet knew of the extent of resistance in Kentucky, for example.[12] The federal government even ignored the sporadic acts of violence that occasionally punctuated the otherwise nonviolent resistance to the tax. Interestingly, by the time Washington finally took military action against the whiskey rebels in western Pennsylvania, the rebellion had already begun to dissolve there anyway.[13]

... & THE TRUTH

Actually, resistance to the whiskey tax was widespread, and the federal government did nothing to curtail it outside Pennsylvania. Frontiersmen continued to evade the tax, until the federal government finally gave up on it entirely.

So why did the president choose western Pennsylvania as the site of a showdown between the federal government and the antitax rebels? For starters, this area was conspicuous because some people there actually dared to be tax collectors. In most other backcountry areas, almost no one enforced the whiskey tax, so for all practical purposes it was neither collected nor paid. The situation was similar to colonial opposition to the Stamp Act in 1765, when anti-British furor among the population dissuaded people from serving as stamp agents and collecting the tax.

Moreover, the federal government had high confidence that it could secure victory in western Pennsylvania. Added to that was Washington's irritation at tax resistance so close to the seat of the federal government (which was in Philadelphia in the 1790s). He was convinced, too, that a successful show of force in one place would bring about speedy compliance elsewhere.

Nevertheless, this episode assuredly did not amount to a victory for the federal government. Evasion of the tax remained widespread throughout the frontier regions, and those tax delinquents who eventually came clean did so only after receiving assurances that the tax would be repealed. Following the election of Thomas Jefferson in 1800, the federal government abandoned the whiskey tax altogether and avoided the use of excise taxes during peacetime until after the War Between the States. Until then the federal government's entire revenue derived from only two sources: a protective tariff and the sale of public lands.

The significance of the Whiskey Rebellion is only now being fully appreciated. A recent study of the rebellion in Kentucky identified it as one of the great movements of civil disobedience in American history:

> The history of the first whiskey tax in Kentucky is thus a history of massive, if largely passive, resistance. There was little violence. . . .
> The spontaneity and tenacity of the movement [are] truly remarkable, especially considering the primitive nature of communication in that era. The near-unanimity with which Kentuckians avoided and evaded the statutes would have astounded even Thoreau, Gandhi, and King.[14]

Astounding as it is, though, this massive resistance to the first American excise tax is all but unknown today. But it is safe to say that the Whiskey Rebellion did not end as a victory for the federal government. Is it too much to say it was a victory for freedom?

QUESTION **21**

WHAT MADE AMERICAN WAGES RISE?
(HINT: IT WASN'T UNIONS OR THE
GOVERNMENT.)

★ ★

E very single mainstream American history textbook on the market
today tells the same story: government has been the savior of the
working class throughout our nation's history. Without government
intervention in favor of the workingman and against big business, the
great bulk of Americans would find themselves in grinding poverty,
working long hours in terrible conditions for subsistence wages. Superficially plausible, this tale is now taken for granted by nearly all
Americans.

It is not enough to say that this tale is false. It is *grotesquely* false.
It praises the very institutions that have held back American pros-
perity and unequivocally reduced the material well-being of the
American population, and it condemns the only forces that have
consistently, and of necessity, raised the standard of living of all
Americans.

To appreciate just how perverse this version of American economic history is, begin by considering the following thought experiment. Suppose some catastrophe should occur today that decimates
the productivity of American labor. All automobiles are destroyed,

165

and with them the knowledge to create new ones. Our entire transportation system reverts to railroads and the horse and buggy. In addition, fax machines, standard and cellular telephones, e-mail, and the Internet all vanish, as do radio and television, and our communications infrastructure is reduced to the telegraph. Likewise, all other capital equipment invented and developed over the course of the past 150 years is wiped out. Many conveniences we take for granted no longer exist at all, and the remainder must be made either by hand or with what from our point of view are the clumsiest and most inefficient machines. Needless to say, this economy is capable of far, far less production than it was before the catastrophe.

Now, in the midst of this disaster, suppose a group of self-proclaimed advocates for the working class declare that even in these radically changed circumstances people should continue to work no more than forty hours a week, and that it should be unlawful to ask any worker to put in additional hours.

What would be the result? Without a doubt, massive impoverishment, malnourishment—and possibly even worse.

Why? Let's say, for simplicity's sake, that before the disaster the American labor force, with each worker employed an average of forty hours a week, was capable of producing 10 trillion consumer goods per year—a figure that would include everything from apples and razors to automobiles, personal computers, and cellular telephones. That same labor force, working the same number of hours but without the benefit of trillions of dollars of advanced capital and modern machinery to help them, can produce only the tiniest fraction of the consumer goods it once made—say, 100 billion goods.

Per capita, therefore, everyone must now be satisfied with one-*hundredth* of the things he used to enjoy. People will have to abandon the purchase of entire categories of goods just to be sure they have enough money for basic necessities. In fact, under these conditions most people will have to be satisfied with the *barest* necessities, if they can acquire even those. The goods they might have purchased and enjoyed in the past *simply do not exist* in the necessary quantities to satisfy everyone, if indeed they exist at all. The American labor force is no longer physically capable of producing them.

Under these circumstances, common sense tells us that we would all have to work much longer and harder in order to produce enough goods to enable us to maintain even a minimally acceptable standard of living. In such a situation, the goods we need would all be unusually scarce, and a great many consumers chasing relatively few goods would inevitably mean high prices. Workers throughout the economy would have to toil long and hard to produce the amount of consumer goods people believed they needed.

If we stubbornly insisted on maintaining a forty-hour workweek even in the face of such changed conditions and such dramatically reduced output per worker, we would not produce anything approaching the amount of consumer goods that most of us would need. By modern standards we would suffer unthinkable deprivation. It is this simple fact of reality, rather than any sinister machinations of greedy businessmen, that would account for our low standard of living in such a case.

In effect, this is something like the situation that people faced in England during the early Industrial Revolution and to a lesser but still considerable extent in the economy in which American workers lived in the latter nineteenth century, the period in which it is routinely alleged that they were unconscionably "exploited" by greedy businessmen.[1] If the disaster described above really occurred today, it is precisely to the conditions of eighteenth- and nineteenth-century England and America that we would revert. People back then could afford far fewer and considerably lower quality consumer goods than we do today because the country's capital-starved workforce could not produce any more.

THE SOURCE OF WAGE INCREASES

Living in a hampered but still basically capitalist economy, we take for granted our ability to feed, clothe, and house more and more people over time, not to mention our enjoyment of a steadily rising life expectancy. The typical critic of capitalism—and needless to say, the standard textbook as well—expects the increased population that capitalism makes possible to enjoy, right away, spacious and commodious homes, fine cuisine, and ample leisure time. If they lack these things, the only explanation our critics can come up with is that greedy businessmen are wickedly depriving the workers of them. That these things might not even exist in any great numbers is not even considered.

How, then, have wages been raised, and how can they continue to rise in the future? Are labor unions and government the heroes of the story?

Not even close.

Here's how Americans' real wages have been raised.[2] (The term *real wages* refers to how much a given dollar amount can buy; a $10 *nominal wage* in 1907 was a much higher *real wage* than was a $10 nominal wage in 2007.) In a free-market economy, businesses invest the vast bulk of their profits in capital goods that make labor more productive. Investing in a forklift, for example, makes it possible for a worker to move and stack far more pallets than before, and to reach heights that would have been impossible with his bare hands. Other kinds of machinery can multiply the efficiency of a single worker many times over, sometimes by orders of magnitude. The amount of goods the economy is capable of producing rises, at times even explodes. This is how wealth is created: we can produce more with the same (or a lesser) amount of labor. (That is one reason that the train was considered an improvement over horse-driven transport, or people having to carry freight on their backs.)

As a result of capital investment, firms can now produce many, many times more goods than before, and at considerably lower cost. Thanks to the pressures of market competition, firms pass on these cost cuts to consumers in the form of lower prices, better quality merchandise, or a combination of both. The ordinary person's standard of living increases, therefore, not because government takes from the rich to give to him or because labor unions "struggle" with employers to win him concessions. His standard of living increases because business firms can invest in machinery that makes it possible for more and more goods to be produced with fewer and fewer hands, thereby increasing the overall amount of material goods available and rendering them less and less expensive. (As economist George Reisman explains, "It is the productivity of labor that determines the supply of consumers' goods relative to the supply of labor, and thus the prices of consumers' goods relative to wage rates.")[3]

We can see this wonderful process at work in our everyday lives. Americans need to work far fewer hours to earn the purchasing power necessary to buy a whole host of goods than they had to in the past. Thus in 1950 Americans had to work 6 minutes to earn the money that would buy them a loaf of bread; in 1999 it was just $3^1/_2$ minutes. It took 21 minutes of labor in 1950 to be able to buy a dozen oranges; by 1999 it was only 9 minutes. For 100 kilowatts of electricity, some-one in 1950 would have had to work for 2 hours. In 1999 the same person would have had to work only 14 minutes. For a 3-minute coast-to-coast telephone call, 104 minutes of labor were required in 1950. By 1999 that was down to 2 minutes.[4]

The statistics are even more dramatic if we use 1900 as one of our baseline years. To buy a pair of jeans, for example, someone in 1900 would have had to work nine hours, as compared with four hours in 1950 and three hours in 1999. For a three-pound chicken, a worker in 1900 would have had to labor for 160 minutes. The amounts of time necessary in 1950 and 1999 were 71 minutes and 24 minutes, respectively.[5] It took the average American two years to earn the money to buy a car in 1908. "Today," writes Tom DiLorenzo in *How Capitalism Saved America,* "a Ford Taurus costs an American worker about eight months of labor, but the car is a technological miracle compared with the cars of yesteryear, with standard air conditioning, power seats, safety devices of all kinds, cruise control, a sunroof, tinted glass, a CD player, and so on."[6]

These ongoing increases in labor productivity will not make America run out of jobs. As long as human wants remain even partially un-fulfilled, there will never be a shortage of jobs. In some fields, such as agriculture, the increase in output made possible by productivity gains will not be met by a proportionate increase in consumption and will therefore result in fewer workers employed. This released labor is now available to produce other goods that we could not have had when it was tied up in agriculture. (In *The Grapes of Wrath* John Stein-beck foolishly condemned the mechanization of agriculture on the grounds that it put people out of work, failing to realize that thanks to the machines, more people were now available to produce other goods and thereby make them more abundant and less expensive.) In other fields, such as automobile manufacturing, productivity increases will make possible a mass market in a product that had once been a mere luxury and will therefore attract more employment. In both cases, consumers are enormously benefited.

George Reisman calls this argument the productivity theory of wages. To say the least, it is not the description of events that we find in the typical history text. Instead, we hear that massive redistribution of wealth from rich to poor was morally necessary and economically indispensable in order to improve the lot of the least wealthy. Reisman reminds us of a little problem with that plan: "There was virtually nothing to redistribute."

> The workers of the early nineteenth century did not lack automobiles and television sets because the capitalists were keeping the whole supply to themselves. There simply were no automobiles or television sets—for anyone. Nor did the workers of those days lack sufficient housing, clothing, and meat because the capitalists had too much of these goods. Very little of such goods could be produced when they had to be produced almost entirely by hand. If the limited supplies of such goods that the capitalists had could have been redistributed, the improvement in the conditions of the workers would hardly have been noticeable. If one person in a thousand, say, is a wealthy capitalist, and eats twice as much and has twenty times the clothing and furniture as an average person, hardly any noticeable improvement for the average person could come from dividing the capitalists' greater-than-average consumption by 999 and redistributing it. At the very best, a redistribution of wealth or income would have been useless as a means of alleviating the poverty of the past.[7]

In fact, such wealth redistribution directly harms the long-term interests of the workers themselves, as well as those of society as a whole. If businessmen wish to stay in business, they must reinvest the vast bulk of their profits in still more additions to their capital stock—which in turn further increase the productivity of labor, thereby increasing the supply of goods that the economy is capable of producing. These increases in the productivity of labor, by increasing the overall amount of output and thus increasing the ratio of consumers' goods to the supply of labor, make prices lower relative to wage rates and thereby raise real wages. The more those profits are taxed away, the less this beneficial process is able to occur.[8]

The cost of the wealth redistribution advocated by fashionable opinion in the universities and the media includes the investment in capital equipment that business must now forgo (because the funds for it have been confiscated by the government) and the lowered incentive to engage in such investment in the future, since businessmen now know its fruits may be taxed away. "The truth," says Reisman, "is that what made possible the rise in real wages and the average standard of living over the last two hundred years is precisely the fact that for the first time in history the redistributors were beaten back long enough and far enough to make large-scale capital accumulation and innovation possible."[9]

THE INTERVENTIONIST MYTHS

The objection is immediately raised: didn't workers in the past have to work very long hours? Without a doubt. By today's standards, people in the nineteenth century worked an exhausting schedule. But again, when output per worker is miserably low, then a supply of consumer goods that most people consider adequate requires people to work correspondingly long hours to produce them all. That, and not the wickedness of big business, accounts for the low standard of living and long hours of work that existed in the past. As the productivity of labor increases, and with it the level of real wages, people can begin to opt for additional leisure rather than continue to work the long hours of the past.

Without the need for any legislation or government coercion at all, a situation will eventually arise in which employers find it in their own economic interest to offer correspondingly fewer hours. If someone who once worked eighty hours per week now wishes to work only sixty (that is, three-fourths as many hours), and is willing to accept a wage less than three-fourths that of his previous wage as a premium on the leisure he will now enjoy, it makes perfect sense for his employer to offer these terms.

To the extent that maximum-hours legislation corresponded with people's desire to work fewer hours, it was superfluous, since such an outcome would have come about by means of the process just described. But to the extent that such legislation was economically premature, forcing fewer hours on workers who needed the wages of their longer hours in order to maintain what they considered an adequate standard of living, it harmed the very people it was allegedly intended to help.

The same can be said for legislation to improve working conditions. Improvements in working conditions that pay for themselves in terms of less workplace damage and disruption will of course be readily adopted by any profit-seeking enterprise. But even improvements that do not pay for themselves will still be adopted in cases in which the wage premium that would have to be offered to attract workers in the absence of the improvement would be higher than the cost of simply introducing the improvement.

THE MYTH ...

The government and labor unions have protected American workers from greedy and exploitative businessmen.

The only nonarbitrary way of introducing an improvement like climate-controlled facilities, and the only way of doing so that does not price workers out of jobs entirely or impoverish society out of proportion to the satisfaction derived by workers now enjoying climate control, is by paying attention to the market. Everyone knows that certain lines of work, because of their difficulty or because of undesirable or unpleasant aspects of the labor involved, carry a wage premium to attract sufficient workers by compensating them for these negative factors. As time goes on and more and more places become climate controlled, the wage premium for non-climate-controlled workplaces will rise. In other words, once more and more businesses install climate control, workers will demand higher and higher wages from firms that still expect them to work without it.

The wage differential that the non-climate-controlled workplace must pay in order to attract workers away from employers with climate-controlled facilities may eventually reach a level at which it would be less expensive for the firm simply to install climate control rather than to go on paying higher wages than their competitors who provide climate control. The market thus allows for rational allocation of resources and helps to ensure that improvements in workplace conditions—which, after all, have no logical limit: who would not want five-hour lunch breaks, the services of a masseuse, and an office with a view of Niagara Falls?—do not come at the expense of other goods that workers and consumers value more. Any improvement in working conditions must come at the expense of something else that must now be forgone. There is no way, in isolation from market exchange, that these forgone opportunities can be rationally compared.

This is why taxes on business and capital are so foolish and counterproductive. Such taxes hamper business investment, which is precisely what raises our standard of living. The vast bulk of high school teachers and college professors, on the other hand, spend their time condemning not the taxes that inhibit investment and hold back American prosperity but rather the wickedness of businessmen and the wealthy. Taxation, according to them, is a righteous method for redistributing the supposedly ill-gotten gains of the wealthy to the oppressed poor.

> ... & THE TRUTH
>
> *Government inter-vention in the economy is counter-productive and ends up hurting the very workers it is supposed to help, as it hampers the very thing—capital investment—that raises our standard of living.*

It so happens that the condition of the poorest is consistently far higher in market societies than in heavily interventionist ones with substantial wealth redistribution.[10] In light of the points raised here, that's no mystery. The only mystery is that anyone could still find it surprising.

QUESTION **22**

DID CAPITALISM CAUSE THE

GREAT DEPRESSION?

★ ★

American history textbooks take for granted that the Great Depression was caused by some inherent flaw in the free market, and that only wise government management of the economy can steer us clear of similar economic catastrophes in the future. This is the mainstream view, held by everyone from Marxists to run-of-the-mill conservatives: the market economy, whatever its benefits, is inherently unstable and susceptible to devastating downturns unless properly managed by central planners of one stripe or another. The business cycle—the boom and bust of prosperity and collapse—is an unavoidable feature of capitalism that can be mitigated by government action but never entirely eliminated.

One major school of economic thought—the so-called Austrian School, named for the country of origin of its principal founders—rejects this casual mainstream assumption and places the blame for boom and bust elsewhere. Significantly, it was economists of this school, practically alone among economists in the 1920s (the rest of whom insisted to their later embarrassment that an age of permanent prosperity had arrived), who predicted the Great Depression. It was his elaborations on this theory that won F. A. Hayek the Nobel Prize in economics in 1974.

Hayek's Nobel sparked renewed interest in the Austrian theory of the business cycle, as did the bust that followed the dot-com boom of the 1990s, which was a textbook example of the Austrian theory in action.[1] But the theory can also shed light on the Great Depression, one of the most catastrophic and least understood episodes in American economic history.

THE REAL CAUSE OF DEPRESSIONS

Any theory that claims to account for the business cycle, wrote economist Murray Rothbard, must be able to reckon with two empirical facts.[2] First, it must be able to explain why, all of a sudden, we should discover that entrepreneurs throughout the economy have made disastrous forecasting errors. Anticipating consumer demand for some product or service is the quintessential entrepreneurial function. Why should entrepreneurs, who have achieved their position thanks to their previous success at anticipating consumer demand, now commit such egregious errors? Not all markets are depressed during the bust period, to be sure—some are flat, some are even countercyclical— but there is a dramatic imbalance toward losses rather than profits. What can account for this sudden cluster of entrepreneurial error?

Second, the theory must explain why economic depressions tend to be considerably worse in so-called producer-goods industries (like construction, machine tools, and raw materials) and relatively mild in consumer-goods industries (like toothbrushes, hats, and magazines). American history texts like to claim that "underconsumption" caused the Great Depression: Americans supposedly could not afford to buy the goods the economy was producing. If that were true, the downturn should have been worse in consumer-goods industries than in producer-goods industries, but the Depression was actually at its *mildest* in consumer-goods industries. "Underconsumption" theories are unable to account for this consistently observed fact about depressions.

The Austrian explanation, which exonerates capitalism of blame for recessions and depressions, begins by reminding us of the role that interest rates play in the economy. Interest rates coordinate production across time. As people consume less and save more, inter-

DID CAPITALISM CAUSE THE GREAT DEPRESSION?

175

est rates come down. That stands to reason: thanks to people's additional saving, the banks now have more funds available to lend, and therefore the price of borrowing—namely, the interest rate—comes down. (On the other hand, if people save relatively little, the interest rate remains high, since in this case the banks have relatively little to lend and the price of borrowing remains high.) Businesses respond to these lower interest rates by taking the opportunity to embark on investment projects, such as building a new physical plant or acquiring additional machinery, that will increase their productive capacity in the future.

When people save more, they reveal a relative decline in their desire to consume *in the present*. That's when it makes the most sense for businesses to carry out time-consuming investment projects with an eye to *future* production. On the other hand, if people possess an intense desire to consume *in the present,* their relatively low amount of saving and the high interest rates that result convey to business that now would not be a good time to shift resources toward projects intended to increase *future* production. The interest rate ensures a compatible mix of market forces: if people want to consume now, businesses respond accordingly; if people want to consume in the future, businesses allocate resources to satisfy that desire as well.

But the interest rate can perform this coordinating function only if it is allowed to fluctuate freely in response to changing conditions. When the central bank—in the American case, the Federal Reserve System—manipulates the interest rate, it introduces systemic problems of discoordination and miscalculation.

Although it cannot do so directly, the Federal Reserve System has various means at its disposal to bring about lower interest rates. When it does so, interest rates are lower not because people have saved more and indicated a desire to consume less in the present, but instead because they have been forced down artificially. They no longer reflect the true state of consumer demand and economic conditions in general. These artificially low interest rates mislead investors. The low rates make investment decisions suddenly appear profitable that under normal conditions would be correctly assessed as unprofitable. As a result, irrational investment decisions are made and investment activity is distorted. The Federal Reserve's policy of cheap credit misleads businesses into thinking that now is a good time to invest in long-term projects, when in fact the public has given no indication of any intention to postpone present consumption and free up resources that investors can devote to long-term projects.

The central bank's lowering of the interest rate therefore creates a mismatch of market forces. *Long-term* investments that will bear fruit *only in the distant future* are encouraged at a time when the public has shown no letup in its desire to consume *in the present*. Resources are therefore being misallocated.

In the short run the result of the central bank's lowering of interest rates is the apparent prosperity of the boom period. New construction is everywhere, businesses are expanding their capacity, and people are enjoying a high standard of living. But the economy is on a sugar high and will inevitably come down. Since the public has not saved as much as the artificially low interest rate makes entrepreneurs think they have saved, insufficient resources have been freed up to make all of these new investment projects sustainable. The complementary goods that businesses need in order to complete these projects turn out to be scarcer and thus more expensive than investors anticipated. Some of these investments will prove to be unsustainable and will have to be abandoned, the resources devoted to them having been partially or completely squandered.

> ... & THE TRUTH
>
> *Despite the capitalism-bashing popular among historians and politicians alike, the free market is not responsible for economic downturns; government intervention in the economy—our supposed savior—is in fact the culprit.*

The Federal Reserve could simply pump still more credit into the economy to keep the boom going, and indeed it usually does just that. But at some point it has to put on the brakes. The more it inflates, the greater the mismatch between consumer preferences and productive capacity. As this becomes more apparent, pressure builds for a liquidation of the malinvestments. If the Fed ignores this pressure and continues inflating the money supply indefinitely, it risks hyperinflation—a galloping inflation so severe as to destroy the currency unit altogether.

The recession or depression is the necessary if unfortunate correction process by which the malinvestments of the boom period, having at last been brought to light, are liquidated. The central bank's cheap credit policy encouraged the initiation of countless investment projects that could not be sustained in the long run. The diversion of resources into unsustainable investments that do not conform with consumer desires and resource availability swiftly ceases as businesses fail and investment projects are abandoned.

We now see how the Austrian theory answers our two original questions. The cluster of entrepreneurial error occurs because economic actors are misled by the interest rate, an economic indicator that enters into the calculations of all serious entrepreneurs. And the downturn is heavier in producer-goods industries because it is that sector in which the artificially low interest rate disproportionately attracts investment.

THE FREE-MARKET SOLUTION

Although this is not the version of the story that Americans get in the standard telling, these are precisely the events that led up to and caused the Great Depression. Contrary to popular belief, the 1920s saw a very substantial inflation of the money supply, which in classic Austrian fashion sowed the seeds of the inevitable collapse.[3] Moreover, just as the Austrian theory would lead us to expect, the economic downturn disproportionately hit producer-goods industries and not the consumer-goods industries that underconsumptionist theories predict will suffer more.

Austrian business cycle theory explains what causes the *initial downturn,* but just how long and severe the depression will be depends on the government's response. If out of misplaced humanitarianism or just plain ignorance the government hinders the liquidation process—by bailing out failing businesses, propping up wages, or artificially stimulating consumption—the recovery will be much slower and more painful. Government-sponsored emergency loans merely prop up the unsound investment projects undertaken during the boom and the misdirected resources being squandered on them, and thus only intensify the problem. Wages and prices must be allowed to fluctuate freely so that labor and capital may be moved rapidly into lines that make sense in terms of prevailing economic conditions.

The initial downturn of the Great Depression occurred in late 1929, but conditions did not reach truly calamitous proportions until 1931, which economist Benjamin Anderson called "the tragic year." Questions 23 and 24 look at the kind of policies that the Herbert Hoover and Franklin Roosevelt administrations pursued that prolonged the downturn of 1929 into a depression that plagued the country throughout the 1930s (and beyond, as Question 24 shows).

The free market, therefore, is responsible neither for the initial downturn nor for the duration of the Great Depression.[4] The culprit in the first case is the Federal Reserve System, a nonmarket institution created by act of Congress, and in the second case is federal government policy that severely hampered the economy's ability to recover and adjust. Unfortunately, the Austrian theory of the business cycle, in spite of winning one of its architects the Nobel Prize, remains one of the best-kept secrets of economics.

QUESTION **23**

DID HERBERT HOOVER SIT BACK AND DO NOTHING DURING THE GREAT DEPRESSION?

★ ★

The version of American history that students learn in school goes something like this: Herbert Hoover, who had the misfortune of being president during the Great Depression, was wedded to an old-fashioned philosophy of rugged individualism that was no longer relevant to the advanced American economy. When the Depression struck, therefore, Hoover did not take decisive action, since as a strict supporter of laissez-faire economics he believed the government should never interfere in the economy.

This depiction of Hoover, which was fashionable among historians in the decades following Franklin Roosevelt's New Deal, has more or less been overturned—finally—in recent years. But while most professional historians have at last come to acknowledge the truth of the matter, the popular rendition of these events continues to portray Hoover as the laissez-faire stooge who could have helped people during a time of great deprivation but callously allowed them to suffer.

First things first: did Hoover in fact believe in the unhampered market economy? Not at all, and he made this point clear time and again during his tenure as secretary of commerce throughout the 1920s. The United States had "abandoned the laissez faire of the 18th century," Hoover explained, and new emphasis had been placed on "social and economic justice." "We have learned," he added, "that the impulse to production can only be maintained at a high pitch if there is a fair division of the product . . . by certain restrictions on the strong and the dominant."[1]

Absolutely free competition, according to Hoover, yielded economic chaos and needed to be replaced by some form of voluntary economic planning. Hoover possessed the typical Progressive confidence in the ability of various classes of experts to plan the economy scientifically and more efficiently than could the aggregate of individuals and their own plans that comprised the unhampered market. But Hoover did not think the federal government should be the primary player in accomplishing this regulation and economic planning, since he believed that government power was difficult to control once unleashed, burdened the private economy, and undermined incentives to produce and innovate. The federal government should instead serve as the great coordinator of the various lesser organizations; in addition to local government, Hoover made specific mention of "the chambers of commerce, trade associations, labor unions, bankers, farmers, [and] propaganda associations." He looked to this kind of government-business cooperation to deal with issues ranging from unemployment to housing, industrial waste, and foreign trade.[2] In normal circumstances (the Great Depression was an exception, as we shall see) the federal government would be confined to this coordinating role.[3]

REJECTING LAISSEZ-FAIRE

The trade associations of which Hoover spoke were voluntary organizations of firms in a particular industry—hundreds of industries had so organized by the 1920s—that were thought to serve a variety of useful social and economic purposes. "As guildlike collectivities led by enlightened and public-spirited men," writes Ellis Hawley, one of the most important scholars of this phenomenon, "these cooperative institutions could develop codes of ethical behavior, desirable patterns of social obligation, and the harmonious productivity of which an integrated and purposeful commonwealth was capable."[4]

These associations were urged to adopt codes of "fair competition" governing their industry that would limit each firm's liberty to some degree in order to stabilize the industry as a whole. Henry S. Dennison, president of Dennison Manufacturing Company, called for exactly that: "We *must* manage ourselves if we are to gain on the past. No laissez-faire, no unchanneled and unimpeded course of nature, no invisible hand will do it for us. . . . We now find ourselves in a period of growing social self-control."[5]

Dennison's comments were typical of what people were hearing from business leaders in the early twentieth century. One trade association executive condemned the businessman who operated his business "in entire disregard of the effects on his competitor and the rest of the industry."[6] Another businessman complained that "our profits are absolutely unprotected." The American Bottlers of Carbonated Beverages declared: "My desire shall not be to undersell my fellow bottlers, but to contend with them for first place in the quality of my products and the service I render my patrons." Business magazines consistently echoed this kind of talk.[7]

In the 1920s the Federal Trade Commission (FTC) held conferences with various industries in order to identify competitive practices that the bulk of existing firms considered unfair.[8] So-called Group I rules governed practices forbidden by the antitrust laws. More interesting were the Group II rules, which dealt with practices that were not strictly illegal but that many firms in an industry simply agreed were unfair. The FTC expected the trade associations to police their own firms, but in many cases the associations issued formal complaints with the FTC over member firms' Group II violations. The FTC sometimes issued cease-and-desist orders against offending firms. (In a study for the *George Washington Law Review,* two scholars concluded that businessmen at the time "were all too prone to regard as 'unfair competition' almost any kind of active competition that discommoded them, particularly if it related to price.")[9] Here was an example of the much-touted government-business cooperation of the 1920s.

"Fair competition" codes hamper newcomers to an industry. Established firms enjoy many advantages, including name recognition and public trust. If newer firms are to have any success against them, they need to be able to compete in particularly vigorous and innovative ways. "But if competitive methods become fairly standardized" through the kinds of agreements established during the 1920s, explains law professor Butler Shaffer, "and the newer firm is required to adhere to the same patterns as the established firm, the newcomer will find itself at an even greater disadvantage: it will have been deprived of the means of offering the necessary inducements to attract customers away from the established firms."[10]

For all their pleasant rhetoric, therefore, these schemes amounted to conspiracies within many American industries to prop up prices and to suppress competition (though historians who in all other situations are willing to ascribe the basest motives to businessmen have typically been rather indulgent in their treatment of these codes). The medieval Scholastics criticized the guilds of their day for doing exactly this; now the same mentality had overtaken the American business community. Adam Smith's observation in the eighteenth century is apropos: "People of the same trade seldom meet together, even for merriment and diversion, but the conversation ends in a conspiracy against the public, or in some contrivance to raise prices."

Now it is true that Hoover did not envision compelling businesses to comply with such schemes. The agreements would be essentially voluntary. But for all of Hoover's protestations to the contrary, journalist John T. Flynn could see where the system of "voluntary" restraints on business was bound to lead: to the government's use of force against firms that refused to comply with the regulations and requirements dreamed up by industry leaders. Trade associations, Flynn said,

are harassed by the unwillingness of those rebellious and adventurous spirits who refuse to accept their rule. They are forever running into the disturbing fact that while a trade may, after a fashion, "rule itself," it cannot rule some other trade which is in collision with it. . . . It is this very weakness which sends trade associations to Congress and the legislatures every year with appeals to the government to join them in some program of regulation. But the practice of regulating others is habit forming. It is a mania. . . . As soon as men find themselves in a game they begin to invent rules for that game, and the more extensive and complicated the rules become. At first they depend upon a certain spiritual pressure operating through the law of honor to support the rules. But very soon they seek more effective means of getting the rules obeyed. This involves a kind of force.[11]

Hoover's support for such "fair competition" schemes reveals his lack of confidence in the unhampered market and thus his refusal to adopt the strict laissez-faire position falsely ascribed to him. The president who first tackled the Great Depression, therefore, was not inclined to trust the free market.

INTERVENTIONISM

When the Depression hit, Hoover certainly did not sit back and do nothing. He called on business leaders to refrain from cutting wages, both in meetings at the White House in November 1929 and in follow-up meetings in the ensuing months. Although the issue of wages was the most pressing, Hoover also called upon business to continue making purchases of raw materials and above all to continue construction and maintenance work.

"What Mr. Hoover is really trying to do," *The Nation* wrote in a November 1929 editorial, "apparently without knowing it, is to create a Supreme Council of National Economy in the United States, and it will be interesting to see how far he can go in our topsey-turvey capitalist economy. He is right in wanting a planned economy." Economist Leo Wolman of the Amalgamated Clothing Workers of America described the Hoover conferences as a "Supreme Economic Council or Americanized Gosplan."[12] No doubt Hoover would have protested such characterizations, but they reveal how significant many observers considered these early presidential interventions.

Hoover's high-wage policy seems reasonable enough to a casual observer—who wouldn't want high wages, after all, and wouldn't they

33 Questions About American History You're Not Supposed to Ask

stimulate the economy, too?—but the idea was in fact terribly ill conceived. Since an artificial boom had distorted the economy's capital structure, wage adjustments were essential if the downturn was to be brought to an end. The necessary readjustments required flexible wage rates in order to direct labor out of areas in which the boom had created unsustainable expansion and into areas that central bank distortions had served to deprive of sufficient labor. Any artificially imposed wage rigidities could only prolong the economy's adjustment process and the suffering that accompanied it.

Hoover believed, wrongly, that reductions in wage rates would harm the economy by depriving wage earners of sufficient "purchasing power" to buy the goods that businesses were producing. This is a common argument, and a superficially plausible one. But it is a fallacy. For our purposes we may at least note that the Depression actually came in the midst of a dramatic *upward* trend in the share of national income devoted to wages and salaries, and a corresponding downward trend in the share going to interest and dividends and entrepreneurial income.[13] In other words, the data shows exactly the opposite of what would need to have happened in order to validate the underconsumption theory of Hoover, and of amateur economists then and now. If depressions are caused by "insufficient consumer purchasing power," how do we account for a Great Depression that appeared at a time when that purchasing power was at a high point?[14]

While the underconsumptionist explanation for unemployment has declined in respectability in recent decades, it has never gone away entirely. In *Out of Work,* one of the most important works of economic history to be published in the late twentieth century, Ohio University economists Richard Vedder and Lowell Gallaway took it head on. They showed that wages are a cost of doing business, and that artificially increasing wage rates beyond the level prevailing on the market will simply create unemployment, as businesses begin to demand less labor and/or to substitute capital for the overpriced labor.[15] (As economist Jacob Viner put it, "An unemployed laborer has no purchasing power at all, however high may be the wage rate he would get if he had a job.")[16]

What that means, in short, is that Hoover's demand for high wages—even in depressed economic conditions—undoubtedly worsened rather than improved the situation. Economist Lionel Robbins observed, "It may prove to be no accident that the depression in which most measures have been taken to 'maintain consumers' purchasing power' is also the depression of the widest extent and most alarming proportions."[17] ("It would be very nice," said another critic, "if simply by doubling or tripling all wage rates overnight, we could end the depression, but its effect would be rather to make unemployment complete rather than partial.")[18]

Although Hoover did not force business to abide by his high-wage policy, the president's appeal nevertheless had substantial impact. Not only did business leaders want to please the president, but in some cases they actually believed that high wages were necessary for their own prosperity. Many contemporary observers commented on the extent of business cooperation with Hoover's request. In early 1930 *Business Week* published an article called "This Time They Did Not Cut Wages." Late that year economist Carter Goodrich observed at a meeting of the American Economic Association: "It seems highly probable that the year 1930 . . . will also show an increase rather than a decrease in the rates of real wages." Leo Wolman said it was impossible to cite any similarly severe depression in which what he called "the wages of prosperity" were maintained for so long. The Alexander Hamilton Institute observed in 1931 that "the efforts to maintain wage scales have been an important factor in prolonging the business depression."[19]

THE MYTH ...

President Herbert Hoover, clinging to an outmoded laissez-faire philosophy, stood idly by while the nation plunged into the Great Depression, an economic disaster he could have offset had the federal government intervened in the economy decisively and immediately.

In 1930, ignoring the all but unanimous advice of economists, Hoover signed the Smoot-Hawley Tariff, which raised tariffs an average of 59 percent on more than 25,000 items. Among other things the tariff damaged the American export sector when other countries retaliated by making it difficult if not impossible for Americans to sell their goods abroad. But another aspect of the tariff, overlooked in nearly every major study of the Hoover years, was at least as important: the contribution the president thought it could make to his high-wage policy. "Tariffs," Vedder and Gallaway point out, "insulate the owners of both labor and capital resources from foreign competition, allowing them higher prices for their output and, in the case of labor, higher wages."[20] They go on to suggest that the unemployment rate would have been 3.8 percent lower by 1932 in the absence of these tariff increases—making the tariff responsible for about 20 percent of the increase in unemployment since 1929.[21]

> ... & THE TRUTH
>
> *Hoover was anything but a believer in the free market; his interventionist efforts to try to stave off the Depression—which, in fact, he thereby prolonged and deepened—laid the groundwork for Franklin Roosevelt's New Deal.*

Overall, Vedder and Gallaway conclude that Hoover's high-wage policy accounts for 77 percent of the observed increase in unemployment from 1929 to 1931.[22]

The high-wage policy by no means exhausted Hoover's anti-Depression program. Public works expenditures also increased dramatically under Hoover, with more money devoted to them in Hoover's four years than during the previous two decades. Substantial tax hikes were also introduced, as federal levies were imposed on countless products and services and income tax rates approached World War I levels. Hoover's interventions to prop up farm prices at a time of general deprivation were a forerunner of Franklin Roosevelt's. Hoover also signed the Norris-LaGuardia Act on behalf of organized labor (more on which in Question 30). He established the Reconstruction Finance Corporation, which extended low-interest loans to businesses in trouble, and extended credit to the states in order to fund public works projects.[23]

How in the world did Herbert Hoover get the reputation as a believer in laissez-faire when he was actually responsible for the greatest peace-time expansion of the federal government in American history to that point? It may have had to do with his hesitation to institute direct federal relief programs, preferring to lend money to the states for relief instead, or with his failure to spend still more money on public works programs. But the answer may also involve Hoover's opposition to Franklin Roosevelt's New Deal in the 1930s. Hoover did not reject the New Deal root and branch—nor could he, if he wanted to be consistent, since so much of the New Deal grew out of his own programs. ("Most of what [Hoover] began would be taken over by Roosevelt and then called the New Deal," later admitted Rexford Tugwell, an important economic adviser to FDR.)[24] He merely rejected the lengths to which FDR's interventions went, making his difference with FDR one of degree, not of kind. Historians have never been particularly good at drawing such distinctions, and thus was born the myth of the laissez-faire Hoover.

Even those who concede that Hoover was far from passive in the midst of the Depression typically conclude that he still did not do enough to address the country's economic woes. But Hoover's much more interventionist successor, Franklin Roosevelt, oversaw continuing double-digit unemployment and similarly dreadful statistics. Moreover, the depression that hit the country in 1920, which was in some ways worse than the Great Depression, was entirely over by 1921, when the country was once again setting production records. All President Warren Harding had done was cut government expenditures—the very opposite of the advice Keynesian economists gave presidents throughout the twentieth century. Dare we propose that Hoover, instead of doing too little, did too much?

QUESTION **24**

DID FRANKLIN ROOSEVELT'S NEW DEAL LIFT THE UNITED STATES OUT OF THE DEPRESSION?

★ ★

In May 2006 historian Ted Widmer warned in the *New York Times* that "a recent spate of books from the right, including Jim Powell's *FDR's Folly* and Thomas E. Woods Jr.'s *Politically Incorrect Guide to American History,* have accused [President Franklin D. Roosevelt] of prolonging the Great Depression and generally screwing up America."[1]

Widmer would have none of this crazy talk, of course. "F.D.R. embodied hope to a people consumed by despair," he hastened to remind us. "Roosevelt reinvented the presidency during his first hundred days in office, through bold policy innovations, brilliant speeches and broadcasts and a personal connection with the American people that has not been equaled since. . . . Through his words, his improvisations and his effortless optimism, Roosevelt resuscitated American capitalism, and in so doing, may have saved democracy as well."[2]

This is prose and analysis fit for a freshman term paper or a fan club newsletter, yet these inane platitudes and clichés were written in the *New York Times* by what we are led to understand is a professional historian. Here once again we confront the model of president-as-demigod: restoring "hope," "saving democracy," taking "bold" action—all in all, just oozing with brilliance. Biographies of Il Duce must read something like this.

The impression Widmer leaves is that were it not for a few oddballs like Powell and Woods, Americans might once again be able to enjoy their undisturbed contemplation of the greatness of Franklin Roosevelt. That there exists a vast and growing body of serious scholarship that debunks the Roosevelt myth is as usual left completely unmentioned.

"THIS WAS FASCISM"

Widmer aside, many on the mainstream Left acknowledge that FDR's New Deal programs did not lift the country out of the Depression. "For all it did, for all it changed, the New Deal never succeeded in its primary goal: ending the Depression," admits historian Robert McElvaine.[3] Even serial plagiarist Doris Kearns Goodwin, dean of the president-as-demigod school of historiography, concedes in her study of the period: "The America over which Roosevelt presided in 1940 was in its eleventh year of depression. No decline in American history had been so deep, so lasting, so far reaching."[4] Most such historians then go on to attribute America's recovery from the Depression to the federal government's expenditures during World War II—an egregious but persistent fallacy that is only now beginning to be abandoned. (See Question 12.)

In 2004 the prestigious *Journal of Political Economy*, which may be the world's top academic economics journal, featured an article by Harold L. Cole and Lee E. Ohanian demonstrating that the Depression persisted not in spite of the New Deal but because of it.[5]

One of the legislative acts that Cole and Ohanian criticize is the National Industrial Recovery Act, which created the National Recovery Administration (NRA). That act finally codified in law the kind of voluntary government-business partnerships that became prevalent in the 1920s. "I do not think we will ever have industry in order," said New York senator Robert Wagner, "until we have a nationally planned economy, and this is the first step toward it."[6] The act called for the organization of the various industries into trade associations that would draft production codes. All member firms of the industry would be expected to abide by the codes, which would deal with minimum prices, minimum wages, hours of production, and other aspects of the production process, and in general tended to restrict production. (The minimum-price requirement meant that you couldn't undersell your competitor too vigorously or you'd be in violation of the code— making it illegal, or at least unpatriotic, to have a sale.) It permitted the creation of industrywide cartels throughout the economy.

As John T. Flynn observed in *The Roosevelt Myth,* FDR's National Recovery Administration was simply a gentler example of the trade associations that Mussolini established in Italy:

> What they liked particularly was his corporative system. He orga-
> nized each trade or industrial group or professional group into a
> state-supervised trade association. He called it a cooperative.
> These cooperatives operated under state supervision and could
> plan production, quality, prices, distribution, labor standards, etc.
> The NRA provided that in American industry each industry
> should be organized into a federally supervised trade association.
> It was not called a cooperative. It was called a Code Authority. But
> it was essentially the same thing. . . . This was fascism.[7]

If the word *fascism* seems over the top, consider that NRA head Hugh Johnson (who once referred to the administration he led as a "Holy Thing . . . the Greatest Social Advance Since the Days of Jesus Christ")[8] gave Secretary of Labor Frances Perkins a copy of Raffaello Viglione's *The Corporate State,* a book that looked sympathetically on Mussolini's policies in Italy.[9]

Cole and Ohanian found that the NRA damaged the economy, and they argued that "New Deal cartelization policies are an important factor in accounting for the failure of the economy to recover back to trend."[10] Later in the 1930s, after the NRA had been declared uncon-stitutional but with some elements of cartelization still lingering, FDR himself came to acknowledge that cartelization policies had played a key role in prolonging the Depression. "The American economy has become a concealed cartel system," he said. "The disappearance of price competition is one of the primary causes of present difficulties."[11]

William Leuchtenburg, a well-known pro-FDR historian, conceded that the NRA "did little to speed recovery, and probably actually hindered it by its support of restrictionism and price raising."[12] Six decades after the program was implemented, further research prompted the even more vigorous criticism of Cole and Ohanian, who concluded:

> New Deal labor and industrial policies did not lift the economy out of the Depression as President Roosevelt had hoped. Instead, the joint policies of increasing labor's bargaining power and linking collusion with paying high wages prevented a normal recovery. . . . Not only did the adoption of these industrial and trade policies coincide with the persistence of depression through the late 1930s, but the subsequent abandonment of these policies coincided with the strong economic recovery of the 1940s.[13]

Many people assume that at least the minimum wages imposed by the NRA codes must have been a good thing. Any minimum wage discourages employment to some degree, but the NRA-imposed wages did so all the more: compared with the minimum wages we know today, these were quite high, averaging 90 percent of the average hourly wage in 1933.[14]

The Agricultural Adjustment Act likewise worsened the position of the vast bulk of Americans, using tax revenues to pay farmers to reduce their acreage or to cease farming altogether. The artificial shortages thus created would increase farm incomes (while making food more expensive for everyone). In 1933 10 million acres of cotton and 6 million pigs were actually destroyed for this purpose. Not only was the nonfarm population looted in order to support this program, but American farm workers suffered as well: with less farming being done, there was less need for their labor. In fact, a 1936 article in the *Atlantic* observed that some 2 million people had been thrown out of work by this program alone.[15]

Beneath the surface of most New Deal programs was the assumption that "purchasing power" needed to be restored if the economy were to return to normal. (Of course, *more production* is needed for that—obviously, nobody can purchase anything without the proceeds of some previous production—but the effect and sometimes the stated purpose of New Deal programs like the NRA was actually to restrict production.) The *Magazine of Wall Street* exposed the fallacy in this line of argument: since the president believed that reducing the workweek and raising wages would help the economy by boosting purchasing power, "why not swell purchasing power still more by establishing a 10-hour week and quadrupling wages?"[16]

THE CONSEQUENCES OF THE NEW DEAL

Each New Deal program had its negative effects, but the collective effect was also substantial. Ohio University economists Richard Vedder and Lowell Gallaway summed it up: "The Great Depression was very significantly prolonged in both its duration and its magnitude by the impact of New Deal programs."[17] Similarly, economist Benjamin Anderson concluded, "The impact of all these multitudinous measures—industrial, agricultural, financial, monetary and other—upon a bewildered industrial and financial community was extraordinarily heavy. We must add the effect of continuing disquieting utterances by the President. He had castigated the bankers in his inaugural speech. He had made a slurring comparison of British and American bankers in a speech in the summer of 1934." That the private sector could survive and even show early signs of recovery "in the midst of so great a disorder is an amazing demonstration of the vitality of private enterprise."[18]

Anderson's point that the Roosevelt administration's arbitrariness and hostility undermined business confidence is reflected in polling data compiled at the time. It was only in the 1930s that organized polling began, and in 1939 American businessmen were first polled about their views on the American economy's present and future. When asked by the American Institute of Public Opinion (AIPO) whether they thought the Roosevelt administration's attitude toward business was responsible for delaying the recovery of the private sector, 54 percent of businessmen polled said yes, 26 percent no, and the rest had no opinion. Some 56 percent expected the American economy a decade hence to be saddled with more government control, with 22 percent expecting less. In another 1939 poll, *Fortune* magazine received much the same answers. The magazine asked executives: "With which of these statements do you come closest to agreeing? (1) The policies of the administration have so affected the confidence of businessmen that recovery has been seriously held back; (2) businessmen generally have been unjustly blaming the administration for their troubles." Nearly two-thirds agreed with the first statement, and only a quarter with the second.[19]

Economic historian Robert Higgs calls this phenomenon "regime uncertainty" and argues that it bears a substantial share of the blame for why the Great Depression lasted as long as it did. He concludes that "given the unparalleled outpouring of business-threatening laws, regulations, and court decisions, the oft-stated hostility of President Roosevelt and his lieutenants toward investors as a class, and the character of the antibusiness zealots who composed the strategists and administrators of the New Deal from 1935 to 1941, the political climate could hardly have failed to discourage some investors from making fresh long-term commitments."[20]

> THE MYTH ...
>
> ___
>
> *Franklin Roosevelt lifted the country out of the Depression and saved American capitalism from its own internal flaws. At the very least he gave people hope at a time of despair.*

Investment data from the period reveals that the kind of sustained, long-term investment needed for any recovery was precisely what uncertain businessmen were moving away from. Long-term bonds carried a substantial risk premium, for example, indicating that business leaders were very uncertain about the future. Higgs's polling data from the 1930s suggest that this uncertainty about the future boiled down to an uncertainty about *future government policy*. Businessmen took seriously the threats and denunciations that ceaselessly issued forth from the White House. The Illinois Manufacturers' Association, in a statement forwarded to Roosevelt via Commerce Secretary Daniel Roper, cautioned that "the principal obstacle to business revival, with accompanying increase in unemployment, is the almost universal attitude of uncertainty and apprehension on the part of business executives regarding the future policies of the federal government on issues directly affecting the welfare of private enterprise."[21] Many similar statements were forthcoming: in 1934 a meeting of more than one hundred business executives and financial experts in New York, under the auspices of the American Management Association, submitted a report to Roosevelt through Treasury Secretary Henry Morgenthau concluding that "uncertainties concerning the fiscal situation likely to result from the Government's borrowing and spending activities, with consequent effects upon monetary and revenue policies, are retarding reemployment and recovery."[22]

> ... & THE TRUTH
>
> *As a growing body of scholarship continues to show, the New Deal actually prolonged the Depression and crippled American capitalism.*

But those activities continued. In June 1935 Roosevelt proposed a series of tax increases that included higher inheritance taxes, gift taxes, and personal income taxes as well as a graduated scale of corporate income taxes. Walter Lippmann, who had once been a supporter of Roosevelt, complained that the tax bill reflected "the absence of any plan and the lack of intellectual effort, the work of tired brains, relying on their wishes and their prejudices and throwing out casual suggestions which they are too hot and bothered to think about." *The New Republic* observed that "the whole conception behind [the tax bill] overlooks the fundamental fact that there is little point in trying to redistribute wealth as long as nothing is done to produce more than a fraction of the wealth we are equipped to create."[23]

"CONFUSED, BEWILDERED"

The New Deal's admirers assure us that FDR's massive spending projects provided jobs and economic stimulus. True, government make-work projects benefit those who get the jobs. But we need to take the analysis further than this single obvious step. When considering the likely outcome of some economic policy, we cannot focus only on the short-run effects on its alleged beneficiaries. It is necessary to think about the *long-term* effects on *the entire economy*. That was the point Henry Hazlitt tried to teach his fellow countrymen more than half a century ago in his bestselling *Economics in One Lesson*.

Economists John Joseph Wallis and Daniel K. Benjamin have estimated that the public sector jobs "created" by the New Deal's make-work programs either simply displaced or actually destroyed private sector jobs.[24] How could this be? Because if people are taxed $10 million to fund some government project, they now have $10 million less to spend on things they need, and that dropoff in spending will cost other people *their* jobs.

Imagine a government-funded bridge project. We can see the bridge being built, and we can see the people doing the building. "The employment argument of the government spenders becomes vivid, and probably for most people convincing," wrote Hazlitt. "But there are other things that we do not see, because, alas, they have never been permitted to come into existence. They are the jobs destroyed by the $10 million taken from the taxpayers. All that has happened, at best, is that there has been a diversion of jobs because of the project. More bridge builders; fewer automobile workers, television technicians, clothing workers, farmers."[25]

The very existence of the bridge, says Hazlitt, is usually enough to win the argument "with all those who cannot see beyond the immediate range of their physical eyes." They cannot see all the things that were never able to come into existence because the necessary resources were diverted to the bridge, like "the unbuilt homes, the unmade cars and washing machines, the unmade dresses and coats, perhaps the ungrown and unsold foodstuffs." Someone who understands how to assess both the direct and the indirect consequences of government programs can indeed see these things in the eye of his imagination, but "to see these uncreated things requires a kind of imagination that not many people have."[26]

These programs did not simply divert jobs from some people to others, or capital from some projects to others, in a zero-sum game. They destroyed wealth and made society worse off. In the private sector, resources must be employed in line with consumer preferences if entrepreneurs wish to see a profit. If they do not employ resources according to consumer desires, they make losses and must either change their business plans or see the rest of their capital slip out of their hands. Government, on the other hand, lacks this crucial feedback mechanism, since it earns its money not by satisfying consumers but by the coercive means of taxation. Without having to pass a profit-and-loss test, it can never know how relatively efficient or destructively uneconomic its projects are. How much of something is needed? Where should it go? What materials should be used? Operating outside the realm of voluntary human relations and answering to no profit-and-loss test to guide them in resource allocation, government is inherently unable to answer these and countless other questions, simply seizing resources from the private sector and employing them arbitrarily.

During the downturn-within-the-downturn that occurred from mid-1937 to mid-1938, one congressional representative confessed: "We Democrats have to admit we are floundering. . . . We are a confused, bewildered group of people."[27] For all the talk of the brilliant leadership of Franklin Roosevelt and his advisers, this is a far truer assessment of the architects of the New Deal.

DOES THE CONSTITUTION'S COMMERCE CLAUSE REALLY GRANT THE FEDERAL GOVERNMENT THE POWER TO REGULATE ALL GAINFUL ACTIVITY?

★ ★

The constitutional clause whose faulty interpretation has caused more mischief than any other is arguably the commerce clause. It is Article I, Section 8, Clause 3 of the Constitution, which grants Congress the power to "regulate Commerce with foreign Nations, and among the several States, and with the Indian Tribes." It is upon this clause that so much of the federal government's involvement in Americans' lives rests. At one time interpreted fairly narrowly, the clause today is used to justify, well, just about anything. And that's why it's so important to figure out what it was really supposed to mean.

First, what does the Constitution mean by "commerce" when it speaks of the power of Congress to "regulate commerce"? Does the word possess a narrow meaning—namely, merely trade or exchange—or was it meant to extend much more broadly to include the production of things that are subsequently exchanged in commerce, such as manufacturing and agriculture? Or, as more modern interpretations would have it, was it meant to include *all gainful activity whatsoever?*

It turns out that it is impossible to find a mention of "commerce" at the Constitutional Convention or in the *Federalist Papers*—where the word appears sixty-three times—that clearly refers to anything other than mere trade.[1] James Madison later observed that "if, in citing the Constitution, the word trade was put in the place of commerce, the word foreign made it synonymous with commerce. Trade and commerce are, in fact, used indiscriminately, both in books and in conversation."[2] Randy Barnett of Georgetown University Law Center writes, "Having examined every use of the term 'commerce' that appears in the reports of the state ratifying conventions, I found that the term was uniformly used to refer to trade or exchange, rather than all gainful activity."[3]

If commerce clearly referred to trade or exchange, what did "among the states" mean? According to the scholarly consensus, the original meaning of this phrase involved commerce between one state and another, not commerce that occurs in one state and merely *concerns or has effects upon* others.[4] So even if the term *commerce* really did include manufacturing, agriculture, and any other gainful activity, it wouldn't matter since none of these things can occur "among the states." (How could a good be manufactured or grown "among the states" or from one state to another?)

Thomas Jefferson was only repeating the intentions of the Framers when he explained that "the power given to Congress by the Constitution does not extend to the internal regulation of the commerce of a State . . . which remains exclusively with its own legislature; but to its external commerce only, that is to say, its commerce with another state, or with foreign nations, or with the Indian tribes."[5] Likewise, James Madison wrote that " '*among* the several States' . . . grew out of the abuses of the power by the importing states in taxing the non-importing, and was intended as a negative and preventive provision against injustice among the States themselves, rather than as a power to be used for the positive purposes of the General Government."[6] In other words, the clause was meant to provide for a giant free-trade zone throughout the United States, and to prevent the states from obstructing commerce by leveling discriminatory taxes and the like against the goods of other states.

FATEFUL STAMP

In the Supreme Court case of *Gibbons v. Ogden* (1824), Chief Justice John Marshall put a fateful stamp on the commerce clause when he observed that the internal commerce of a state was a matter reserved to the state itself, *unless that commerce "affects other states."* That proviso had not a shred of support in the history of the commerce clause. Marshall's position, wrote legal scholar Raoul Berger, was "a naked assertion unaccompanied by legislative history or precedential explanation."[7] It opened up a potentially limitless field of power for the federal government, since anything can be said to "affect" anything else.[8]

> THE MYTH . . .
>
> ---
>
> *When the Constitution grants the federal government the power of Congress to "regulate commerce," it means the government can regulate virtually all gainful activity and almost anything that "affects" interstate commerce.*

By the time of Franklin Roosevelt's presidency, the commerce clause was being cited to justify federal powers that the Framers could scarcely have believed. The best-known example is the case of *Wickard v. Filburn* (1942). There the Supreme Court concluded that a farmer growing wheat on his own land for his own use was subject to regulation under the commerce clause. Why? Because if he hadn't consumed his own wheat, he might have purchased wheat in the open market. His abstention from purchasing wheat in the market therefore affected interstate commerce and thus made him subject to federal regulation.

The *Wickard* case made perfectly clear that the commerce clause would no longer restrain the federal government in any serious way. Anything that might affect interstate commerce in some way had now become subject to federal regulation. The trick now became trying to define all of life as somehow affecting interstate commerce so the federal government would have the authority to regulate it. (When Supreme Court nominee Samuel Alito was up for confirmation in 2005–6, his stance on the commerce clause was one of New York senator Chuck Schumer's consistent talking points. Would Alito take us back to the bad old days when every aspect of human life didn't qualify as interstate commerce?)

SOME LIMITS AT LAST

Only very recently has the Supreme Court begun to rethink, albeit timidly, the liberties the federal government has taken with the commerce clause. An important recent case involved the Gun-Free School Zones Act, passed in 1990, which criminalized the possession of a firearm within a thousand feet of a school. (Forty states already had such legislation on the books at the time.) Particularly significant is how the federal government justified its involvement in this issue from a constitutional standpoint. An educated population is important to the American economy, the government's argument began. If guns are present in schools, the educational process will be disrupted and the American population will end up less educated. If the American population is less educated, interstate commerce will be impaired. Therefore, the federal government has the power to legislate on the issue of guns in schools.

> ... & THE TRUTH
>
> *The courts have ignored the Framers' stated aims in order to grant the federal government extraordinary power to interfere in Americans' lives.*

This reasoning was too much even for the Supreme Court, which had previously indulged the federal government in all sorts of bizarre readings of the commerce clause. In a 5–4 decision the Court declared in *United States v. Lopez* (1995) that not every conceivable federal power could be justified under some strained interpretation of the commerce clause. The majority's decision, though, kept intact the precedent in *Wickard,* whereby the federal government could regulate anything that had "substantial effects" on interstate commerce; its argument was simply that the government could not demonstrate that those substantial effects existed in this case.[9]

More recently, in the 2005 case of *Gonzales v. Raich,* the federal government challenged a California law that legalized marijuana for medical use. The federal government argued that medical marijuana was subject to federal regulation because its use affected interstate commerce, in particular the interstate marijuana market—a market the same government has made illegal. (For all their supposed concern for personal liberty, incidentally, the liberals on the Court, in particular Justices Ruth Bader Ginsburg and Stephen Breyer, eagerly embraced this *Wickard*-influenced interpretation of the commerce clause in finding against the two patients involved. Enforcing federal supremacy always comes first.)

In his dissent, Justice Clarence Thomas noted that the two patients around whom the case revolved had used

> marijuana that has never been bought or sold, that has never crossed state lines, and that has had no demonstrable effect on the national market for marijuana. If Congress can regulate this under the Commerce Clause, then it can regulate virtually anything— and the Federal Government is no longer one of limited and enumerated powers. . . . By holding that Congress may regulate activity that is neither interstate nor commerce under the Interstate Commerce Clause, the Court abandons any attempt to enforce the Constitution's limits on federal power.[10]

The logic of Justice Thomas's argument is inescapable. If the broad interpretation of the commerce clause is correct, then no aspect of American life is exempt from government oversight. Why not regulate human reproduction while we're at it? The number of people born in the United States every year has a much more direct effect on interstate commerce than does a farmer consuming his own wheat. If we are to accept modern interpretations of the commerce clause, on what logical grounds could it be argued that the federal government could *not* regulate reproduction?[11] (Justice Oliver Wendell Holmes actually anticipated this *reductio ad absurdum:* "Commerce depends upon population, but Congress could not, on that ground, undertake to regulate marriage and divorce.")[12]

HUMAN NATURE

The Constitution was sold to Americans as a device that would keep government restrained. The commerce clause, Americans were promised, applied only to a very limited range of activities. Now Americans are essentially being told that the commerce clause means what the Supreme Court says it means—even if these new interpretations are completely at odds with the clear statements of the Framers, and even if they lead to infringements on American liberties that no state voting to ratify the Constitution could possibly have imagined.

The federal government's manipulation of the commerce clause— to say nothing of its obviously indefensible readings of other parts of the Constitution—raises an important but often sidestepped question: can constitutions, in the long run, really restrain governments? Imagine giving a group of people a legal monopoly on the use of force as well as the power to levy taxes on an entire population. Then imagine telling them that their powers will be limited by a document that they themselves have the exclusive power to interpret.

Human nature being what it is, what in the long run should we expect to happen?[13]

CAN THE FEDERAL GOVERNMENT DO WHATEVER IT THINKS WILL PROVIDE FOR THE "GENERAL WELFARE" OF AMERICANS?

★ ★

Another of the phrases by which the Constitution's limitations on the federal government have been circumvented is the so-called general welfare clause. Article I, Section 8 of the Constitution speaks of the power of Congress to lay taxes "to provide for the common defence and general welfare of the United States." All too often the clause is said to authorize the federal government to appropriate funds for a wide array of purposes—well beyond the powers specifically granted to the federal government in the rest of Article I, Section 8—that have the "general welfare" of the American population as their aim.

Does this popular rendition accurately portray the meaning of the general welfare clause?

Certainly there was disagreement over the meaning of the clause in early American history. In his 1791 *Report on Manufactures* Treasury Secretary Alexander Hamilton adopted an expansive reading of the clause. According to Hamilton, the general welfare clause granted a broad spending power to Congress that was not limited by or confined to the enumerated powers of Congress that followed it in Article I, Section 8. Supreme Court justice Joseph Story adopted Hamilton's position in his *Commentaries on the Constitution* (1833). Story's argument was historically weak, however, and rested by and large on debatable inferences from the text of the Constitution.[1] (In formulating his opinion, Story also lacked James Madison's all-important notes of the proceedings of the Constitutional Convention.)

Hamilton was bold enough to advance his broad interpretation even though he had rejected that position himself in 1787–88. Prior to ratification Hamilton had written in *Federalist* No. 17 that "supervision of agriculture and of other concerns of a similar nature . . . can never be desirable cares of a general jurisdiction," and in *Federalist* No. 34 that "encouragement of agriculture and manufactures" were "objects of state expenditure." Then in 1791 he suddenly announced that "there seems to be no room for a doubt that whatever concerns the general Interests of *learning,* of *Agriculture,* of *Manufactures,* and of *Commerce* are within the sphere of the national Councils *as far as regards an application of Money.*"[2] Law professor Robert Natelson writes, "This sort of contradiction is one reason I have often wondered why some take Hamilton's Report on Manufactures seriously as a source of 'original understanding.' As a *post eventum* statement, it is inherently less reliable as evidence of agreement than statements (including Hamilton's) issued to induce ratification."[3]

As he himself admitted, Hamilton was very far from the mainstream of the Constitutional Convention. In an unpublished paper two weeks after the close of the convention, he spoke of his desire to see the central government "triumph altogether over the state governments and reduce them into an entire subordination." This put him completely at odds with the stated views of practically everyone, not to mention the positions advanced in the *Federalist.* If anything, Hamilton's postconvention statements are a good indication of the *opposite* of the common understanding of the Constitution.[4]

Hamilton's broad interpretation of the clause flew in the face of assurances given to the Constitution's Anti-Federalist opponents, who had been persuaded to ratify that document on the basis of a far narrower interpretation of the term "general welfare." Skeptics like Patrick

Henry, who feared the clause would one day transform the new government into one of unlimited powers, were assured that the clause could never be interpreted that way since the federal government would have only those powers "expressly delegated" to it.[5] The general welfare clause, Anti-Federalists were told, did not constitute an additional grant of power to the federal government, which was limited to its enumerated powers.

That the Framers took the trouble to enumerate the federal government's powers testifies against a broad interpretation of the general welfare clause. What point would there be in specifically listing the federal government's powers if the general welfare clause had already provided that government with an essentially boundless authority to enact whatever it thought would contribute to the people's well-being? If the clause really did bestow plenary spending power upon the new government, what was the purpose of including specific grants of power to "establish Post Offices and Post Roads," "constitute Tribunals inferior to the supreme Court," or purchase "dock-Yards, and other needful Buildings"?[6] The Framers were astute enough to realize that just about anything, however oppressive, that a government might choose to do could be justified on the basis of a contrived appeal to the general welfare. (Interestingly, the Confederate Constitution of 1861 dropped the general welfare clause entirely, fearful of its potential interpretations by ambitious politicians.)[7]

These were the very arguments that the likes of James Madison and Thomas Jefferson raised against the expansive interpretation of the clause. In *Federalist* No. 41, for example, Madison wrote:

> It has been urged and echoed that the power "to lay and collect taxes, duties, imposts, and excises, to pay the debts, and provide for the common defense and general welfare of the United States," amounts to an unlimited commission to exercise every power which may be alleged to be necessary for the common defense or general welfare. . . . But what color can the objection have, when a specification of the objects alluded to by these general terms immediately follows, and is not even separated by a longer pause than a semicolon? . . . *For what purpose could the enumeration of par-*

33 Questions About American History You're Not Supposed to Ask

ticular powers be inserted, if these and all others were meant to be included in the preceding general power? Nothing is more natural nor common than first to use a general phrase, and then to explain and qualify it by a recital of particulars. But the idea of an enumeration of particulars which neither explain nor qualify the general meaning, and can have no other effect than to confound and mislead, is an absurdity.[8]

Years later Madison explained, "With respect to the words general welfare, I have always regarded them as qualified by the detail of powers [enumerated in the Constitution] connected with them. To take them in a literal and unlimited sense would be a metamorphosis of the Constitution into a character which there is a host of proofs was not contemplated by its creators."[9] In 1792 Madison stated that the Constitution had created "not an indefinite Government, deriving its powers from the general terms prefixed to the specified powers, but a limited Government, tied down to the specified powers which explain and define the general terms." "It would be absurd," he went on,

to say, first, that Congress may do what they please, and then that they may do this or that particular thing. . . . In fact, the meaning of the general terms in question must either be sought in the subsequent enumeration which limits and details them, or they convert the Government from one limited, as hitherto supposed, to the enumerated powers, into a Government without any limits at all.[10]

Toward the end of his presidency Madison vetoed a bill that would have appropriated federal funds for the construction of roads, canals, and other "internal improvements." Although he favored such expenditures, he could not find them authorized in the Constitution. More to the point, he rejected the claim that the general welfare clause was all the authorization they needed. So expansive an interpretation of that clause would render "the special and careful enumeration of powers which follow the clause nugatory and improper," he said. "Such a view of the Constitution would have the effect of giving to Congress a general power of legislation instead of the defined and limited one hitherto understood to belong to them."[11]

Thomas Jefferson likewise stood firmly against an expansive reading of the general welfare clause. In his 1791 commentary on the controversial issue of a federally chartered national bank, he explained that the power to lay taxes to provide for the general welfare did not authorize Congress "*to do anything they please* to provide for the general welfare, but only to *lay taxes* for that purpose. To consider the latter phrase, not as describing the purpose of the first, but as giving a distinct and independent power to do any act they please, which might be for the good of the Union, would render all the preceding and subsequent enumerations of power completely useless." Moreover, such a reading "would reduce the whole instrument to a single phrase, that of instituting a Congress with power to do whatever would be for the good of the United States; and, as they would be the sole judges of the good or evil, it would be also a power to do whatever evil they please."[12]

Jefferson argued that if the general welfare clause had really been intended to have the broad meaning that people like Hamilton claimed for it, the clause would have deprived the other parts of the Constitution of meaning. "It is an established rule of construction," Jefferson explained, "where a phrase will bear either of two meanings, to give it that which will allow some meaning to the other parts of the instrument, and not that which would render all the others useless."[13] Therefore the broad interpretation could not be the correct one.

The testimony of history is also strongly in favor of the limited interpretation. Jefferson's victory in the presidential election of 1800 was in part a repudiation of Hamilton's broad interpretation of the Constitution in general and especially its general welfare clause. (And the election of 1800, writes law professor John Eastman, "was not a revolution in thought about the expanse of the spending power, but a return to what had been the common understanding of the phrase employed and the underlying principle it codified.")[14] In addition, just about every president from Thomas Jefferson to James Buchanan adopted a Madisonian interpretation of the clause; Buchanan held that the power of the federal government to spend money was "confined to the execution of the enumerated powers delegated to Congress."[15] If anything, the general welfare clause, far from being a grant of power to the federal government, was often understood to be a *limitation* on government power, in that the word "general" restricted federal spending only to those purposes whose benefits were national in scope rather than purely local or confined to a single interest group.[16]

> ... *&* THE TRUTH
>
> *A broad reading of the general welfare clause makes no logical sense and contradicts the stated intentions of the Framers.*

In case the dangers of a broad interpretation of the general welfare clause are not obvious, consider this: in the 1990s Supreme Court justice Antonin Scalia asked Bill Clinton's solicitor general if he could name a single activity on which the Congress might choose to legislate that in his view would go beyond its legitimate powers under the Constitution.[17]

He could not.

DOES THE CONSTITUTION REALLY

CONTAIN AN "ELASTIC CLAUSE"?

★ ★

In its listing of the powers of Congress, Article I, Section 8 of the Constitution includes the power to "make all laws which shall be necessary and proper for carrying into execution the foregoing powers, and all other powers vested by this Constitution in the Government of the department or officer thereof." This "necessary and proper" clause has proven to be a particular favorite among people and politicians who would expand the federal government's powers beyond those delegated to it. The typical high school social studies class presents it as an "elastic clause" that can be pressed into service to authorize just about anything.

To understand what the clause was intended to mean, it may help to consider first what it was plainly *not* intended to mean. At the Constitutional Convention Gunning Bedford proposed a clause that would have granted the federal government sweeping, open-ended power to legislate "in all cases for the general interests of the Union." That proposal was rejected. Instead, the Constitution would enumerate a finite list of powers, followed by a clause authorizing those powers that were "necessary and proper" in order to carry them out.[1] The necessary and proper clause, therefore, was intended to be different from and more limited than the sweeping clause that Bedford had proposed and that the Convention had rejected. But the necessary and proper clause has come to be interpreted so broadly as to amount to the open-ended clause the Convention chose not to adopt.

In the state ratifying conventions supporters of the Constitution reassured Anti-Federalist skeptics that the clause would not be used, and was not intended to be used, to permit the federal government to exercise a broad range of unspecified powers. George Nicholas told the Virginia ratifying convention that the necessary and proper clause "only enables them [Congress] to carry into execution *the powers given to them,* but gives them *no additional power*." James Madison held the same view.[2]

In *Federalist* No. 33 Alexander Hamilton argued that the necessary and proper clause, along with the supremacy clause (Article VI, Clause 2), only made explicit what was logically and unavoidably implied in the very nature of the Constitution, and that it added nothing other than simple clarification. "It may be affirmed with perfect confidence," wrote Hamilton, "that *the constitutional operation of the intended government would be precisely the same, if these clauses were entirely obliterated,* as if they were repeated in every article. They are only declaratory of a truth which would have resulted by necessary and unavoidable implication from the very act of constituting a federal government, and vesting it with certain specified powers."[3]

It was also argued that in light of the limits that the Constitution intended to place on government, the necessary and proper clause could not have the expansive meaning some feared. If the Constitution held that the government could do whatever was necessary to carry out its enumerated powers, but the government itself determined what constituted necessity, the clause would be a recipe for unlimited government, an outcome nobody wanted. That was the view of Virginia representative William Branch Giles, who asked: "If expediency constituted constitutionality; the House judged of the expediency; then every measure they could possibly enter into would be ipso facto constitutional: And what would then be the weight it was intended the Constitution should have; and where were its limits?"[4]

In the debates over the national bank, Thomas Jefferson argued in 1791 that if "necessary and proper" simply meant "convenient," then the result would be a government of unlimited powers:

> The Constitution allows only the means which are "*necessary*," not those which are merely "convenient" for effecting the enumerated powers. If such a latitude of construction be allowed to this phrase as to give any non-enumerated power, it will go to every one, for there is not one which ingenuity may not torture into a *convenience* in some instance *or other,* to *some one* of so long a list of enumerated powers. It would swallow up all the delegated powers, and reduce the whole to one power, as before observed. Therefore it was that the Constitution restrained them to the *necessary* means, that is to say, to those means without which the grant of power would be nugatory.[5]

St. George Tucker, a judge and professor of law, developed the Jeffersonian position further in his highly regarded *View of the Constitution of the United States* (1803). Tucker feared that some would attempt "to expound these phrases in the constitution, so as to destroy the effect of the particular enumeration of powers, by which it explains and limits them." The necessary and proper clause, he explained, "neither enlarges any power specifically granted, nor is it a grant of new powers to congress, but merely a declaration, for the removal of all uncertainty, that the means of carrying into execution those otherwise granted, are included in the grant."[6] Tucker concluded by noting that his discussion of the words "necessary and proper" was "not only consonant with that which prevailed during the discussions and ratification of the constitution, but is

THE MYTH ...

The Constitution includes an "elastic clause" that gives the federal government sweeping power to do what it considers to be useful or convenient.

33 Questions About American History You're Not Supposed to Ask

absolutely necessary to maintain their consistency with the peculiar character of the government, as possessed of particular and defined powers, only."[7]

But then the Supreme Court intervened. In *McCulloch v. Maryland* (1819), one of the most significant decisions in American history, Chief Justice John Marshall in effect adopted the view that "necessary" meant "convenient" or "useful"—the very position that Jefferson, Madison, and others had expressly rejected. In one of the most significant passages in the decision, Marshall held that the word "necessary" often "imports no more than that one thing is convenient, or useful, or essential to another. To employ the means necessary to an end, is generally understood as employing any means calculated to produce the end, and not as being confined to those single means, without which the end would be entirely unattainable."[8]

Although perhaps the best-known critic of *McCulloch* was James Madison, who believed the Court's reasoning threatened to undermine the limited nature of the federal government, Judge Spencer Roane wrote an especially thoughtful and lengthy reply. Judge Roane, all but unknown today, was a respected and important legal thinker of the early republic. With a reputation as one of the country's finest jurists, Roane would certainly have been Thomas Jefferson's choice for chief justice of the United States had John Adams not nominated John Marshall in the waning hours of his presidency.

In a series of articles in 1819 published in the *Richmond Enquirer* under the name Hampden, Roane set forth a detailed critique of the Court's reasoning in *McCulloch*. The *Enquirer*'s editor, Thomas Ritchie, opened the series by commending the articles to his readers and noting: "We solemnly believe the opinion of the supreme court in the

> ... & THE TRUTH
>
> *The Framers explicitly and repeatedly affirmed that the Constitution granted the federal government only the authority to carry out its specifically enumerated powers. The Supreme Court ignored that history to grant the federal government far more expansive powers.*

case of the bank to be fraught with alarming consequences, the federal constitution to be misinterpreted, and the rights of the states and the people to be threatened with danger."[9] Roane recalled that according to the *Federalist* the words "necessary and proper" had been added "for greater caution, and are tautologous and redundant," and cited James Madison's Report of 1800 as contending that "these words do not amount to a grant of new power, but for the removal of all uncertainty, the declaration was made that the means [of carrying out the delegated powers] were included in the grant [of powers to the federal government]." Roane wrote, "I do not object to them, considered as merely declaratory words, and inserted for greater caution: I only deny to them an extension to which they are not entitled, and which may be fatal to the reserved rights of the states and of the people. . . . The state governments being originally in possession of all the legislative powers, are still to retain such as are not *shewn* to have been relinquished."[10]

The following year John Taylor of Caroline, whose career included service both in the Virginia House of Delegates and in the U.S. Senate, set forth a similar understanding of the necessary and proper clause in his book *Construction Construed and Constitutions Vindicated* (1820). "These words," according to Taylor, "far from enlarging, restrict the legislative power of Congress," since they "expressly limit the legislative power of Congress to laws necessary and proper for executing the *delegated* powers, and bestow no authority to assume powers *not delegated*."[11]

WHEN THE TRUTH DOESN'T MATTER

The reasoning and arguments in *McCulloch* are often cited as the complete and definitive interpretation of the necessary and proper clause. UCLA law professor Stephen Gardbaum describes *McCulloch* as "one of the handful of foundational decisions of the Supreme Court that are automatically cited as original sources for the propositions of constitutional law that they contain. But *McCulloch* has the further (and even rarer) distinction of being treated as providing a full and complete interpretation of a particular clause of the Constitution.

Analysis of the Necessary and Proper Clause has historically begun and ended with *McCulloch*."[12] But the reasoning that John Marshall used in reaching his decision was disputed immediately by numerous thinkers of distinction and contradicts the assurances about the clause that were made at the time of ratification.

None of that matters anymore. Law students today read Marshall and *McCulloch*. If they have even heard of Roane or Taylor, or know about the objections of Jefferson and Madison, it is only by accident.

DID THE FOUNDING FATHERS BELIEVE JURIES COULD REFUSE TO ENFORCE UNJUST LAWS?

★ ★

How much power did the Founding Fathers want juries to have? The answer will surprise most Americans: by and large the Founders believed in jury nullification, a position that is considered radical today but had become quite mainstream in America by the late eighteenth century.

A jury nullifier upholds not only a jury's right to decide the *fact* of whether an accused is guilty of breaking the law, but also its right to determine whether the *law* itself is just. (Stated more briefly, the jury nullifier believes the jury has the right to judge both the fact and the law, while the opponent of jury nullification believes in the jury's power to judge fact only.) Thus even if someone is found guilty of breaking the law, according to the theory of jury nullification he would escape punishment if the jury found the law itself obnoxious or unjust. The same line of reasoning would permit juries to refuse to convict someone in cases in which they believe the law to be invalidly applied to the defendant, or in which the particular circumstances of the case would make enforcement of the law repugnant to the average person's natural sense of justice. Jury nullification is, in the last resort, a way for the people to see right prevail when the government seems indifferent or even hostile to the cause of justice.

LANDMARK CASE

One of the most celebrated legal cases from the colonial period, and the most prominent example of jury nullification from that time, involved a case of criminal libel against New York printer John Peter Zenger in 1735. Zenger printed the *New York Weekly Journal,* which contained criticisms both of the royally appointed governor of New York and of that governor's appointments to New York's Supreme Court. The colony's attorney general, who could not prove who exactly had written the critical passages, brought charges against the paper's printer.

Zenger had the good fortune of being represented by Andrew Hamilton (not to be confused with Alexander Hamilton), one of the most skilled and credentialed lawyers in the colonies. Hamilton noted that the accusation against his client accused him of publishing "a certain false, malicious, seditious and scandalous libel," and he countered that everything the paper had printed about government officials, although perhaps not terribly flattering, was *true.* The word *false* was contained in the accusation, Hamilton explained, and therefore it fell to the prosecution to prove that the statements in question were in fact false.[1] Hamilton even offered to prove that the statements were true.

Chief Justice James Delancey, on the other hand, instructed the jury that truth was no defense in libel cases. At that point Hamilton called on the jury to decide for itself whether the truth of his statements exonerated Zenger.

> Then, gentlemen of the jury, it is to you we must now appeal, for witnesses to the truth of the facts we have offered, and are denied the liberty to prove; and let it not seem strange, that I apply myself to you in this manner; I am warranted so to do, both by law and reason. The law supposes you to be summoned out of the neighbourhood where the fact is alleged to be committed; and the

reason of your being taken out of the neighbourhood is, because you are supposed to have the best knowledge of the fact that is to be tried. And were you to find a verdict against my client, you must take upon you to say, the papers referred to in the information, and which we acknowledge we printed and published, are false, scandalous and seditious; but of this I can have no apprehension. You are citizens of New York; you are really, what the law supposes you to be, honest and lawful men; and according to my brief, the facts which we offer to prove were not committed in a corner; they are notoriously known to be true; and therefore in your justice lies our safety.[2]

Chief Justice Delancey responded that it was the jury's task only to determine whether or not Zenger was the printer of the paper in question; it was then up to the Court to judge whether the words published had been libelous. Thus it was up to the jury to determine the matter of *fact* of whether Zenger was the printer, and up to the Court to decide whether as a matter of *law* the published matter qualified as libel. The jury, Delancey said, should "leave the matter of law to the Court."

"I know, it may please your honour, the jury may do so," Hamilton replied, "but I do likewise know they may do otherwise. I know they have the right, beyond all dispute, to determine both the law and the fact; and where they do not doubt of the law, they ought to do so. Leaving it to the judgment of the Court, whether the words are libellous or not, in effect renders juries useless (to say no worse) in many cases." Appalled that the truth of the statements made in the *Journal* was off limits to the jury—who were in fact told that the truth of the statements would make Zenger's offense even more grave— Hamilton appealed directly to jurors to judge of the law themselves and to acquit his client: "It is your right to do so, and there is much depending upon your resolution, as well as upon your integrity."[3]

> THE MYTH ...
>
> ———
>
> *The only role of a jury is to determine the facts of a case, not whether the relevant law is just.*

Not only was Zenger acquitted, but Hamilton's arguments on behalf of the powers of juries became influential throughout the American colonies. The power of jury nullification arguably made its way into the U.S. Constitution.

A DUTY

Clay Conrad, author of *Jury Nullification: The Evolution of a Doctrine,* suggests that the right of jury nullification is implied in the Sixth Amendment to the Constitution, which guarantees the right to a jury trial. It is reasonable to suppose that the framers of that amendment would use the definition of the word *jury* that was then current in the colonies. According to *Jacob's Law Dictionary,* the British text that was the most frequently consulted legal dictionary in colonial Virginia, "Juries are fineable, if they are unlawfully dealt with to give their verdict; but they are not fineable for giving their verdict contrary to the evidence, or against the direction of the court; for the law supposes the jury may have some other evidence than what is given in court, and they may not only find things of their own knowledge, but they go *according to their consciences.*" We may conclude that the right of jurors to judge matters "according to their consciences" was therefore part of the colonial legacy that the Framers, in guaranteeing the right of a jury trial, intended to hand down to future generations of Americans.[4] "Colonial Americans," Conrad writes, "had found jury service to be one of their most effective protests against the unjust laws imposed by Parliament, and they had only limited confidence in their own legislature and public officials."[5]

> ... *&* THE TRUTH
>
> *The Founding Fathers frequently argued that juries had the right to decide both fact and the law itself.*

There is no shortage of testimonies from important early Americans in favor of jury nullification. John Adams once wrote, "It is not only [the juror's] right, but his duty . . . to find the verdict according to his own understanding, judgment, and conscience, though in direct opposition to the direction of the court."[6] John Jay, the first chief justice of the United States, gave the following instructions to a jury in a 1794 civil case:

> On questions of fact, it is the province of the jury, on questions of law, it is the province of the court to decide. But it must be recognized that by the same law, which recognized this reasonable distribution of jurisdiction, you have nevertheless a right to take upon yourselves to judge of both, and to determine the law as well as the fact in controversy. On this, and on every other occasion, we have no doubt, you [the jury] will pay that respect, which is due to the opinion of the court: For, as on the one hand, it is presumed, that juries are the best judges of facts it is, on the other hand, presumable, that the courts are the best judge of the law. But still both objects are lawfully within your power of decision.[7]

Thomas Jefferson, in his *Notes on the State of Virginia,* also argued that juries had the right to decide both fact and the law.[8] Likewise, he was speaking on behalf of juries and their power of nullification when he wrote, "Were I called upon to decide, whether the people had best be omitted in the legislative or judiciary department, I would say it is better to leave them out of the legislative. The execution of laws is more important than the making of them."[9]

Alexander Hamilton spoke with particular urgency about the right of juries "to decide the law as well as the fact." Certainly the court should direct the jury in matters of law, and the jury should respectfully and attentively receive that instruction. "But," Hamilton said, "it is also their duty to exercise their judgments upon the law, as well as the fact; and if they have a clear conviction that the law is different from what is stated to be by the court, the jury are bound, in such cases, by the superior obligations of conscience, to follow their own convictions. It is essential to the security of personal rights and public liberty, that the jury should have and exercise the power to judge both of the law and of the criminal intent."[10] The court "are the constitutional advisers of the jury, in matters of law who may compromit [*sic*] their consciences by lightly or rashly disregarding that advice; but may still more compromit their consciences by following it, if, exercising their judgments with discretion and honesty, they have a clear conviction that the charge of the court is wrong."[11]

A FAMILIAR STORY

Despite the Founding Fathers' support of the right of jury nullification, merely to express support for that position today is enough to disqualify a potential juror in all but a handful of states. But in some cases a jury's power to exercise its right to nullify is the only way justice can truly be served. Here again a principle that was once taken for granted and known by everyone is now virtually forgotten—and when it is known, it is positively reviled. Sadly, this is a familiar story in America.

IS THE U.S. GOVERNMENT TOO STINGY WITH FOREIGN AID (OR NOT STINGY ENOUGH)?

★ ★

When the terrible Asian tsunamis hit in 2004, some people in the United States and abroad took the opportunity to lecture the U.S. government not only for its alleged stinginess in disaster relief but also for its supposedly inadequate commitment to development aid for the Third World in general. Conservatives typically responded to these criticisms by noting that of the $108.5 billion in combined foreign aid given by the nations of the world in 2003, the United States had contributed $37.8 billion—more than a third of the total.

But this argument, true as it was, missed the point. "Development aid" from the West to less-developed nations is not a good thing in the first place. It was in fact one of the more expensive failures of the latter half of the twentieth century.

By the end of the Cold War more than $2 trillion in inflation-adjusted dollars had been given to less-developed countries. And what did the recipients have to show for it? Not much. The U.S. Agency for International Development (AID) acknowledged in a 1989 report that "only a handful of countries that started receiving U.S. assistance in the 1950s and 1960s has ever graduated from dependent status." A Clinton administration task force later in the decade conceded that "despite decades of foreign assistance, most of Africa and parts of Latin America, Asia and the Middle East are economically worse off today than they were 20 years ago."[1] Looking back on the world's experience with foreign aid, a 1997 World Bank report recalled: "Governments embarked on fanciful schemes. Private investors, lacking confidence in public policies or in the steadfastness of leaders, held back. Powerful rulers acted arbitrarily. Corruption became endemic. Development faltered, and poverty endured."[2] (The economic arbitrariness encouraged by foreign aid was to be expected: since governments do not have to pass the profit-and-loss test that private investors do, they can get away with allocating money toward economically dubious projects that yield high-profile jobs, and therefore support for the regime, in the short run.)[3]

WASTED MONEY

Individual examples of economic stagnation and retrogression among recipient countries are everywhere. Over the past decade Egypt's percentage of people in extreme poverty has remained unchanged despite the billions that country has received; Egypt is the second-largest beneficiary of U.S. aid.[4] When Zambia became independent in 1964, its people's annual income per capita was $540 (in 2001 dollars). By 2000 they were making only $300—despite $6 billion in foreign aid from 1980 to 1996 alone.[5] And the list goes on and on like this, for scores of countries.

Economist Peter Boone compiled data for ninety-seven countries receiving aid over a twenty-year period and found no significant correlation between aid and poverty reduction. He likewise found nothing to indicate that aid increases life expectancy figures or primary school enrollment in countries receiving it.[6]

Foreign aid has likely slowed the process of economic reform; even the World Bank concedes that governments are more likely to pursue such reforms when they are feeling economic pressures.[7] In a separate study the World Bank concluded that "reform is more likely to be preceded by a decline in aid than an increase in aid."[8] (South Korea, Taiwan, and Chile, when faced with a cutoff in U.S. aid, embraced the free market and prospered.) Author Tom Bethell suggests that foreign aid has retarded economic development by masking the destructive consequences of these governments' economic policies.[9]

Even basic humanitarian assistance has severely disrupted Third World economies. Sending free goods to these countries has devastated local producers, who cannot compete against a price of zero, and has therefore all but destroyed local incentives to produce. A study of the UN World Food Program's response to eighty-four emergencies found that it took the world body an average of 196 days to respond to a crisis, and that the European Economic Community took more than twice as long. Agricultural expert Dennis Avery contends that aid arrived "too late to relieve hunger but in time to depress prices for local farmers who tried their best to respond."[10]

Governments receiving such assistance, moreover, very often use the food not to feed the hungry but to build support for their regimes by making food available to groups whose political support they need. (According to economist Peter Bauer, "The poor, particularly the rural poor who are the great majority, are politically ineffective and thus of little interest to the rulers.")[11] The *Wall Street Journal* writes:

> No wonder the effectiveness of food aid around the world is under suspicion in the United States. Some critics have concluded that this low-cost food is merely a device for keeping elites in power by propping up foreign-government budgets and feeding influential middle classes. Food aid has discouraged food production, these analysts say, and has failed to address the basic challenge of helping the poor earn enough to buy the food already available.

In Bangladesh the food never reaches the hungry because it is distributed by the regime according to calculations of political gain:

> It comes as a surprise to a layman, but not at all to the experts that food aid arriving in Bangladesh and many other places isn't used to feed the poor. Governments typically sell the food on local markets and use the proceeds however they choose. Here, the govern-

ment chooses to sell the food in cut-rate ration shops to members of the middle class.[12]

Someone buying food in a cut-rate ration shop needs a ration card. The poor have no way to get one.[13]

CORRUPTION

Americans who have grown cynical about foreign aid because it seems correlated with corruption are on to something, according to the latest research. A study published in the *American Economic Review* in 2002 argued that "increases in aid are associated with contemporaneous increases in corruption" and that "corruption is positively correlated with aid received from the United States."[14] Not long ago *Parade* magazine published a ranking of the twenty worst dictators currently in power. The U.S. government, it turns out, has contributed aid to all but one of them (Saudi Arabia's King Abdullah).[15] According to a Brookings Institution report, "The history of U.S. assistance is littered with tales of corrupt foreign officials using aid to line their own pockets, support military buildups, and pursue vanity projects. It is no wonder that few studies show clear correlations between aid flows and growth."[16]

The situation is especially serious in Africa. African government officials have become so well known for their attachment to fancy automobiles that Swahili now has a word, *wabenzi,* for "men of the Mercedes-Benz."[17] "Since independence in Africa," explains Kenyan human rights activist Makau Wa Mutua, "government has been seen as the personal fiefdom a leader uses to accumulate wealth for himself, his family, his clan. He cannot be subjected to criticism by anyone, and everything he says is final."[18]

It has been said that what Africa needs is its own Marshall Plan— a reference to the aid package that the United States bestowed on Western Europe in the wake of World War II. I have elsewhere argued that the Marshall Plan, praised to this day by liberals and conservatives alike, does not deserve the credit for Western Europe's economic recovery, as is carelessly (if frequently) assumed.[19] But even if we assume that the Marshall Plan was appropriate and wise, the fact is that Africa has already received the financial equivalent of five Marshall Plans, and it continues to receive annual aid packages comparable to what Western Europe received in each of the four years of the original Marshall Plan.[20] The results are there for anyone to see.

Even the *New York Times* admitted during the 1990s that "three decades of foreign development assistance in the Third World has failed to lift the poorest of the poor in Africa and Asia much beyond where they have always been." It had simply "fattened political elites."[21]

That may have come as a big surprise to the *New York Times* but not to anyone who knows anything about the subject.

WARNINGS IGNORED

The *Times* gave its readers the impression that no one could have known the dismal results of Third World development programs funded by the West. Well, somebody did know, and he tried for decades to warn people of the effects these policies would have: Peter Bauer, who taught economics at Cambridge University and later at the London School of Economics, where he spent the bulk of his career. For years, Bauer once observed, the field of development economics had remained "immune to inconvenient evidence."[22] By the last two decades of his life, that had begun to change, thanks in no small part to Bauer's work.

> THE MYTH ...
>
> ———
>
> *Foreign aid can play an important role in lifting countries out of poverty. The United States should increase its foreign aid expenditures accordingly.*

The fact is, foreign aid has propped up brutal and corrupt regimes and sheltered them from the economic consequences of their destructive policies. It has delayed or derailed essential economic reforms. It has subsidized programs (e.g., "import substitution") that have destroyed developing countries' export sectors. It has politicized life in these countries, as hostile groups struggle with each other to seize control of the increasingly lucrative coffers of the state apparatus. It has led to violence—"even massacre," as Bauer noted—as ethnic and other groups compete for control of the state apparatus and its foreign largesse; violence has escalated in such countries as Burundi, Kampuchea, Ethiopia, Indonesia, Iraq, Nigeria, Pakistan, Tanzania, Uganda, Vietnam, and Zaire.[23]

After more than five decades of foreign assistance, the results are essentially all bad.

It wasn't supposed to happen this way, of course. In the decades following World War II foreign aid was sold to Western taxpayers as a profound moral obligation that no person of good will could oppose. Outside aid, according to the conventional wisdom, was absolutely essential to the prosperity of the world's less-developed countries. These countries were said to be trapped in a "vicious circle of poverty." A high savings rate was necessary in order to fund the capital investment that would increase these countries' productive capacities and lift them out of poverty. But since they were so poor, they could not produce adequate savings in the first place and thus could not get this salutary process started. Foreign aid programs were intended to provide the capital.[24]

Bauer insisted from the beginning that this argument was invalid, even laughable. If it were really true that infusions of outside capital were necessary to spur economic development, then how did the *first* countries to develop manage to do so? By definition, they did so at a time when there were *no* developed countries to provide them with the capital, in the form of foreign aid, that developing economies supposedly needed in order to break out of the circle of poverty. As Bauer himself put it, if the "vicious circle of poverty" theory were correct, it would have been impossible for any country to develop, and everyone would still be living in the Stone Age.[25]

> ... & THE TRUTH
>
> *Some $2 trillion later foreign aid programs have essentially nothing to show for themselves, apart from propping up corrupt regimes, introducing perverse and destructive incentives, and postponing economic reform.*

Bauer contended that there was not "a single instance in history when external donations were required for the economic development of a country." Economic prosperity depends on "people's attributes, attitudes, motivations, mores and political arrangements. . . . If the conditions for development other than capital are present, the capital required will either be generated locally or be available commercially from abroad to governments or to businesses. If the required conditions are not present, then aid will be ineffective and wasted."[26]

Over the course of his many books and articles, Bauer showed that cultural attitudes and institutional arrangements have played a decisive role in determining a nation's economic performance. A people who believe in fatalism or collectivism rather than in personal responsibility, for instance, will be less likely to undertake the risks associated with capitalist entrepreneurship. Hernando de Soto demonstrated the importance of institutions when he investigated the poor economic performance of his native Peru. He found that insecure or poorly defined property rights were at the root of much of what ailed his country. He also showed that the suffocating effects of regulation, a factor almost entirely neglected in the development literature, had played a substantial role in Peru's woes. (He found, for instance, that it took "the equivalent of 289 work days, 81 meters of forms, and eight overt bribes to legally establish a small clothing factory.")[27]

THE PLATITUDES ENDURE

In spite of all this scholarly work and the second thoughts that so many former supporters of foreign aid had begun to have as the last century came to a close, by the early years of the twenty-first century the old, long-exploded platitudes of foreign aid advocates were back in force once again. Even the "vicious circle of poverty" made a comeback. According to the United Nations Millennium Project, "Many reasonably well governed countries are too poor to make the investments to climb the first steps of the ladder." Jeffrey Sachs, supposedly one of the world's greatest experts on the subject of international development, likewise contended that outside aid was necessary to fund a "big push" in public investments essential to ending African poverty. ("The claim that Africa's corruption is the basic source of the problem does not withstand practical experience or serious scrutiny," Sachs assures us.)[28]

One of the most effective critics of this renewed confidence in foreign aid is William Easterly. Easterly left the World Bank following the controversy surrounding his 2002 book *The Elusive Quest for Growth,* which criticized traditional foreign aid programs. Now a professor at New York University, Easterly consistently throws cold water on the propaganda:

> Sachs said that large aid increases would finance ". . . a 'big push' in public investments to produce a rapid 'step' increase in Africa's underlying productivity, both rural and urban." Over 1970–94, there is good data on public investment for 22 African countries. These countries' governments spent $342 billion on public investment. The donors gave these same countries' governments $187 billion in aid over this period. Unfortunately, the corresponding "step" increase in productivity, measured as per capita growth over this period, was zero.[29]

Still, proponents of what has been called the new economics of foreign aid remain confident that aid can work wonders so long as it is directed at countries with good policy environments; greater selectivity by donors can ensure that only trustworthy and responsible regimes are awarded with loans or grant money. Those regimes, in turn, will direct the aid money to fruitful and worthwhile enterprises.

A major difficulty is that this new confidence in foreign aid and what it can accomplish given greater selectivity is based entirely on a small number of studies conducted by the World Bank, whose conclusions have proven impossible to verify by outside researchers or else, when the Bank's data *can* be independently evaluated, are flatly contradicted by other scholars.[30] For example, much research suggests that even when aid is directed toward countries with relatively sound economic policies, the overall result is still negative.[31] A recent International Monetary Fund study concluded that there is "no evidence that aid works better in better policy or geographical environments," and that "no sub-categories [of aid] have any significant impact . . . on growth."[32]

But even if, after more than half a century of missteps, aid could somehow be channeled only to the best-behaved and least predatory regimes, that would not solve the fundamental problem: that "foreign aid is *inherently bad*," as Alan Waters, former chief economist for U.S. AID, so aptly put it.

> It retards the process of . . . economic growth and the accumulation of wealth (the only means of escape from poverty and degradation); it weakens the coordinating effect of the market process; it pulls entrepreneurship and intellectual capital into non-productive and administrative activities; it creates a moral ethical tone which denies the hard task of wealth creation. Foreign aid makes it possible for . . . societies to transfer wealth from the poor to the rich.[33]

A FAMILIAR REFRAIN

Despite such warnings about the problems with foreign aid, in 2002 the administration of President George W. Bush began to adopt the new selectivity approach. In March of that year President Bush agreed to attend a United Nations summit on global poverty to be held in Monterrey, Mexico. Perhaps to disarm some of his detractors (Bush had spoken against foreign aid numerous times in the past), shortly before leaving for Monterrey the president announced his intention to increase foreign aid by $5 billion over the next three years.

But instead of the global huzzahs it expected, the White House heard only crickets.

Author James Bovard tells what happened next:

> The White House was chagrined when Bush's proposal did not generate massive international applause. So on the day before he left for Mexico, White House officials revealed that there had been a glitch in the original announcement and that Bush actually planned to give away more than twice as much money under the new program. White House spokesman Ari Fleischer said the mistake was simply a result of "confusing" math. National Security

Adviser Condoleezza Rice explained, "We didn't want to go out there with essentially false or phony numbers." The *New York Times* noted that "skeptics said the White House was just adding on billions to make sure that the president was a hit in Monterrey."[34]

In his speech in Monterrey, Bush echoed the familiar refrain of the new economics of foreign aid: greater selectivity in identifying recipients of aid would set the developing world on the road to prosperity. This new program, in which foreign aid would be more selectively disbursed than in the past, would be known as the Millennium Challenge Account (MCA). (Congress had been consulted about none of this, naturally; legislation establishing the new program did not reach the legislative branch until early the following year.)

In fact, there was nothing new about calls for selectivity in determining recipients of foreign aid. We had heard all this before— again and again. In 1963 John F. Kennedy outlined "objective No. 1: To apply stricter standards of selectivity . . . in aiding developing countries." The Pearson Commission called for the same thing six years later. In 1985 the Cassen Development Committee Task Force on Foreign Aid declared that "the relief of poverty depends both on aid and on the policies of the recipient countries." In 1992, nearly thirty years after Kennedy's original statement, the Wapenhans Report, an internal review of the World Bank's lending portfolio, was still noting, "Even very well designed projects cannot succeed in a poor policy . . . environment."[35]

WE NEVER LEARN

If programs that have entrenched human misery and consistently failed for five decades cannot be called *failures,* nothing can. If history is any guide, no one should place his hopes in yet another new-and-improved foreign aid program. But there are some things Westerners *can* do for their brethren in the developing world: give sound economic advice; showcase success stories like Hong Kong, which has prospered fantastically without foreign aid; and repeal their agricultural subsidies and tariff restrictions, which would do more for the developing world's standard of living than all the foreign aid programs put together. This is not brain surgery: economist Mancur Olson noted in 1993 that the world's economically successful countries all possessed relatively secure property and contract rights, while all the unsuccessful ones did not.[36]

Even with all the talk about a new approach to foreign aid, incidentally, the older view is still very much present: the U.S. government still disburses about the same amount of standard foreign aid and will continue to ship some $10 billion abroad annually in the age of the MCA.[37] There, in case anyone needed it, is more evidence that the only thing we learn from history is that nobody learns from history.

DID LABOR UNIONS MAKE AMERICANS

MORE FREE?

★ ★

Visitors to Homestead, Pennsylvania, just outside of Pittsburgh, can expect to see a monument commemorating a famous strike that took place there in 1892. It reads: "Erected by the members of the Steel Workers Organization Committee Local Unions in memory of the iron and steel workers who were killed in Homestead, Pennsylvania, on July 6, 1892, while striking against the Carnegie Steel Company in defense of their American rights." Although most labor histories would say the same thing, in fact the strikers were themselves violating the American rights of others.

At the conflict's height the strikers' advisory committee took full control of the town, monitoring people's movement and even censoring the press. Nonunion workers hired as replacements, thinking they had the right to work for whatever employer offered them satisfactory terms, were beaten or had their living quarters bombed or burned down. The strikers also opened fire on the Homestead plant's guards, killing one, and spent the night trying to destroy the barges that carried them, at one point trying to set them on fire and another time setting off dynamite.[1] What "American rights" are these, exactly?

As late as the 1920s labor law in America went something like this. First, freedom of contract and association were essential principles. A laborer was perfectly free to reject any offer of compensation that an employer might make to him, and an employer was likewise entitled to reject any offer made by a laborer. An employee was free to withhold his labor services if unsatisfied with his employer's terms; likewise, a group of laborers jointly exercising this individual right were permitted to do so. No one, however, was allowed to prevent individuals who wished to work from exercising their right to do so. Strikers, like anyone else, were forbidden to interfere with consumers' right to shop where they liked. And strikes could not obstruct suppliers from making deliveries, since to do so would again violate the rights of others. Finally, since the employer's plant was private property, the employer had the absolute right to decide who would be permitted to enter, and complete strangers who wished to enter for the purpose of agitating his employees could be lawfully excluded altogether.[2]

Unions, therefore, were not prohibited in and of themselves— they were simply not permitted to engage in violence, threaten violence, or interfere in any way with the rights of other workers or of employers. This principle had been spelled out nearly a century earlier in the New York case of *People v. Fisher* (1835), which involved an attempt by a union to prevent Pennock, an independent bootmaker, from underselling them. The court ruled:

> The man who owns an article of trade or commerce is not obliged to sell it for any particular price, nor is the mechanic obliged to labor for any particular price. He may say that he will not make coarse boots for less than one dollar per pair, but he has no right to say that no other mechanic shall make them for less. . . . If one individual does not possess such a right over the conduct of another, no number of individuals can possess such a right. All combinations therefore to effect such an object are injurious not only to the individual particularly oppressed, but to the public at large. . . . It may be that Pennock, from greater industry or greater skill, made more profit by making boots at seventy-five cents per pair than the defendants at a dollar. He had a right to work for what he pleased.

His employer had a right to employ him for such a price as they could agree upon. The interference of the defendants was unlawful; its tendency is not only to individual oppression, but to public inconvenience and embarrassment.[3]

STACKING THE DECK FOR THE UNIONS

This approach to labor unionism began to give way with the Norris-LaGuardia Act, signed by President Herbert Hoover in 1932. First, the legislation made "yellow dog" contracts—in which an employee could be required to promise to refrain from union activity as a condition of employment—unenforceable in the courts.[4] In addition to exempting labor unions from prosecution under the Sherman Antitrust Act, the act also prohibited the federal courts from issuing injunctions against labor unions in some cases and seriously crippled their ability to do so in others.

Injunctions had been used to put a stop to union violence and property destruction when local authorities seemed unwilling or unable to protect life and property. Unions hated them. "An injunction," explains labor economist Morgan Reynolds, "temporarily restrained union actions pending a trial and this explains the intense union campaign against its use in labor disputes because once violence-ridden strikes were enjoined for a few days, they were difficult to revive, reorganize, and rekindle."[5]

It is one of the many myths of American labor history that the courts issued injunctions frequently and indiscriminately. Labor economist Sylvester Petro, who undertook a thorough study of the period from 1880 to 1932, found injunctions to be exceedingly rare: federal injunctions were issued in not even 1 percent of all work stoppages, while state injunctions were issued in less than 2 percent of all work stoppages. And these few injunctions were issued not to thwart labor union activity per se but to put a stop to violence against persons and property.[6] Now even this protection of the employer's rights—yes, employers have rights, too—would henceforth be absent.

Franklin Roosevelt's New Deal added the National Labor Relations Act of 1935, more commonly known as the Wagner Act, to the mix. It had once been the case that a worker who did not wish to join a union or pay its dues refrained from joining and was not obligated to pay dues. Thanks to the Wagner Act, that individual freedom disappeared. From then on, if a majority of workers in a given bargaining unit chose to unionize, then that union represented all the workers and could force them either to join or at least to pay dues. This is the principle of exclusive representation. The usual defense of such coercion is that since the Wagner Act called for a single certified bargaining agent to represent all workers in a given bargaining unit, requiring all workers to contribute something to the union was only fair. After all, it is argued, since all workers gain from the union's activities on their behalf, it would be wrong for each of them not to contribute to it.

This objection overlooks the real problem, which is the idea of having an exclusive bargaining agent in the first place. If unions were content to bargain solely on behalf of their own members, there would be no problem of nonmembers getting union benefits for free. If individuals were allowed to represent themselves and to enter into contracts with their employers on their own terms, those who wished to remain nonunion would not be "free riding" on the benefits bestowed by labor unions, since the union would simply not bargain on behalf of those individuals. But federal labor law no longer guarantees workers this freedom.

Interestingly enough, President Roosevelt had publicly opposed the principle of exclusive representation just one year before signing the Wagner Act into law. In order to avoid a strike by the United Auto Workers (UAW) that would have shut down the auto industry, FDR intervened in the dispute and settled it on the basis of proportional representation—that is, the UAW would represent only its own voluntary members instead of being the exclusive bargaining agent for all industry workers. In a national radio broadcast FDR even said that proportional representation was the only organizational principle for unionism that was compatible with the American commitment to liberty.[7]

Although it has become second nature to Americans, exclusive representation is rather uncommon as a system of labor-management interaction. In fact, the only other democratic country to mandate exclusive representation is Canada, which learned the principle from the United States. Other countries operate on the principle that in their private affairs individuals should be free to act in accordance with what they perceive to be their best interests and not be forced to accept the will of some majority. The idea that a majority should be able to bind a minority, this line of reasoning goes, is acceptable only in matters of politics and government. But since selling one's labor services to an employer is not a governmental matter but an exchange between two private parties, forcing individuals to accept the arbitration services of an organization they did not choose and do not want violates their right of freedom of contract.[8]

Once it is officially designated by a majority of workers as the exclusive bargaining agent for all workers, the union is never required to stand for reelection. Even after all the workers who originally voted for the union have died or retired, the union is simply assumed to have the support of a majority of workers. The new slate of workers has no say in the matter at all.

> ... & THE TRUTH
>
> *Americans are actually less free as a result of changes in American labor law since the 1930s. It is simply a myth that workers have little to no bargaining power if they are not unionized.*

The Wagner Act also forced employers to bargain "in good faith" with unions that were established by a majority of workers. The National Labor Relations Board (NLRB) would determine whether an employer had complied with this requirement. Moreover, the Wagner Act interfered with employers' freedom of speech by making it an "unfair labor practice" to attempt to influence their employees' decision whether to unionize or not. Employers were likewise required to permit total strangers to use company property for the purpose of persuading employees to unionize.

FREE SPEECH?

When an election campaign is under way to certify a union, employers are sharply restricted in what they are allowed to say. The Taft-Hartley Act of 1947 in effect amended the Wagner Act—which contained no protections of the employer's freedom of speech—by declaring that the "expressing of any views, argument, or opinion, or the dissemination thereof . . . shall not constitute or be evidence of an unfair labor practice under any of the provisions of this Act, if such expression contains no threat of reprisal or force or promise of benefit."[9]

This well-intentioned effort to protect employers' free speech rights did not fully work out in practice, since just about anything an employer might say to discourage unionism could be interpreted as a "threat of reprisal or force." Consider the case of *NLRB v. Gissel Packing Co., Inc.* (1969). Gissel Packing Company had had two of its plants shut down for several months in 1952 as a result of a strike; when they reopened, they did so on a nonunion basis. In 1965 enough interest in unionization had developed that a certification election on behalf of the Teamsters was set to be held. The employer reminded his employees of the consequences of union activity in the past and warned that certifying another union could result in more plant closings. And if workers should become unemployed as a result, their advanced age and low level of education would make it hard to find other work. According to the Supreme Court, these statements amounted to threats of reprisal. Thus, even though the workers ended up voting not to certify the Teamsters, the Court overturned the election results and imposed a bargaining order on Gissel Packing.[10]

The Wagner Act also allows strikers to use the picket line to try to prevent their employer from gaining access to other workers, as well as to prevent the arrival of deliveries and the entry of customers onto his property. Employers can even be compelled to rehire strikers guilty of violence. According to an NLRB ruling, whether strikers accused of such offenses should get their jobs back depends on whether their conduct "is so violent or of such serious character as to render the employees unfit for further service," or whether it amounted to only a "trivial rough incident" perpetrated in "a moment of animal exuberance." Such cases of "impulsive behavior" were "normal outgrowths of the intense feelings developed on picket lines." According to labor economist Charles Baird, excused cases of "animal exuberance" have included "beatings, stabbings, bombings, threatening of nonstrikers' families, destruction of property, blocking entrances to struck firms with broken glass and nails, and hurling brickbats."[11]

In practice, during strikes the police have typically stood aside and done nothing in the face of union intimidation and even violence against nonunion workers or those who simply wish to continue working. This is one reason that the court injunction had so often been sought against violent strikes. Labor unions can thus deprive employers of labor if they do not accede to union demands. (As economist Henry George wrote in the nineteenth century, "Those who tell you of trades unions bent on raising wages by moral suasion alone are like those who would tell you of tigers that live on oranges.")[12] And the NLRB is not exactly known for even-handedness in its rulings; in an all-too-typical arbitration decision in 1975, for example, the board determined that although the company in question "had a legal right to keep the plant open, its decision to do so gives it some share of responsibility for creating an environment conducive to violence."

Harvard University's Edward Chamberlin once described the unique legal status that twentieth-century labor law had granted to unions:

> If A is bargaining with B over the sale of his house, and if A were given the privileges of a modern labor union, he would be able (1) to conspire with all other owners of houses not to make any alternative offer to B, using violence or the threat of violence if necessary to prevent them, (2) to deprive B himself of access to any alternative offers, (3) to surround the house of B and cut off all deliveries, including food (except by parcel post), (4) to stop all movement from B's house, so that if he were for instance a doctor he could not sell his services and make a living, and (5) to institute

a boycott of B's business. All of these privileges, if he were capable of carrying them out, would no doubt strengthen A's position. But they would not be regarded by anyone as part of "bargaining"— unless A were a labor union.[13]

No wonder Nobel Prize–winning economist F. A. Hayek once said, "We have now reached a state where [unions] have become uniquely privileged institutions to which the general rules of law do not apply."[14]

THE LABOR MYTHS ENDURE

There is no denying that Americans are less free as a result of American labor law since Herbert Hoover and FDR. Most Americans probably assume that the loss of certain freedoms has been necessary in order to raise wages. But the empirical evidence simply does not bear out the conventional wisdom regarding unions. For one thing, if labor is "exploited" in a free labor market and employers can typically pay workers far below their marginal revenue product, we should expect labor-intensive industries—where by definition there would be more of this kind of exploitation—to be more profitable than capital-intensive industries. But no evidence exists to confirm this expectation.[15]

Moreover, if employers could really impose whatever wage rate they wished, then why in the decades prior to large-scale labor unionism did wages not diminish to near zero? (In fact, real wages rose substantially in the decades before modern labor law took shape.) For that matter, why did skilled workers earn more than unskilled workers? If firms were really in a position to tell workers to take or leave whatever pathetic wage they might choose to offer, why would they have felt a need to pay skilled workers more than unskilled workers? Why not just pay them both the same pittance?

Notwithstanding the claim that employers in the nineteenth century could force workers to accept low wages because they lacked assets and savings to sustain them during their job search or their period of unemployment, research has turned up no difference in wage rates between workers with substantial savings and workers with little to none. Workers, moreover, were increasingly mobile, and their variety of alternatives gave them substantial bargaining power, says Charles Baird.

> This idea, that workers without unions inherently have a bargaining power disadvantage relative to employers, is picked up again in the Wagner Act. But it is a hoary myth. A worker's bargaining power depends on the worker's alternatives. If a worker either works for Employer A or he doesn't work, i.e., if Employer A is a monopsonist, the worker has little bargaining power. If the worker has several employment alternatives, he has strong bargaining power. There may have been instances of monopsony or oligopsony in the nineteenth century, but they were short-lived. . . . It was Henry Ford, not Samuel Gompers, who did the most to increase worker bargaining power. By making the automobile inexpensively available to working people, Henry Ford increased every worker's effective job search area.[16]

Unfortunately, the vast bulk of the existing scholarship on American labor history is essentially unreadable. It takes for granted all the economic myths of unionism, the essential righteousness of the union cause, and the moral perversity of anyone who would dare to oppose it. Major incidents in the history of American unionism, like the Haymarket incident of 1886, the Homestead Strike of 1892, and the Pullman Strike of 1894, are often misleadingly described in order to conform to the ideological demands of this one-dimensional morality play. Having read in 2006 of the devastation of General Motors, essentially destroyed by the cumulative effects of the United Auto Workers' absurd demands, have we not reached an opportune moment to revisit the received version of American labor history?

SHOULD AMERICANS CARE ABOUT HISTORIANS' RANKINGS OF THE PRESIDENTS?

★ ★

Every so often the American public must endure another poll of professional historians ranking U.S. presidents in order of their "greatness." The practice began in 1948 when historian Arthur Schlesinger Sr. polled fifty-five historians and published his results in *Life* magazine. He did the same for *The New York Times Magazine* fourteen years later, and his son, Arthur Schlesinger Jr., published yet another such poll, for the same publication, in 1996.[1] Numerous other polls, up through a *Wall Street Journal* survey published in 2005, would be added to the list as well.

Who comes out on top in these polls? George Washington, Abraham Lincoln, and Franklin Delano Roosevelt are consistently the top three. Also toward the top in most polls are Theodore Roosevelt, Harry Truman, and Woodrow Wilson. Given the political views of the vast bulk of historians, presidents who strengthen the federal government by means of sweeping new domestic programs or foreign wars fare quite well, while those who exercise their power more modestly often find themselves relegated to the designation of "average" or worse.

Recall Woodrow Wilson's comment that the president is "at liberty, both in law and conscience, to be as big a man as he can."[2] If he accepts this invitation, he can expect to be richly rewarded by our court historians.

PRESIDENTIAL POWER GROWS

There was a time in American history when a powerful presidency was viewed with suspicion rather than held up as an ideal. Libertarian commentator Lew Rockwell describes the older view as one in which "the president is mostly a figurehead and a symbol, almost invisible to myself and my community. He has no public wealth at his disposal. He administers no regulatory departments. He cannot tax us, send our children into foreign wars, pass out welfare to the rich or the poor, appoint judges to take away our rights to self-government, control a central bank that inflates the money supply and brings on the business cycle, or change the laws willy-nilly according to the special interests he likes or seeks to punish."[3]

Elections and election campaigns were not the be-all and end-all of American liberty. "For those who do not vote and do not care about politics, their liberty is secure. They have no access to special rights, yet their rights to person, property, and self-government are never in doubt."

> For that reason and for all practical purposes, they can forget about the president and, for that matter, the rest of the federal government. It might as well not exist. People do not pay direct taxes to it. It doesn't tell them how to conduct their lives. It doesn't send them to foreign wars, regulate their schools, pay their retirement, much less employ them to spy on their fellow citizens. The government is almost invisible.[4]

Alexis de Tocqueville, the nineteenth century's most perceptive foreign observer of the United States, noted in the 1830s that "in some countries a power exists which, though it is in a degree foreign to the social body, directs it, and forces it to pursue a certain track. In others the ruling force is divided, being partly within and partly without the ranks of the people. But nothing of the kind is to be seen in the United States; there society governs itself for itself." The president "has but little power, little wealth, and little glory to share among his friends; and his influence in the state is too small for the success or ruin of a faction to depend upon his elevation to power." Foreign as it is to us today, that was how the presidency was viewed by the Framers of the Constitution. "The people who ratified the original Constitution never intended the presidency to be a powerful office spawning 'great men,'" writes Robert Higgs. "Article II, Sections 2–4, which enumerate the powers of the president, comprise but four paragraphs, most of which deal with appointments and minor duties."[5]

In the twentieth century this relatively minor position was transformed into a larger-than-life office whose occupant is expected to exude "vision," "leadership," and "greatness." This view of the president is what we might hear in Mussolini's Italy, or in any fascist regime, where The Leader is expected to exert bold leadership on behalf of the people. (Adolf Hitler once told a *New York Times* correspondent, "I have sympathy for Mr. [Franklin] Roosevelt because he marches straight toward his objectives over Congress, lobbies and bureaucracy"; he later described himself as the only European leader who expressed "understanding of the methods and motives of President Roosevelt.")[6] The one idea that is absolutely anathema to all such regimes is that society is capable of running its own affairs without the paternal custodianship of a Great Leader and his "vision."

THE MYTH ...

Our greatest presidents have been those who had "vision" and exercised their power to the fullest to lead the nation and serve the American people.

The historians consulted in these rankings of the presidents welcome this expansion of the presidency and conceive of the ideal president as a far-seeing demigod rather than a humble executor of the laws. Question 17 offered a great many good reasons not to celebrate the legacy of Theodore Roosevelt, for example, since he was largely the architect of the new kind of presidency and the superstitious reverence that Americans

33 Questions About American History You're Not Supposed to Ask

were expected to show for the chief executive. Yet there he is at number four in C-Span's 2000 poll of historians—and probably for some of the very reasons he has come in for *criticism* in this book. That poll ranked the presidents on their "vision" and on "setting an agenda"; other categories included "public persuasion," "crisis management," "economic management," "moral authority," "international relations," "administrative skills," "relations with Congress," "pursued equal justice for all," and "performance within the context of the times." That's funny: nothing on "fidelity to the Constitution" or "commitment to liberty."

And there is a pretty big difficulty. The polls take for granted that there exists an objective, apolitical, nonideological basis upon which such a ranking of the presidents may be compiled. But there is no such thing. To evaluate whether someone has been a good president requires a standard of measurement—philosophical, moral, economic, and constitutional. What constitutes good "economic management," for instance? A Keynesian will say one thing and a free-marketeer another. What does "equal justice for all" mean? Jacksonian Democracy intended the phrase "equal rights" to mean that no individual or group of individuals deserved a government-granted privilege at the expense of his fellow men. Today the awarding of government-granted privileges to certain favored groups is exactly what "equal rights" has come to mean.

> ### ... *&* THE TRUTH
>
> *The Framers never intended the presidency to be an all-powerful, all-important office, yet those who do best in presidential rankings tend to be those who grew the federal government and grabbed more power for themselves. Polls of historians reveal more about the historians themselves than about the presidents.*

THE VAN BUREN LESSON

Historian Jeff Hummel has argued that from a libertarian point of view the greatest president in American history was actually the relatively obscure Martin Van Buren, elected in 1836.[7] (A strong runner-up, surely, is Grover Cleveland.) Van Buren resolutely supported the free market and the Constitution at a time when every incentive existed for him to do otherwise. His support for the Independent Treasury, which separated government from banking, gave the U.S. a system that many economists—in spite of much foolish criticism by historians in the past—"are coming to agree . . . was the best monetary system the United States has ever had."[8] Van Buren also managed to avoid not one but two unnecessary wars (one with Mexico and one with Britain), a fact of particular significance when we recall the Founders' oft-repeated concerns about war and its tendency to undermine free societies.

Now, where does Van Buren wind up in the major presidential polls for his commitment to the Constitution? In 1948 he was 15 out of 29 presidents; in 1962 he was 17 out of 31; and in 2005 he was 27 out of 41. Arthur Schlesinger Jr. complained that Van Buren lacked "executive energy"; another historian described Van Buren's inaugural address as "essentially a charter for inaction."[9] (It hardly needs pointing out that those are Bad Things to the official historians who rank our presidents for us.)

The consistently low rankings of presidents like Ulysses Grant and Warren Harding are due in part to the corruption associated with their administrations. To a certain degree that is all well and good, but what is the Teapot Dome scandal compared to Woodrow Wilson's catastrophic decision, in the face of strong popular opposition, to involve the United States in World War I, a horrific conflict in which American security was in no way threatened?[10] At the very least Wilson's decision paved the way for the ultranationalistic politics of Adolf Hitler and the Nazis, who protested a punitive Versailles Treaty that the Allies would never have been in a position to impose without American assistance. Yet Wilson is consistently ranked among America's best presidents. Forget the foreign policy disasters he was responsible for, the historians polled seem to be saying, and forget the American deaths his decisions caused. The man had *vision*.

QUESTION **32**

WHO WAS S. B. FULLER?

★ ★

S tudents in African-American studies courses are unlikely to encounter S. B. Fuller's name. But Fuller's is an extraordinary story:
in 1935, in the middle of the Great Depression, he took twenty-five
dollars and made it into a large and fantastically successful cosmetic
company, in the process making himself reportedly the wealthiest
black man in America. In addition to his Fuller Products Company,
Fuller went on to own or control eight other corporations.[1] Historian
David Beito has described Fuller as "a remarkable illustration of business success and self-help" and a man whose business ventures "gave
inspiration and training to countless aspiring entrepreneurs and other
future leaders."[2]

Born into poverty in Louisiana in 1905 and attaining only a sixth-
grade education, Fuller began his career as a door-to-door salesman.
From the beginning he believed in old-fashioned bourgeois values.
"My mother died when I was 17 years old," Fuller later recalled. "She
left six children besides myself. The relief people came and offered us
relief, but we did not accept it, because it was something of a shame
for people to receive relief in those days. We were embarrassed just
because the relief lady came to talk to us. We did not want our neighbors to know we couldn't make it for ourselves. So we youngsters
made it for ourselves."[3]

By rights, Fuller should have been a hero among blacks—and

indeed to a great many he was. But in 1963 Fuller delivered a speech before the National Association of Manufacturers that all but guaranteed his slide down the Orwellian memory hole.

FULLER'S WAKE-UP CALL—UNHEEDED

In his controversial speech Fuller argued that even if blacks did suffer under legal disabilities, there was much they could do to improve their condition here and now. Fuller did not claim that blacks faced no obstacles; he was all too aware of them.[4] His point was that blacks themselves constituted a market, and that the black entrepreneur could enrich himself, employ his fellow blacks, and build up his community by launching businesses catering to the black community.

Fuller believed that winning the vote would go a long way toward removing the disabilities under which blacks lived, but he also knew that politics and electing fellow blacks were not enough. (If they were, today's Detroit would be a paradise for blacks.) Fuller was on to something here: the Irish, the American ethnic group that most embraced politics as a means of advancement, lagged consistently behind other groups that were less politically involved or that shunned politics altogether. Chinese Americans, on the other hand, who faced substantial racial obstacles of their own, avoided politics or entered the political arena only after they had attained prosperity (and even then they typically did so not as advocates for the Chinese-American community but on behalf of the common good of society generally).[5]

Fuller argued that much of what ailed blacks could be traced to a lack of entrepreneurial energy and imagination:

> If the Negro had the amount of initiative, courage, and imagination required, he could control the retail selling in his own community. Since he represents ten percent of the population of America today, he would be able to employ 1,065,000 people. There are 1,788,325 retail establishments in America and yet in New York City, where there are over 1,000,000 Negroes, they do not own over fifteen businesses which employ over ten people.[6]

Establishment civil rights organizations went berserk. Fuller was "blaming the victim." He was saying his fellow blacks lacked initiative, courage, and imagination. And by emphasizing economic independence and initiative rather than political activism as the more fruitful avenue in terms of bringing about substantial, long-term prosperity for blacks, Fuller had crossed a forbidden line. He was condemned by the National Urban League, the National Association for the Advancement of Colored People (whose Chicago South Side branch Fuller himself had once briefly headed), and the Congress of Racial Equality. Jackie Robinson, who had broken the color line in major league baseball, spoke of boycotting any of Fuller's business activities. "As far as I am personally concerned," he said, "I have already begun my one-man 'selective buying' program with regard to Fuller Products."[7]

Of course, Fuller's blunt words were intended not to be insulting but to serve as a wake-up call to the black community. Several months earlier, in fact, Fuller had told *U.S. News & World Report* that black Americans had been slow to embrace the capitalist system as a means of liberation at least partly because white condescension and contempt had produced a sense of helplessness among them. "The Negroes have been free for 100 years," Fuller said, "but, during that time, the white man has not told Negroes the truth. He has always taught the Negroes that they were at a disadvantage. He never told Negroes that they should do business for themselves, that they should clean up their own community and that they should accept community responsibility."[8]

Revered Harlem personality Vincent Baker, looking back on the controversy, sympathized with Fuller:

> Although Fuller may not have emphasized fully the extent of racial discrimination in that speech, and may have oversimplified some things, he was right in his notion that when someone has something to sell, he has greater bargaining power. If you have products and services and skills to sell, you have greater tools in the struggle to end racism. Fuller wasn't the first black to teach us this. A half century earlier, Booker T. Washington had said essentially the same thing, and we know what happened to him. It is not that

we have not had prophets but, as so often happens in history, they are not listened to.[9]

At the time many blacks jumped to Fuller's defense against Robinson. New York businessman Carl Offord asked in the *Amsterdam News,* "Why in the name of sanity, or in the name of the lowest animalistic sense of group identity and self-preservation, have you elected to begin a 'private' boycott of Mr. Fuller's products? Do you believe, really, that bankrupting the Fuller Products Company would 'thrust' the Civil Rights Movement forward? Do you honestly think that Mr. Fuller is standing in your way to freedom?"[10]

<table>
<tr><td>

THE MYTH ...

The only way forward for a disadvantaged people, whether Irish American, Chinese American, or black, is through political activism.

</td><td>

Another supporter pointed to the *New York Courier,* the influential black newspaper Fuller had helped to rescue when it was on the verge of closing its doors. Fuller became owner and publisher of the *Courier* "to save a vitally needed organ for the Negro national and local community. He stepped in when the jobs of over 150 people were at stake and no financing group—and no Negro civil rights group—could or would help." Among other things, bailing out the *Courier* meant that Fuller saved the very paper "that played such a prominent and singularly significant role in getting the Negro

</td></tr>
</table>

ballplayer into organized baseball. This should be a fairly easy point of recall, shouldn't it, Jackie?"[11]

IGNORED

Why has there been such hostility toward Fuller, and so little attention paid to him, in the black community? "There are a number of people in leadership positions who fear the coming of the truth," explained Vincent Baker, "because the truth might make black people free, free of the necessity of following a false leadership. . . . Fuller used to talk about blacks standing before the white man with 'a hand-

33 Questions About American History You're Not Supposed to Ask

ful of gimmes and a mouthful of much obliged.' He wanted to see blacks free themselves from this endless begging."[12]

In spite of the controversy his comments generated, S. B. Fuller earned the respect even of those who may have disagreed with his philosophy. At a certain level you can't argue with success. At Fuller's seventieth birthday celebration photographs reveal Jesse Jackson himself taking a major part in the proceedings.

Still, as Beito rightly notes, "professional historians have pretty much ignored Fuller's life."[13] But as information continues to trickle out about the man and his legacy, scholars are bound to become curious. Elizabeth Wright, editor of *Issues & Views,* writes, "There is no doubt that the life of S. B. Fuller will stand out as a remarkable achievement, not only in the annals of black history, but as part of the history of free enterprise."[14]

... *&* THE TRUTH

S. B. Fuller, all but forgotten today, was a great example of the use of economic means to bring prosperity and independence to a disadvantaged people.

DID BILL CLINTON REALLY STOP A
GENOCIDE IN KOSOVO?

★ ★

To this day Bill Clinton considers his military intervention in Kosovo, a province of Serbia, to be one of his presidency's most important legacies. Clinton wrote in his memoir of the "enormous relief and satisfaction" he felt the day hostilities officially ended in Kosovo. "The burning of villages and killing of innocents was history," he declared.[1] He was equally dramatic at the time, as he made the case for launching a military campaign in Kosovo in 1999: "What if someone had listened to Winston Churchill and stood up to Adolf Hitler earlier? How many people's lives might have been saved? And how many American lives might have been saved? . . . If you don't stand up to brutality and the killing of innocent civilians, you invite them to do more."[2]

In Clinton's portrayal, the Kosovo conflict was a horrific case of "ethnic cleansing" on the part of Serbs against the Albanians (and in particular Albanian Muslims) who made up most of the province's population. According to this view, the Serbs were a hopeless obstacle to peace, and the United States and its allies needed to put a stop to their grotesque campaign of violence.

But this account of the Kosovo war badly misstates what happened in the Balkans and what the U.S. military intervention achieved. The

Clinton administration, together with the American and British press, condemned the Serbs almost exclusively, when in fact the Kosovo Liberation Army (KLA) conducted repeated assaults on Serbian and Albanian civilians in the course of a bloody civil war. The KLA, which had links to Albanian organized crime and to radical Islamic groups, had been condemned by the Clinton administration as a "terrorist group" as recently as 1997.[3] That story suddenly changed when President Clinton declared his intention in 1999 to put a stop to what he described as an ongoing act of genocide, and to ensure the success of a multiethnic Kosovo that would be tolerant of ethnic minorities, allow religious freedom, and abide by modern Western values.

Such happy talk proved a deadly case of willful self-delusion.

"AN EXCUSE TO START BOMBING"

A civil war had begun to rage in Kosovo in 1998. Throughout the conflict the KLA employed guerrilla tactics with the aim of establishing Kosovo as an independent state, or possibly annexing it to neighboring Albania. The Serbs refused to consent to this territorial dismemberment in light of Kosovo's profound religious and historical significance.

Despite having condemned the KLA just a couple of years earlier, the Clinton administration in 1999 began calling for bombing the Serbs in effect on behalf of the KLA, in order to force them to accede to the latter's demands. The administration and others in the West argued that the Serbs were blocking international peace efforts, when in fact it was the Serbs and not the Albanians who promptly accepted what NATO called its supposedly "non-negotiable principles." Those principles were "an immediate end to hostilities, broad autonomy for Kosovo, an executive legislative assembly headed by a president, a Kosovar judicial system, a democratic system, elections under the auspices of the OSCE [Organization for Security and Cooperation in Europe] within nine months of the signing of the agreement, respect of the rights of all persons and ethnic groups, and the territorial integrity of the Federal Republic of Yugoslavia, with Kosovo remaining within the country."[4] The Albanians rejected these principles as insufficient and came around only when a NATO peacekeeping force was added to the mix, as well as a promise that within three years the disposition of Kosovo would be decided by means of a mechanism reflecting "the will of the people." Of course, such a vote, given the demographics of Kosovo, could mean only one outcome.[5]

The Clinton administration and its NATO supporters claimed to want to bring peace to Kosovo and prevent further bloodshed, and they said that the so-called Rambouillet agreement would have done just that. But the terms that were included under the heading "Implementation II," a late addition to the draft agreement, were impossible for any sovereign nation to accept. Among other things, they would have granted NATO "free and unrestricted passage and unimpeded access throughout the Federal Republic of Yugoslavia"—that is, not just Kosovo but all of Serbia and Montenegro. They likewise demanded absolute immunity for NATO soldiers "from all legal process, whether civil, administrative, or criminal" and from all laws "governing any criminal or disciplinary offenses which may be committed by NATO personnel in the Federal Republic of Yugoslavia." One State Department official boasted that the U.S. government "deliberately set the bar higher than the Serbs could accept."[6] He added, "They need some bombing, and that's what they are going to get."[7] Former secretary of state Henry Kissinger described the Rambouillet text as "a provocation, an excuse to start bombing."[8]

HOW TO JUSTIFY A WAR: FABRICATE

By any reasonable standard, Kosovo prior to the bombing was a brutal local conflict, but it was hardly a blip on the radar screen compared to countless outrages in the rest of the world that were either ignored or even condoned by the West. But in order to gain public support for the bombing of Serbia, the Clinton administration consistently employed fabricated casualty figures that were orders of magnitude removed from reality. According to the State Department, the Serbs were "conducting a campaign of forced population movement not seen in Europe" since World War II; a U.S. Information Agency release suggested that as many as 400,000 Albanians may have been

33 Questions About American History You're Not Supposed to Ask

massacred. David Scheffer, U.S. envoy for war crimes issues, repeatedly cited a figure of more than 225,000 ethnic Albanian men missing. Clinton himself spoke of "100,000 people who are still missing," and his secretary of defense, citing the same figure, ominously declared, "They may have been murdered."[9]

Writing in May 2006, Ed Herman and David Peterson looked back at the true and false numbers of the conflict:

> As regards the numbers problem, here too mainstream media protectiveness of the demonizing narrative was at a high level. For Kosovo, the U.S. Defense and State Departments had claimed at various times during the bombing war that 100,000, 225,000 and in one press release 500,000 Kosovo Albanians had been killed by the Yugoslav army. This was eventually pared to 11,000, although after a uniquely intensive search only some 4,000 bodies were found, including unknown numbers of fighters and victims of NATO and KLA actions; and as of early March, 2006, only 2,398 people remain listed by the Red Cross as still missing. There has never been any hint of criticism in the mainstream media of the inflated numbers given by U.S. officials, nor have there been any doubts expressed as to the accuracy of the 11,000 figure, although it came from sources of proven unreliability and was 70 percent higher than the official body count plus list of missing (6,398). In the *New York Times,* Michael Ignatieff explained that if the number of bodies found was less than 11,000 it must have been because the Serbs moved them out. He never explained why the bodies plus missing total fell far short of 11,000, but he didn't have to worry: in dealing with a demonized enemy anything goes.[10]

The lurid claims of war supporters typically proved unfounded. The British press, for instance, referred to the Trepca mines as another Auschwitz. "Trepca—the name will live alongside those of Belsen, Auschwitz, and Treblinka," reported the *Mirror.*[11] Inspection turned up no bodies there at all: Hague War Crimes Tribunal spokeswoman Kelly Moore said investigators had found "absolutely nothing."[12] One of the worst atrocity sites was supposed to be the village of Ljubenic, which was said to hold 350 bodies in a mass grave. Seven bodies were found.[13] On the eve of Serb leader Slobodan Milosevic's war crimes trial at The Hague, the fantastic figures once bandied about had been reduced to the claim that "at least four and a half thousand people died, but estimates rise to ten"—a terrible situation to be sure, but not exactly the 400,000 deaths intimated at the start.[14]

THE MYTH ...

By standing up to the Serbs in 1999, President Bill Clinton stopped a genocide from occurring in Kosovo. Thanks to the Western military intervention, "the burning of villages and killing of innocents was history," as Clinton himself proudly recalled.

Indeed, it was only after the bombing began that the Serbs began a massive expulsion of Albanians—an awful and indefensible act, perpetrated on the grounds that NATO was providing air cover for the terrorist KLA. The CIA had warned Clinton that such a humanitarian catastrophe was likely if he decided to bomb, but he went ahead anyway and then pretended to be shocked at the result. The bombing led to a humanitarian disaster of its own, destroying hospitals and schools, wreaking environmental havoc, and claiming as many as 2,000 lives. The cost to rebuild was estimated at $100 billion. In May, in the midst of the bombing, John Pilger reported in the *Guardian*:

> Eighteen hospitals and clinics and at least 200 nurseries, schools, colleges and students' dormitories have been destroyed or damaged, together with housing estates, hotels, libraries, youth centres, theatres, museums, churches, and fourteenth-century monasteries on the World Heritage list. Farms have been bombed, their crops set on fire. As Friday's bombing of the Kosovo town of Korisa shows, there is no discrimination between Serbs and those being "saved." Every day, three times more civilians are killed by NATO than the daily estimate of deaths in Kosovo in the months prior to the bombing.[15]

The American media could hardly have been more in lockstep with the Clinton administration's version of events—from the negotiations at Rambouillet to the NATO bombing itself—than if Al Gore had written the news reports himself. It was one of the worst cases of yellow journalism in recent memory, in which the Western press almost without exception portrayed the conflict as a simple matter of good against evil. In many cases the unsavory KLA was simply not mentioned at all. The *New York Times* managed to write an entire prowar editorial on the first day of the bombing (March 24, 1999) without once referring to the KLA— a practice the *Times* maintained in numerous later articles as well. Entire network news broadcasts managed to cover the issue without so much as a reference to the KLA or even to the fact that a civil war was in progress. Omitting one of the two contending parties from the discussion of Kosovo, wrote two critics, helped "to simplify the conflict so that those without additional information will see that the side supported by Washington are the 'good guys,' and the other side are the 'bad guys.' "[16]

Not everyone cheered the bombing of Kosovo. Conservatives like Robert Novak and leftists like Noam Chomsky condemned it, with Pope John Paul II even describing it as an "act of diabolical retribution."[17]

But all in all Western liberals loved the war. C. Raja Mohan, the strategic and military correspondent for India's *Hindu*, wondered aloud: "Where have all the Western liberals gone? Nearly two weeks into NATO's war against Serbia, there is barely a whimper

> ... & THE TRUTH
>
> *The Clinton administration used fabricated casualty figures to obscure what was taking place in Kosovo— not "genocide" but a brutal civil war that had claimed several thousand lives. The Kosovo Liberation Army, which the Clinton administration itself had previously called a "terrorist group," proved resistant to peace efforts and actually conducted ethnic cleansing of its own—not that anyone consulting the Western media would know anything about it.*

of protest in either Europe or North America. But then you can't expect Western peaceniks to protest against a war they themselves are waging."[18] Alexander Cockburn and Jeffrey St. Clair, leftist writers themselves, said the Kosovo campaign "was the Liberals' War waged by social democracy's best and brightest, intent on proving once again that wars can be fought with the best and most virtuous of intentions: the companion volume to Hillary Clinton's 'It Takes a Village' turns out to be 'It Takes an Air Force.' "[19]

THE REST OF THE STORY

For all the Clinton administration's alleged concern about saving people from ethnically based violence and displacement, it stood mute as the KLA began a massive ethnic cleansing campaign of its own against all non-Albanians after the NATO bombing ended in June 1999. By the second half of the year, long after most of the Western press had lost interest in the issue, Serbs in Kosovo found themselves subject to the ethnic Albanians' desire for revenge. Before long, even with a UN presence there, more Serbs had been killed than Albanians before the bombing. Serbs were forced from their homes in huge numbers, with more than 200,000 fleeing Kosovo altogether. In Pristina, Kosovo's capital city, a mere 120 Serbs out of 40,000 remain.[20]

And it wasn't only Serbs: some 100,000 Roma Gypsies—three quarters of the population—were driven out of Kosovo in the course of the KLA's ethnic cleansing program. Sani Rifati, a Romani activist, recalls the day—May 2, 2002—when conditions at last seemed safe enough that he could return to the Pristina neighborhood where he had lived for twenty-seven years. He found that "that place—where I grew up with my four brothers and one sister, cousins, relatives, neighbors, friends—no longer existed. Everything had been wiped away. The new and renovated houses, villas, gas stations, motels, all built in the past three years by the triumphant ethnic Albanians, made Kosovo look like a foreign country to me." That story never made it to the Western media, either—"the media and the international 'humanitarian' community are silent," Rifati says.[21]

This is the part of the story that is typically left out, attracting far less media attention than Serbian crimes in 1998–99, and to this day even most educated Americans are probably unaware of the ethnic cleansing and the overall humanitarian catastrophe that occurred in the wake of the Clinton-sponsored bombing of Serbia. But here and there the truth has managed to leak out. In early 2004 Senator Sam Brownback wrote a letter to President George W. Bush deploring the crimes against Serb Kosovars following the cessation of the NATO bombing campaign: "We should not consider advancing the cause of independence of a people whose first act when liberated was to ethnically cleanse a quarter of a million of their fellow citizens and destroy over a hundred of their holy sites."[22] In March of that year, after nearly five years of United Nations rule, a UN official described the situation thus: "Kristallnacht is under way in Kosovo. What is happening in Kosovo must unfortunately be described as a pogrom against Serbs: churches are on fire and people are being attacked for no other reason than their ethnic background."[23] Those Serbs who do remain in Kosovo are confined to certain enclaves under NATO protection and have continued to suffer from ethnically motivated aggression.[24] No multicultural utopia has yet emerged.

But the delusion of a tolerant Kosovo continues to be entertained by some people even now. "At the time when the prospective 'clash of civilizations' between the West and Islam is widely feared," claims the Alliance for a New Kosovo, "the creation of a Muslim-majority secular state, tolerant of all ethnic peoples regardless of personal creed, would be viewed as a victory for the national values espoused by the United States and the nations of the European Union." Writing in *The National Interest,* Damjan de Krnjevic-Miskovic observes rather more accurately that "some in the Kosovo Albanian leadership believe that by cleansing all remaining Serbs from the area . . . and destroying Serbian cultural sites, they can present the international community with a *fait accompli.*"[25] The International Crisis Group has likewise been more realistic than either the Clinton administration or the Alliance for a New Kosovo: "With no vision for the future of Serbs in Kosovo, one might suspect that the latent Albanian hope is that they will all eventually sell out and leave."[26] Yes, one might suspect that.

Since NATO took control of the province, those few Serbs still living there have seen thousands of their homes looted and vandalized and 150 Christian churches and monasteries destroyed. There is the real Clinton legacy in Kosovo.

Conclusion: Schools and Superstition

> But the whole thing, after all, may be put very simply. I believe that it is better to tell the truth than to lie. I believe that it is better to be free than to be a slave. And I believe that it is better to know than to be ignorant.
>
> —H. L. MENCKEN

We began with Mencken, and with Mencken we shall conclude.

The most dangerous man, to any government, is the man who is able to think things out for himself, without regard to the prevailing superstitions and taboos. Almost inevitably he comes to the conclusion that the government he lives under is dishonest, insane and intolerable, and so, if he is romantic, he tries to change it. And even if he is not romantic personally he is very apt to spread discontent among those who are.[1]

What purpose—apart from condom distribution, of course—does the public school monopoly serve today if not to indoctrinate young people precisely in the "prevailing superstitions and taboos"?

It is a genuine miracle when a public school student graduates today with anything but the most conventional views about important issues involving (in particular) history, economics, and religion. As far as he knows, the Middle Ages were a time of backwardness and superstition, the Church contributed nothing to Western civilization (except perhaps ignorance and repression), the Industrial Revolution was a disaster for the lower classes, Third World poverty is the West's fault, and capitalism impoverishes workers—the list goes on and on.[2] (The fact that most if not all of these statements may sound plausible to the casual reader is an indication of how well the system has worked; recall Mencken's definition of a platitude as an idea "[a] that is admitted to be true by everyone, and [b] that is not true.") It's not the student's fault that his knowledge is a tissue of bumper-sticker slogans: his teachers never gave him so much as a hint that entire bodies of scholarship contradicted these slogans, or that in some cases practically *no professional scholar* any longer held the clichéd positions he was being taught in school.

In the case of American history in particular, the conclusion that students are expected to draw isn't terribly subtle: the private sector is the realm of exploitation and greed, and we should seek relief from the government sector, which is populated by idealistic crusaders for justice. This progovernment prejudice is clear even in the choice of subject matter: students leave school knowing all about how a bill becomes a law, for instance, but not the first thing about how markets work.

No matter where in the country they live, American public school students learn one and the same perspective on topics as diverse as the Constitution, labor unions, Franklin Roosevelt, states' rights, and capitalism. Try teaching the conclusions of some of the chapters of this book in such a school, and—regardless of the mountain of scholarly evidence you can cite in their favor—see how long it takes before what will inevitably happen to you happens to you.

You almost have to give the architects of this system credit for the cleverness of the racket they have going: the same group of people who hold a monopoly on the power to tax and the power to initiate force also wield an effective monopoly on the power to educate future generations of Americans. And what a surprise: the education that the system imparts just happens to consist of flattering descriptions of government and all its works, laundry lists of all the terrible things that would surely happen to us in its absence, and—of course—the depiction of U.S. presidents as larger-than-life demigods whose "vision" has made our lives so much better.

"The ruling elite," wrote Murray Rothbard, "whether it be the monarchs of yore or the Communist parties of today, are in desperate need of intellectual elites to weave *apologias* for state power. The state rules by divine edict; the state insures the common good or the general welfare; the state protects us from the bad guys over the mountain; the state guarantees full employment; the state activates the multiplier effect; the state insures social justice, and on and on. The *apologias* differ over the centuries; the effect is always the same."[3]

For this reason alone the state's official version of history, which is always and everywhere another such apologia on behalf of itself, deserves not the benefit of the doubt but an abiding and informed skepticism. No free people ever survived on a consistent diet of official propaganda. Hayek was right: how we understand the past dramatically influences how we view the present. That is why, for the sake of American freedom, there should be no question about American history you're not supposed to ask.

NOTES

INTRODUCTION

1. The article appears in H. L. Mencken, *The Bathtub Hoax and Other Blasts & Bravos from the Chicago Tribune,* ed. Robert McHugh (New York: Alfred A. Knopf, 1958), 4–10.
2. Ibid., 17.
3. Ibid., 15.
4. Ibid., 11.
5. Ibid., 12.
6. F. A. Hayek, "History and Politics," in *Capitalism and the Historians,* ed. F. A. Hayek (Chicago: University of Chicago Press, 1954), 3–29.

QUESTION 1

1. The issue of immigration has been opened up again among American libertarians. The summer 1998 issue of the *Journal of Libertarian Studies* was dedicated to this debate. Murray Rothbard, who was known as "Mr. Libertarian," rethought the question toward the end of his life and became convinced that libertarian theory did not demand open borders as presently understood. See Murray N. Rothbard, "Deconstructing the Nation State," *Journal of Libertarian Studies* 11 (Fall 1994): 1–10. Hans-Hermann Hoppe questions prior libertarian orthodoxy in *Democracy—the God That Failed: The Economics and Politics of Monarchy, Democracy, and Natural Order* (New Brunswick, N.J.: Transaction, 2001), chs. 7–8. See also Thomas E. Woods Jr., "Liberty and Immigration," *Freeman* 45 (December 1995): 775–77.
2. John Bigelow, ed., *The Complete Works of Benjamin Franklin* (New York: G. P. Putnam's Sons, 1887), 2:231.
3. Thomas Jefferson, *Notes on the State of Virginia,* ed. David Waldstreicher (Boston: Bedford/St. Martin's, 2002), 138.
4. Ibid., 139.
5. Ibid.

6. Ibid.

7. Henry Cabot Lodge, ed., *The Works of Alexander Hamilton* (New York: G. P. Putnam's Sons, 1904), 8: 217; the entire set is available online at http://oll .libertyfund.org/Home3/Set.php?recordID=0249.

8. M. Grant and C. S. Davison, eds., *The Founders of the Republic on Immigration, Naturalization and Aliens* (New York: Charles Scribner's Sons, 1928), 47. This volume contains many of the excerpts used here; for the convenience of readers I have included the primary source information in the notes.

9. Ibid., 49–50.

10. Ibid., 50.

11. Worthington Chauncey Ford, ed., *The Writings of George Washington* (New York: G. P. Putnam's Sons, 1889), 12:489.

12. Charles R. King, ed., *The Life and Correspondence of Rufus King* (New York: G. P. Putnam's Sons, 1894–1900), 2:371.

13. *The Federalist Papers,* ed. Clinton Rossiter (New York: Penguin, 1961), 38.

14. Thomas G. West, *Vindicating the Founders: Race, Sex, Class, and Justice in the Origins of America* (Lanham, Md.: Rowman & Littlefield, 1997), 155.

15. Grant and Davison, eds., *Founders of the Republic,* 81.

QUESTION 2

1. This chapter is based on an article I wrote for *The Free Market* in September 2001.

2. Michael Eric Dyson, *I May Not Get There With You: The True Martin Luther King, Jr.* (New York: Free Press, 2001), 21.

3. Ibid., 23.

4. Ibid., 24.

5. Martin Luther King Jr., *Why We Can't Wait* (New York: Signet Classics, 2000), 128.

6. Dyson, *I May Not Get There With You,* 40.

7. Ibid., 39.

8. Ibid., 88.

9. Ibid.

10. Ibid., 87.

11. Jack M. Bloom, *Class, Race, and the Civil Rights Movement* (Bloomington: Indiana University Press, 1987), 212.

QUESTION 3

1. Quoted in William M. Denevan, "The Pristine Myth: The Landscape of the Americas in 1492," *Annals of the Association of American Geographers* 82 (1992): 369–83.

2. Fergus M. Bordewich, *Killing the White Man's Indian: Reinventing Native Americans at the End of the Twentieth Century* (New York: Doubleday, 1996), 212.

3. Ibid.; see also Gordon M. Day, "The Indian as an Ecological Factor in the Northeastern Forest," *Ecology* 34 (April 1953): 329–44.

4. Terry L. Anderson, *Conservation Native American Style* (PERC Policy Series, July 1996).

5. Shepard Krech III, *The Ecological Indian: Myth and History* (New York: Norton, 1999), 120–21.

6. Ibid., 121.

7. Anderson, *Conservation Native American Style.*

8. Krech, *Ecological Indian,* 170–71.

9. Ibid., 188.

10. Al Gore, *Earth in the Balance* (New York: Houghton Mifflin, 2000 [1992]), 259.

11. Denise Low, "Contemporary Reinvention of Chief Seattle: Variant Texts of Chief Seattle's 1854 Speech," *American Indian Quarterly* 19 (Summer 1995): 409.

12. William S. Abruzzi, "The Myth of Chief Seattle," *Human Ecology Forum* 7 (2000): 73.

13. Bordewich, *Killing the White Man's Indian,* 133.

14. Abruzzi, "Myth of Chief Seattle," 73–74.

15. Low, "Contemporary Reinvention of Chief Seattle," 411.

16. Abruzzi, "Myth of Chief Seattle," 72–73; see also Low, "Contemporary Reinvention of Chief Seattle," 408.

17. Kay Milton, *Environmentalism and Cultural Theory: Exploring the Role of Anthropology in Environmental Discourse* (London: Routledge, 1996), 113.

18. Ibid.

19. Terry L. Anderson and Peter J. Hill, *The Not So Wild, Wild West: Property Rights on the Frontier* (Stanford, Calif.: Stanford University Press, 2004), 40–41.

20. Anderson, *Conservation Native American Style.*

21. Robert Higgs, "Legally Induced Technical Regress in the Washington Salmon Fishery," *Research in Economic History* 7 (1982): 59.

22. Ibid. Higgs concludes that the Indians' property-based system was far more sophisticated, sensible, and efficient than what replaced it.

23. Anderson, *Conservation Native American Style.*

QUESTION 4

1. Thomas Fleming, *The Politics of Human Nature* (New Brunswick, N.J.: Transaction, 1993), ch. 8.

2. Thomas Jefferson to Charles Hammond, August 18, 1821, http://yamaguchy.netfirms.com/jefferson/1821.html.

3. In his exposition of the Virginia Resolutions in 1833, Virginia legal thinker Abel Upshur argued very precisely that the Virginia Resolutions did in fact call for nullification, Madison's later protests to the contrary notwithstanding. Kevin Gutzman writes, "The distinction so often drawn between Jefferson's strident and Madison's moderate tone seems strained; there is no difference between 'null, void, and of no force or effect' and 'invalidity,'

between 'nullifying' a statute and 'interpos[ing]' to prevent its enforcement." Kevin R. Gutzman, "A Troublesome Legacy: James Madison and 'the Principles of '98,'" *Journal of the Early Republic* 15 (Winter 1995): 581. Again: "One of Madison's most notable 'tactical adjustments' had been his campaign, as a retired former president, to becloud the events of 1798 by denying they had meant what they plainly had meant." K. R. Constantine Gutzman, "'Oh, What a Tangled Web We Weave . . .': James Madison and the Compound Republic," *Continuity* 22 (Spring 1998): 22.

4. For a brief overview of these ideas, see Thomas E. Woods Jr., *The Politically Incorrect Guide to American History* (Washington, D.C.: Regnery, 2004), ch. 4; for a lengthier elaboration see William J. Watkins Jr., *Reclaiming the American Revolution: The Kentucky and Virginia Resolutions and Their Legacy* (New York: Palgrave Macmillan, 2004).

5. Watkins, *Reclaiming the American Revolution,* 87; see also H. Arthur Scott Trask, "Thomas Jefferson: Classical Liberal Statesman of the Old Republic," in *Reassessing the Presidency,* ed. John V. Denson (Auburn, Ala.: Ludwig von Mises Institute, 2001), 88, 89.

6. James J. Kilpatrick, *The Sovereign States: Notes of a Citizen of Virginia* (Chicago: Regnery, 1957), 128, 129–30.

7. Ibid., 130.

8. Forrest McDonald, *States' Rights and the Union: Imperium in Imperio, 1776–1876* (Lawrence: University Press of Kansas, 2000), 64.

9. Ibid.

10. Watkins, *Reclaiming the American Revolution,* 88.

11. Kilpatrick, *Sovereign States,* 131.

12. Ibid.

13. Edward James Wagner II, "State-Federal Relations During the War of 1812" (Ph.D. diss., Ohio State University, 1963), 35–36.

14. Watkins, *Reclaiming the American Revolution,* 90.

15. Ibid., 90–91; Kilpatrick, *Sovereign States,* 135; Wagner, "State-Federal Relations," 31.

16. Kilpatrick, *Sovereign States,* 137.

17. On fugitive-slave legislation as just one example of how the federal government socialized the costs of slaveholding (and thus enhanced slavery's profitability), see Mark Thornton, "Slavery, Profitability, and the Market Process," *Review of Austrian Economics* 7, no. 2 (1994): 21–48. Thornton pursues this line of argument further in Mark A. Yanochik, Bradley T. Ewing, and Mark Thornton, "A New Perspective on Antebellum Slavery: Public Policy and Slave Prices," *Atlantic Economic Journal* 29 (September 2001): 330–40. The same group of scholars also notes that *government-subsidized railroad production* likewise artificially stimulated slave prices in the 1850s, a phenomenon that has typically been cited by less rigorous scholars as a spontaneous phenomenon that (supposedly) illustrated the economic vigor and profitability of slavery. See Mark A. Yanochik, Mark Thornton, and

Bradley T. Ewing, "Railroad Construction and Antebellum Slave Prices," *Social Science Quarterly* 84 (September 2003): 723–37.

18. On the constitutional argument against the Fugitive Slave Act of 1850, see Stanley W. Campbell, *The Slave Catchers: Enforcement of the Fugitive Slave Law, 1850–1860* (Chapel Hill: University of North Carolina Press, 1968), ch. 2.

19. Ibid., 42.

20. Ibid., 170–71.

21. Kilpatrick, *Sovereign States,* 214–15.

22. Ibid., 154.

23. Ibid., 157.

24. See Thomas E. Woods Jr., "Cobden on Freedom, Peace, and Trade," *Human Rights Review* 5 (October–December 2003): 77–90; Ralph Raico, "The Theory of Economic Development and the 'European Miracle,'" in *The Collapse of Development Planning,* ed. Peter Boettke (New York: New York University Press, 1994), 37–58; Hans-Hermann Hoppe, *Democracy—the God That Failed: The Economics and Politics of Monarchy, Democracy, and Natural Order* (New Brunswick, N.J.: Transaction, 2001).

25. See Felix Morley, *Freedom and Federalism* (Indianapolis: Liberty Press, 1981 [1959]), 142–44; Thomas J. DiLorenzo, *Lincoln Unmasked* (New York: Crown Forum, 2006), 81–84.

QUESTION 5

1. Srdja Trifkovic, "Jihadist Hotbed in the Balkans: The Truth Is Out," January 10, 2004, available online at http://www.chroniclesmagazine.org/News/Trifkovic04/NewsST011004.html.

2. Srdja Trifkovic, "Obituary of Alija Izetbegovic," *Chronicles,* October 22, 2003, available online at http://www.chroniclesmagazine.org/News/Trifkovic/NewsST102203.html.

3. Mick Hume, "Nazifying the Serbs, from Bosnia to Kosovo," in *Degraded Capability: The Media and the Kosovo Crisis,* ed. Philip Hammond and Edward S. Herman (London: Pluto Press, 2000), 76.

4. Charles G. Boyd, "Making Peace with the Guilty," *Foreign Affairs* 74 (September–October 1995): 22–38.

5. Srdja Trifkovic, "The Balkan Terror Threat," *Chronicles,* March 2004, 42.

6. Trifkovic, "Obituary of Alija Izetbegovic."

7. Boyd, "Making Peace with the Guilty."

8. David Binder, "U.S. Policymakers on Bosnia Admit Errors in Opposing Partition in 1992," *New York Times,* August 29, 1993.

9. Trifkovic, "Obituary of Alija Izetbegovic."

10. David Binder, "Thoughts on United States Policy Towards Yugoslavia," *South Slav Journal* 16 (Autumn–Winter 1995).

11. Michael Mandel, *How America Gets Away with Murder* (London: Pluto Press, 2004), 67.

12. Boyd, "Making Peace with the Guilty."

13. A. M. Rosenthal, "For American Worth—Stop Bombing Bosnian Serbs," *New York Times,* September 12, 1995.
14. "How We Trained Al Qaeda," *Spectator* [U.K.], September 12, 2003.
15. K. Gajendra Singh, "Turkey: 'Sow War and Reap Terror,'" *Asia Times,* November 22, 2003.
16. Diana Johnstone, *Fools' Crusade: Yugoslavia, NATO, and Western Delusions* (New York: Monthly Review Press, 2002), 62.
17. Trifkovic, "Balkan Terror Threat," 41.
18. Srdja Trifkovic, "Richard A. Clarke, a Liar," *Chronicles,* April 2, 2004, available online at http://www.chroniclesmagazine.org/News/Trifkovic04/NewsST040204.html.
19. Craig Pyesjosh Meyer and William C. Rempe, "Bosnia: Bin Laden's Terrorist Base," *Los Angeles Times,* October 7, 2001.
20. Rade Maroevic and Daniel Williams, "Terrorist Cells Find Foothold in Balkans," *Washington Post,* December 1, 2005, A16.
21. Meyer and Rempe, "Bosnia: Bin Laden's Terrorist Base."
22. Trifkovic, "Jihadist Hotbed in the Balkans."

QUESTION 6

1. Terry L. Anderson and Peter J. Hill, *The Not So Wild, Wild West: Property Rights on the Frontier* (Stanford, Calif.: Stanford University Press, 2004).
2. See Andrew P. Morriss, "Miners, Vigilantes & Cattlemen: Overcoming Free Rider Problems in the Private Provision of Law," *Land and Water Law Review* 33 (1998): 619.
3. Ryan W. McMaken, "The American West: A Heritage of Peace," Mises.org, February 12, 2004; Terry L. Anderson and P. J. Hill, "An American Experiment in Anarcho-Capitalism: The *Not* So Wild, Wild West," *Journal of Libertarian Studies* 3 (Fall 1979): 14.
4. McMaken, "American West: A Heritage of Peace."
5. Anderson and Hill, "American Experiment in Anarcho-Capitalism," 14.
6. Quoted in P. J. Hill, "Old West Violence Mostly Myth," *Arizona Republic,* July 17, 2005.
7. John Tierney, "The Mild, Mild West," *New York Times,* June 25, 2005.
8. Ibid.
9. McMaken, "American West: A Heritage of Peace."
10. Anderson and Hill, "American Experiment in Anarcho-Capitalism," 21, quoting Ray Allen Billington, *The Far Western Frontier, 1830–1860* (New York: Harper & Bros., 1956), 99.
11. Anderson and Hill, *Not So Wild, Wild West,* 120.
12. Hill, "Old West Violence Mostly Myth."
13. McMaken, "American West: A Heritage of Peace."
14. Andrew P. Morriss, "Hayek & Cowboys: Customary Law in the American West," *NYU Journal of Law & Liberty* 1 (2005): 36.
15. Anderson and Hill, *Not So Wild, Wild West,* 160.

16. Anderson and Hill, "American Experiment in Anarcho-Capitalism," 15.
17. Anderson and Hill, *Not So Wild, Wild West,* 163–66.
18. Morriss, "Miners, Vigilantes & Cattlemen," 595n48.
19. Otis E. Young Jr., *Western Mining,* 112, quoted in Morriss, "Miners, Vigilantes & Cattlemen," 600. Placer mining involved gold that was mixed with gravel and soil and that needed to be separated from those substances with the use of water. Anderson and Hill, *Not So Wild, Wild West,* 112.
20. Morriss, "Miners, Vigilantes & Cattlemen," 598–99.
21. Hill, "Old West Violence Mostly Myth."
22. Cited in Morriss, "Hayek & Cowboys," 48.
23. Morriss, "Miners, Vigilantes & Cattlemen," 596ff.
24. Ibid., 598. See also Morriss, "Hayek & Cowboys," 48ff.
25. Morriss, "Miners, Vigilantes & Cattlemen," 607.
26. Ibid., 606–7.
27. Ibid., 625.

QUESTION 7

1. William E. Leuchtenburg, "Progressivism and Imperialism: The Progressive Movement and American Foreign Policy, 1898–1916," *Mississippi Valley Historical Review* 39 (December 1952): 485.
2. Ibid., 486.
3. Ibid. Emphasis added.
4. Herbert Croly, *The Promise of American Life* (New York: Macmillan, 1909), 169.
5. Arthur A. Ekirch Jr., *The Decline of American Liberalism* (New York: Atheneum, 1967), 189.
6. Leuchtenburg, "Progressivism and Imperialism," 500–501.
7. Richard M. Weaver, "The South and the American Union," in *The Southern Essays of Richard M. Weaver,* ed. George M Curtis III and James J. Thompson Jr. (Indianapolis: Liberty Press, 1987), 247.
8. August Heckscher, *Woodrow Wilson: A Biography* (New York: Charles Scribner's Sons, 1991), 551.
9. Walter Karp, *The Politics of War* (New York: Harper & Row, 1979), 337; Sigmund Freud and William C. Bullitt, *Thomas Woodrow Wilson: A Psychological Study* (New York: Avon, 1966), 285.
10. Freud and Bullitt, *Thomas Woodrow Wilson,* 240.
11. See Richard M. Gamble, *The War for Righteousness: Progressive Christianity, the Great War, and the Rise of the Messianic Nation* (Wilmington, Del.: ISI Books, 2003).
12. Murray N. Rothbard, "World War I as Fulfillment: Power and the Intellectuals," in *Reassessing the Presidency,* ed. John V. Denson (Auburn, Ala.: Ludwig von Mises Institute, 2001), 203–53.
13. Ibid., 226.
14. Ibid., 227.

15. Ralph Raico, "Harry Truman: Advancing the Revolution," in Denson, ed., *Reassessing the Presidency,* 552; Justin Raimondo, *Reclaiming the American Right* (Burlingame, Calif.: Center for Libertarian Studies, 1993); Murray N. Rothbard, "The Transformation of the American Right," *Continuum* 2 (Summer 1964): 220–31.

16. Walter A. McDougall, *Promised Land, Crusader State: The American Encounter with the World Since 1776* (Boston: Houghton Mifflin, 1997), 188.

17. Ibid., 183; see also Lloyd C. Gardner, *Pay Any Price: Lyndon Johnson and the Wars for Vietnam* (Chicago: Ivan R. Dee, 1995), xiv–xv and ch. 9.

18. Arthur Schlesinger, *The Bitter Heritage: Vietnam and American Democracy, 1941–1966* (New York: Houghton Mifflin, 1967), 76; quoted in H. W. Crocker III, *Don't Tread on Me* (New York: Crown Forum, 2006).

19. McDougall, *Promised Land, Crusader State,* 178.

20. Justin Raimondo, "Hillary the Hawk," *American Conservative,* March 27, 2006.

21. Robert Nisbet, *Conservatism: Dream and Reality* (Minneapolis: University of Minnesota Press, 1986), 103.

22. Robert Nisbet, *Twilight of Authority* (New York: Oxford University Press, 1975), 163.

23. Quoted in Ralph Raico, "American Foreign Policy—The Turning Point, 1898–1919," in *The Failure of America's Foreign Wars,* ed. Richard M. Ebeling and Jacob G. Hornberger (Fairfax, Va.: Future of Freedom Foundation, 1996), 75.

24. Weaver, "South and American Union," 235.

QUESTION 8

1. Philip A. Levy, "Exemplars of Taking Liberties: The Iroquois Influence Thesis and the Problem of Evidence," *William and Mary Quarterly* 53 (July 1996): 589.

2. Samuel B. Payne Jr., "The Iroquois League, the Articles of Confederation, and the Constitution," *William and Mary Quarterly* 53 (July 1996): 606.

3. Michael Newman, "Founding Feathers," *New Republic,* November 7, 1988, 17.

4. Quoted in Payne, "Iroquois League," 611.

5. Quoted in ibid., 607.

6. Benjamin Franklin to James Parker, March 20, 1750, in *The Writings of Benjamin Franklin,* ed. Albert Henry Smyth (New York: Macmillan, 1907), 3:42.

7. Quoted in Payne, "Iroquois League," 613.

8. Ibid., 612–13.

9. Elisabeth Tooker, "Reply to Johansen," *Ethnohistory* 37 (Summer 1990): 292. Internal footnote omitted.

10. Elisabeth Tooker, "The United States Constitution and the Iroquois League," *Ethnohistory* 35 (Fall 1988): 312; Newman, "Founding Feathers," 17.

11. Donald A. Grinde and Bruce E. Johansen, *Exemplar of Liberty: Native America and the Evolution of Democracy* (Berkeley: University of California Press, 1991), 202.

QUESTION 9

1. This was known in the social science literature as the harm-and-benefit thesis.
2. Abigail Thernstrom and Stephan Thernstrom, *No Excuses: Closing the Racial Gap in Learning* (New York: Simon & Schuster, 2003), 13.
3. Ibid., 17.
4. Ibid., 19–20.
5. Thomas Sowell, *Affirmative Action Around the World: An Empirical Study* (New Haven: Yale University Press, 2005), 184.
6. Thernstrom and Thernstrom, *No Excuses,* 130.
7. Ibid., 130, 138–39.
8. Ibid., 140.
9. Ibid., 138.
10. Ibid., 89, 127–29.
11. On Shaker Heights, see ibid., 121–23.
12. Ibid., 94.
13. David J. Armor, *Forced Justice: School Desegregation and the Law* (New York: Oxford University Press, 1995), 72.
14. Ibid., 94–95.

QUESTION 10

1. James McPherson, *For Cause and Comrades: Why Men Fought in the Civil War* (New York: Oxford University Press, 1997).
2. Jeffrey Rogers Hummel, *Emancipating Slaves, Enslaving Free Men: A History of the American Civil War* (Chicago: Open Court, 1996), 352.
3. Ibid., 353.
4. For Livingston's views, see Donald W. Livingston, *Philosophical Melancholy and Delirium* (Chicago: University of Chicago Press, 1998), ch. 14.
5. Ralph Raico, "The Theory of Economic Development and the 'European Miracle': The Vindication of P. T. Bauer," manuscript in possession of the author; a shorter version appeared in *The Collapse of Development Planning,* ed. Peter J. Boettke (New York: New York University Press, 1993), 37–58.
6. Jean Baechler, *The Origins of Capitalism* (New York: St. Martin's Press, 1976), ch. 7.
7. Livingston, *Philosophical Melancholy and Delirium,* 380.
8. Richard M. Weaver, *The Southern Tradition at Bay: A History of Postbellum Thought* (New Rochelle, N.Y.: Arlington House, 1968), 128.
9. Robert E. Lee to Lord Acton, December 15, 1866, in *Selected Writings of Lord Acton: Essays in the History of Liberty,* ed. J. Rufus Fears (Indianapolis: Liberty Fund, 1985), 1: 364.
10. Donald W. Livingston, "A Moral Accounting of the Union and the Confederacy," *Journal of Libertarian Studies* 16 (Spring 2002): 88–92.
11. Ibid., 88–89.
12. Lord Acton to Robert E. Lee, November 4, 1866, in Fears, ed., *Selected Writings of Lord Acton,* 277.

13. See Lysander Spooner, "No Treason," in *The Lysander Spooner Reader,* ed. George W. Smith (San Francisco: Fox & Wilkes, 1992), 53–122; Murray N. Rothbard, "America's Two Just Wars: 1775 and 1861," in *The Costs of War: America's Pyrrhic Victories,* ed. John V. Denson (New Brunswick, N.J.: Transaction, 1997), 119–33.

QUESTION 11

1. David Gray Adler, "Clinton, the Constitution, and the War Power," in *The Presidency and the Law: The Clinton Legacy,* ed. David Gray Adler and Michael A. Genovese (Lawrence: University Press of Kansas, 2002), 20.

2. Indeed, at the Constitutional Convention, the delegates expressly disclaimed any intention to model the American executive exactly after the British monarchy. James Wilson, for example, remarked that the powers of the British king did not constitute "a proper guide in defining the executive powers. Some of these prerogatives were of a Legislative nature. Among others that of war & peace." Edmund Randolph likewise contended that the delegates had "no motive to be governed by the British Government as our prototype." David Gray Adler, "The Constitution and Presidential Warmaking: The Enduring Debate," *Political Science Quarterly* 103 (Spring 1988): 3–4.

3. James Madison to Thomas Jefferson, April 2, 1798; available online at http://press-pubs.uchicago.edu/founders/documents/a1_8_11s8.html.

4. See Jane E. Stromseth, "Understanding Constitutional War Powers Today: Why Methodology Matters," *Yale Law Journal* 106 (December 1996): 845n1. Madison later warned that even the legitimate powers of the executive during wartime were exceedingly dangerous: "No nation can preserve its freedom in the midst of continual warfare. War is in fact the true nurse of executive aggrandizement. In war, a physical force is to be created; and it is the executive will, which is to direct it. In war, the public treasuries are to be unlocked; and it is the executive hand which is to dispense them. In war, the honors and emoluments of office are to be multiplied; and it is the executive patronage under which they are to be enjoyed; and it is the executive brow they are to encircle. The strongest passions and most dangerous weaknesses of the human breast; ambition, avarice, vanity, the honorable or venal love of fame, are all in conspiracy against the desire and duty of peace." Robert W. Tucker and David C. Hendrickson, *Empire of Liberty: The Statecraft of Thomas Jefferson* (New York: Oxford University Press, 1990), 39–40.

5. Louis Fisher, *Presidential War Power* (Lawrence: University Press of Kansas, 1995), 7–8.

6. *The Federalist Papers,* ed. Clinton Rossiter (New York: Penguin, 1961), 417–18.

7. Abraham Lincoln to William H. Herndon, February 15, 1848, in *Abraham Lincoln: Speeches and Writings, 1832–1858,* ed. Don E. Fehrenbacher (New York: Classics of Liberty Library, 1992), 175–76; emphasis in original.

8. Fisher, *Presidential War Power,* 7.

9. Ibid., 15.

10. Adler, "Constitution and Presidential Warmaking," 35.
11. Ibid., 18. Emphasis in original.
12. Fisher, *Presidential War Power,* 24–25.
13. Adler, "Constitution and Presidential Warmaking," 19.
14. Fisher, *Presidential War Power,* 26.
15. Ibid., 26–27.
16. Walter A. McDougall, *Promised Land, Crusader State: The American Encounter with the World Since 1776* (Boston: Houghton Mifflin, 1997), 34–35.
17. Adler, "Constitution and Presidential Warmaking," 21.
18. Fisher, *Presidential War Power,* 32.
19. Adler, "Constitution and Presidential Warmaking," 24.
20. Walter LaFeber, *The Cambridge History of American Foreign Relations,* vol. 2, *The American Search for Opportunity, 1865–1913* (Cambridge: Cambridge University Press, 1993), 177.
21. Fisher, *Presidential War Power,* 87–88.
22. See Department of State, Office of the Legal Adviser, "The Legality of United States Participation in the Defense of Viet Nam," *Yale Law Journal* 75 (June 1966): 1085–108.
23. Fisher, *Presidential War Power,* 88.
24. Robert A. Taft, *A Foreign Policy for Americans* (Garden City, N.Y.: Doubleday, 1951), 33.
25. Louis Fisher and David Gray Adler, "The War Powers Resolution: Time to Say Goodbye," *Political Science Quarterly* 113 (Spring 1998): 11.
26. Ibid., 16–17.
27. Ibid., 17.
28. Ibid., 16.
29. Ibid., 17.
30. For a legal critique of Clinton's 1994 intervention in Haiti, for example, see Michael L. Glennon, "Too Far Apart: Repeal the War Powers Resolution," *University of Miami Law Review* 50 (1995): 22–27.
31. Adler, "Clinton, the Constitution, and the War Power," 19.

QUESTION 12

1. Jonathan Weisman, "Across America, War Means Jobs," *Washington Post,* May 11, 2004, A1.
2. Gene Smiley, *The American Economy in the Twentieth Century* (Cincinnati, Ohio: South-Western Publishing, 1994), 196.
3. Cf. Murray N. Rothbard, *Man, Economy, and State: A Treatise on Economic Principles* (Auburn, Ala.: Ludwig von Mises Institute, 1993 [1962]), 791–93.
4. George Reisman, *Capitalism* (Ottawa, Ill.: Jameson Books, 1996), 591.
5. Quoted in Robert Higgs, "Wartime Prosperity? A Reassessment of the U.S. Economy in the 1940s," *Journal of Economic History* 52 (March 1992): 41–60; available online at http://www.independent.org/newsroom/article.asp?id=138. Thus even Melman, whose analysis of wartime economics is usually

quite sound, is taken in by the persistent fallacy about alleged prosperity during World War II.

6. Robert Higgs, "From Central Planning to the Market: The American Transition, 1945–1947," *Journal of Economic History* (1999), footnotes omitted; available online at http://www.independent.org/newsroom/article.asp?id=109.

7. Smiley, *American Economy in the Twentieth Century,* 199.

8. Richard K. Vedder and Lowell Gallaway, "The Great Depression of 1946," *Review of Austrian Economics* 5, no. 2 (1991): 5.

9. Higgs, "Wartime Prosperity?"

10. Robert Higgs, private correspondence with the author, April 7, 2006.

11. Higgs, "From Central Planning to the Market."

12. Robert Higgs, *Depression, War, and Cold War: Studies in Political Economy* (New York: Oxford University Press, 2006), 106.

13. Ibid.; Vedder and Gallaway, "Great Depression of 1946," 3.

QUESTION 13

1. Gregory Bresiger, "The Revolution of 1935: The Secret History of Social Security," *Essays in Political Economy,* (Aubum, Ala.: Ludwig von Mises Institute, 2002), 58; available at Mises.org.

2. Andrew Achenbaum, *Social Security: Visions and Revisions* (Cambridge: Cambridge University Press, 1986), 28.

3. John Attarian, *Social Security: False Consciousness and Crisis* (New Brunswick, N.J.: Transaction, 2002), 89. The Supreme Court upheld the Social Security program in *Helvering v. Davis* (1937). The fact that the Court's position was so poorly argued, combined with the failure of the two dissenters to so much as write an opinion, raises the possibility that the Court approved the program out of fear of reprisals by Roosevelt; the case was heard shortly after the failure of Roosevelt's notorious court-packing scheme. Ibid., 97, 101.

4. William E. Leuchtenburg, *Franklin Roosevelt and the New Deal, 1932–1940* (New York: Harper, 1963), 133.

5. Attarian, *Social Security,* 68–70.

6. Bresiger, "Revolution of 1935," 29–30.

7. Attarian, *Social Security,* 209.

8. Ibid., 210–11. Emphasis in original.

9. Ibid., 213.

10. See Abraham Ellis, *The Social Security Fraud* (Irvington-on-Hudson, N.Y.: Foundation for Economic Education, 1996), esp. ch. 4.

11. John Attarian, "The Roots of the Social Security Myth," *Essays in Political Economy* (Ludwig von Mises Institute, 2002), 38.

12. On the Amish, see ibid., 223–25.

13. Ibid., 265.

14. Ibid., 267.

15. Ibid., 293–96; quotations on 295.

16. Thanks to the Mises.org blog for the example in this paragraph and the one following.
17. Attarian, *Social Security,* 123.
18. Ellis, *Social Security Fraud,* 58–59.

QUESTION 14

1. The exact year is a matter of dispute. See Linda O. McMurry, *George Washington Carver: Scientist and Symbol* (New York: Oxford University Press, 1981), 9–10.
2. Barry Mackintosh, "George Washington Carver: The Making of a Myth," *Journal of Southern History* 42 (November 1976): 511–12.
3. Barry Mackintosh, "George Washington Carver and the Peanut: New Light on a Much-Loved Myth," *American Heritage,* August 1977, 70.
4. Mackintosh, "George Washington Carver: Making of a Myth," 515.
5. Ibid., 519.
6. Ibid., 521, 524–25.
7. McMurry, *George Washington Carver,* 306.
8. Ibid., 313.
9. Ibid., 308.
10. Mackintosh, "George Washington Carver: Making of a Myth," 527.
11. Mackintosh, "George Washington Carver and the Peanut," 72.

QUESTION 15

1. Bruce Ackerman, *We the People: Foundations* (Cambridge, Mass.: Harvard University Press, 1991); Bruce Ackerman, *We the People: Transformations* (Cambridge, Mass.: Belknap, 1998).
2. A. R. Myers, *Parliaments and Estates in Europe to 1789* (New York: Harcourt Brace Jovanovich, 1975), 29.
3. James Otis, "The Rights of the British Colonies Asserted and Proved," in *The American Republic: Primary Sources,* ed. Bruce Frohnen (Indianapolis: Liberty Fund, 2002), 126.
4. Jack P. Greene, *Peripheries and Center: Constitutional Development in the Extended Polities of the British Empire and the United States, 1607–1788* (New York: W. W. Norton, 1986), 71.
5. Ibid., 100.
6. John Adams, "Braintree Instructions," in Frohnen, ed., *American Republic,* 115.
7. Greene, *Peripheries and Center,* 120–21.
8. John Dickinson, Letter V of "Letters from a Farmer in Pennsylvania," in Frohnen, ed., *American Republic,* 146.
9. See the argument in Greene, *Peripheries and Center,* 115–16, 120, and ch. 6.
10. Raoul Berger, "Judicial Manipulation of the Commerce Clause," *Texas Law Review* 74 (March 1996): 696.

QUESTION 16

1. Charles C. Mann, *1491: New Revelations of the Americas Before Columbus* (New York: Alfred A. Knopf, 2005), 60–61.
2. Lynn Ceci, "Fish Fertilizer: A Native North American Practice?" *Science* 188 (4 April 1975): 26–30.
3. Lynn Ceci, "Squanto and the Pilgrims: On Planting Corn 'in the manner of the Indians,'" in *The Invented Indian: Cultural Fictions and Government Policies,* ed. James A. Clifton (New Brunswick, N.J.: Transaction, 1990), 76.
4. William Cronon, *Changes in the Land: Indians, Colonists, and the Ecology of New England* (New York: Hill and Wang, 2003 [1983]), 45.
5. Ceci, "Squanto and the Pilgrims," 71.
6. Ibid., 82–83.
7. Ibid., 83.
8. Mann, *1491,* 365n34.
9. Lynn Ceci, "Letters," *Science* 189 (19 September 1975): 949.
10. Neal Salisbury, *Manitou and Providence: Indians, Europeans, and the Making of New England, 1500–1643* (New York: Oxford University Press, 1982), 252n39.
11. Mann, *1491,* 365n34.

QUESTION 17

1. Robert Nisbet, *Twilight of Authority* (New York: Oxford University Press, 1975), 34, 46–47.
2. Ibid., 29.
3. Ibid., 33–34.
4. Ibid., 35–36.
5. Ibid., 36.
6. One of the few reliable, nonhagiographical studies of Theodore Roosevelt is Jim Powell, *Bully Boy: The Truth About Theodore Roosevelt's Legacy* (New York: Crown Forum, 2006).
7. Clinton Rossiter, *The American Presidency* (New York: New American Library, 1960), 97.
8. Walter LaFeber, "The Making of a Bully Boy," *Inquiry,* June 11 and 25, 1979, 15.
9. Emmet John Hughes, *The Living Presidency: The Resources and Dilemmas of the American Presidential Office* (New York: Coward, McCann & Geoghegan, 1973), 91.
10. Edmund Morris, *The Rise of Theodore Roosevelt* (New York: Coward, McCann & Geoghegan, 1979).
11. John Milton Cooper Jr., *The Warrior and the Priest: Woodrow Wilson and Theodore Roosevelt* (Cambridge, Mass.: Harvard University Press, 1983), 69.
12. Michael P. Riccards, *The Ferocious Engine of Democracy: A History of the American Presidency,* vol. 2, *Theodore Roosevelt Through George Bush* (Lanham, Md.: Madison Books, 1995), 5–6.
13. John Morton Blum, *The Republican Roosevelt* (New York: Atheneum, 1962 [1954]), 107–8.

14. Theodore Roosevelt to John St. Loe Strachey, February 12, 1906, in *The Letters of Theodore Roosevelt,* ed. Elting E. Morison, vol. 5, *The Big Stick, 1905–1907* (Cambridge, Mass.: Harvard University Press, 1952), 151.
15. This discussion of executive orders is indebted to the excellent study by William J. Olson and Alan Woll, "Executive Orders and National Emergencies: How Presidents Have Come to 'Run the Country' by Usurping Legislative Power," Cato Institute Policy Analysis No. 358, October 28, 1999.
16. Edmund Morris, *Theodore Rex* (New York: Modern Library, 2002), 165.
17. Ibid.
18. W. Stull Holt, *Treaties Defeated by the Senate: A Study of the Struggle Between President and Senate over the Conduct of Foreign Relations* (Gloucester, Mass.: Peter Smith, 1964 [1933]), 216.
19. Ibid., 215–16.
20. Forrest McDonald, *The American Presidency: An Intellectual History* (Lawrence: University Press of Kansas, 1994), 390.
21. Ibid., 389–90.
22. Hughes, *Living Presidency,* 93.
23. Theodore Roosevelt to George Otto Trevelyan, June 19, 1908, in Morison, ed., *Letters of Theodore Roosevelt,* vol. 6, *The Big Stick, 1907–1909,* 1087.
24. Gabriel Kolko, *The Triumph of Conservatism: A Reinterpretation of American History, 1900–1916* (New York: Free Press, 1963), 207.
25. Woodrow Wilson, *Constitutional Government in the United States* (New York: Columbia University Press, 1908), 68.
26. Ibid., 70.
27. Arthur A. Ekirch Jr., *The Decline of American Liberalism* (New York: Atheneum, 1967), 193.
28. Ibid.

QUESTION 18

1. Thomas Sowell, *Civil Rights: Rhetoric or Reality?* (New York: William Morrow, 1985), 43.
2. Ibid., 42–43, 46, 59–60.
3. Thomas Sowell, *Affirmative Action Around the World: An Empirical Study* (New Haven: Yale University Press, 2005), 175.
4. Ibid.
5. Sowell, *Civil Rights: Rhetoric or Reality,* 20–21.
6. Ibid., 21.
7. Sowell, *Affirmative Action Around the World,* 188; Sowell, *Civil Rights: Rhetoric or Reality,* 49–50.
8. Marianne Bertrand and Sendhil Mullainathan, "Are Emily and Greg More Employable Than Lakisha and Jamal? A Field Experiment Evidence on Labor Market Discrimination," National Bureau of Economic Research Working Paper, 2003.

9. Steven D. Levitt and Stephen J. Dubner, *Freakonomics* (New York: William Morrow, 2005), 186–87. Thanks to economist Robert P. Murphy for this reference.

10. Jared Taylor, *Paved with Good Intentions: The Failure of Race Relations in Contemporary America* (New York: Carroll & Graf, 1992), 153–55, 161.

11. Sowell, *Civil Rights: Rhetoric or Reality,* 45, 57–58.

12. Abigail Thernstrom, "On the Scarcity of Black Professors," *Commentary,* July 1990, 22–26.

13. Taylor, *Paved with Good Intentions,* 170.

14. Shelby Steele, *The Content of Our Character: A New Vision of Race in America* (New York: HarperPerennial, 1991), 138–39.

15. John McWhorter, *Losing the Race: Self-Sabotage in Black America* (New York: Free Press, 2000), x, xi.

16. Dinesh D'Souza, *Illiberal Education* (New York: Free Press, 1998 [1991]), 39.

17. Sowell, *Affirmative Action Around the World,* 174.

18. Taylor, *Paved with Good Intentions,* 181.

19. Ibid.

20. Lew Rockwell, *Speaking of Liberty* (Auburn, Ala.: Ludwig von Mises Institute, 2003), 101–2.

21. Ibid., 95.

22. Ibid., 105.

QUESTION 19

1. The classic development of this position is Adrienne Koch and Harry Ammon, "The Virginia and Kentucky Resolutions: An Episode in Jefferson's and Madison's Defense of Civil Liberties," *William and Mary Quarterly* 5 (April 1948): 147–76.

2. Kevin R. C. Gutzman, "Edmund Randolph and Virginia Constitutionalism," *Review of Politics* 66 (Summer 2004): 491.

3. K. R. Constantine Gutzman, "The Virginia and Kentucky Resolutions Reconsidered: 'An Appeal to the *Real Laws* of Our Country,' " *Journal of Southern History* 66 (August 2000): 476.

4. Gutzman, "Edmund Randolph and Virginia Constitutionalism," 491–92.

5. Ibid., 473.

6. Gutzman, "Virginia and Kentucky Resolutions Reconsidered," 485.

7. Gutzman, "Edmund Randolph and Virginia Constitutionalism," 473; see also Gutzman, "Virginia and Kentucky Resolutions Reconsidered," 477–78.

QUESTION 20

1. I first became aware of the newer scholarship on the Whiskey Rebellion thanks to Murray N. Rothbard, "The Whiskey Rebellion: A Model for Our Time?" in *Making Economic Sense* (Auburn, Ala.: Ludwig von Mises Institute, 1995), 157–60.

2. Mary K. Bonsteel Tachau, "The Whiskey Rebellion in Kentucky: A Forgotten Episode of Civil Disobedience," *Journal of the Early Republic* 2 (Fall 1982): 240.
3. Thomas P. Slaughter, *The Whiskey Rebellion: Frontier Epilogue to the American Revolution* (New York: Oxford University Press, 1986), 5.
4. Ibid., 117–18, 206–11.
5. Bonsteel Tachau, "Whiskey Rebellion in Kentucky," 241.
6. Leland D. Baldwin, *Whiskey Rebels* (Pittsburgh: University of Pittsburgh Press, 1939), 25, 28.
7. Slaughter, *Whiskey Rebellion,* 24.
8. Ibid., 104; see also 25, 99.
9. Ibid., 104.
10. Ibid., 13.
11. Bonsteel Tachau, "Whiskey Rebellion in Kentucky," 240 and passim; Slaughter, *Whiskey Rebellion,* 118.
12. Bonsteel Tachau, "Whiskey Rebellion in Kentucky," 247.
13. Lauren Gallo, "The Whiskey Rebellion: Internal Taxation Versus Secession," paper presented at the Austrian Student Scholars Conference, Grove City College, Grove City, Pa., November 2005.
14. Bonsteel Tachau, "Whiskey Rebellion in Kentucky," 259.

QUESTION 21

1. For a reply to the myth of the Industrial Revolution as a catastrophe for workers, see Thomas E. Woods Jr., *The Church and the Market* (Lanham, Md.: Lexington, 2005), 169–74.
2. What follows is a brief exposition of George Reisman's productivity theory of wages. See George Reisman, *Capitalism* (Ottawa, Ill.: Jameson Books, 1996), 603–72.
3. Ibid., 621.
4. Thomas J. DiLorenzo, *How Capitalism Saved America* (New York: Crown Forum, 2004), 98; DiLorenzo is citing Michael Cox and Richard Alm, *Myths of Rich and Poor* (New York: Basic Books, 1999), 43.
5. DiLorenzo, *How Capitalism Saved America,* 98.
6. Ibid., 99.
7. Reisman, *Capitalism,* 653.
8. In an economy with an expanding money supply, such as our own, it is conceivable for everyone to earn more money at the same time, and for the prices of all goods to rise consistently. With prices and wages both typically on the rise, it is not as easy to see the process described by Reisman—in which Americans grow more prosperous because the prices for the goods they buy consistently decline—at work. In such an economy, the rise in real wages described here is at work when *the rise in wages outstrips the rise in prices.* (Naturally, the cumulative effect of untold thousands of government interventions and distortions obstructs this process.)
9. Reisman, *Capitalism,* 653.

10. Robert A. Lawson, "We're All Rawlsians Now!" *Ideas on Liberty,* June 2002, 49–50.

QUESTION 22

1. See Gene Callahan and Roger W. Garrison, "Does Austrian Business Cycle Theory Help Explain the Dot-Com Boom and Bust?" *Quarterly Journal of Austrian Economics* 6 (Summer 2003): 67–98.
2. Murray N. Rothbard, "Economic Depressions: Their Cause and Cure," in *The Austrian Theory of the Trade Cycle and Other Essays,* comp. Richard M. Ebeling (Auburn, Ala.: Ludwig von Mises Institute, 1996 [1978]), 71–73.
3. Melchior Palyi, *The Twilight of Gold, 1914–1936: Myths and Realities* (Chicago: Regnery, 1972), 302; Murray N. Rothbard, *America's Great Depression,* 4th ed. (New York: Richardson & Snyder, 1983), 86. An increased supply of goods resulting from productivity gains during the 1920s offset the price rise that ordinarily accompanies an inflationary monetary policy; the price level appeared relatively stable in the 1920s and masked the substantial inflation that occurred.
4. Rothbard's *America's Great Depression,* now in a fifth edition, is the standard work that applies the Austrian theory to the American case.

QUESTION 23

1. Marc Allen Eisner, *From Warfare State to Welfare State: World War I, Compensatory State Building, and the Limits of the Modern Order* (University Park: Pennsylvania State University Press, 2000), 107–8.
2. Ellis W. Hawley, "Herbert Hoover, the Commerce Secretariat, and the Vision of an 'Associative State,' 1921–1928," *Journal of American History* 61 (1974): 122.
3. Eisner, *From Warfare State to Welfare State,* 108–9.
4. Ellis W. Hawley, "Herbert Hoover and American Corporatism, 1929–1933," in *The Hoover Presidency: A Reappraisal,* ed. Martin L. Fausold and George T. Mazuzan (Albany, N.Y.: State University of New York Press, 1974), 103; Naomi Lamoreaux, "From Antitrust to Supply-Side Economics: The Strange History of Federal Intervention in the Economy," in *Essays in Supply Side Economics,* ed. David G. Raboy (Washington, D.C.: Institute for Research on the Economics of Taxation, 1982), 158–59.
5. Butler Shaffer, *In Restraint of Trade: The Business Campaign Against Competition, 1918–1938* (Lewisburg, Pa.: Bucknell University Press, 1997), 92.
6. Ibid.
7. For a critique of this system and its spiritual cousins, the medieval guilds, see Thomas E. Woods Jr., *The Church and the Market* (Lanham, Md.: Lexington, 2005).
8. On these conferences, see Shaffer, *In Restraint of Trade;* see also Eisner, *From Warfare State to Welfare State,* 128–33.
9. Shaffer, *In Restraint of Trade,* 85.

10. Ibid., 72.

11. Quoted in ibid., 77–78.

12. Eisner, *From Warfare State to Welfare State,* 275.

13. C. A. Phillips, T. F. McManus, and R. W. Nelson, *Banking and the Business Cycle: A Study of the Great Depression in the United States* (New York: Macmillan, 1937), 76.

14. For a more theoretical reply to the underconsumption fallacy, see Ludwig von Mises, *Human Action,* Scholar's Edition (Auburn, Ala.: Ludwig von Mises Institute, 1998 [1949]), 298–99; see also George Reisman, *Capitalism* (Ottawa, Ill.: Jameson Books, 1996), 580–91. Thanks to Jeff Herbener for directing me to Mises's discussion.

15. Phillips et al., *Banking and the Business Cycle,* 225. See also the important refinements in William Barnett II and Walter Block, "On Gallaway and Vedder on Stabilization Policy," *Quarterly Journal of Austrian Economics* 9 (Spring 2006): 57–81.

16. Phillips et al., *Banking and the Business Cycle,* 225.

17. Ibid., 72.

18. Ibid., 229.

19. Richard K. Vedder and Lowell E. Gallaway, *Out of Work: Unemployment and Govrnment in Twentieth-Century America* (New York: Holmes & Meier, 1993), 93.

20. Ibid., 95.

21. Ibid., 97.

22. Ibid., 96.

23. The most systematic indictment of Hoover's interventionist policies is Murray N. Rothbard, *America's Great Depression,* 4th ed. (New York: Richardson & Snyder, 1983).

24. Rexford Tugwell, *FDR, Architect of an Era* (New York: Macmillan, 1967), 71.

QUESTION 24

1. Ted Widmer, "Magic Man," *New York Times,* May 7, 2006.

2. Ibid.

3. Robert McElvaine, *The Great Depression: America, 1929–1941* (New York: Times Books, 1984), 337; cited in Gregory Bresiger, "The Revolution of 1935: The Secret History of Social Security," *Essays in Political Economy* (Auburn, Ala.: Ludwig von Mises Institute, 2002), 43; available at Mises.org.

4. Doris Kearns Goodwin, *No Ordinary Time* (New York: Simon & Schuster, 1994), 42.

5. Harold L. Cole and Lee E. Ohanian, "New Deal Policies and the Persistence of the Great Depression: A General Equilibrium Analysis," *Journal of Political Economy* 112 (August 2004). Thanks to Tom DiLorenzo for first bringing this article to my attention in 2004.

6. William E. Leuchtenburg, *Franklin D. Roosevelt and the New Deal, 1932–1940* (New York: Harper & Row, 1963), 58.

7. Quoted in Thomas J. DiLorenzo, "Franklin Delano Roosevelt's New Deal: From Economic Fascism to Pork-Barrel Politics," in *Reassessing the Presidency*, ed. John V. Denson (Auburn, Ala.: Ludwig von Mises Institute, 2001), 436.

8. Butler Shaffer, *In Restraint of Trade: The Business Campaign Against Competition, 1918–1938* (Lewisburg, Pa.: Bucknell University Press, 1997), 106.

9. Alan Brinkley, *The End of Reform: New Deal Liberalism in Recession and War* (New York: Vintage, 1996), 39.

10. Cole and Ohanian, "New Deal Policies," 779.

11. Ibid., 787, 793.

12. Leuchtenburg, *Franklin D. Roosevelt and the New Deal,* 69.

13. Cole and Ohanian, "New Deal Policies," 813; see also Gary Dean Best, *Pride, Prejudice, and Politics: Roosevelt Versus Recovery, 1933–1938* (New York: Praeger, 1991), 63–64.

14. Richard K. Vedder and Lowell E. Gallaway, *Out of Work: Unemployment and Government in Twentieth Century America* (New York: Holmes & Meier, 1993), 137.

15. Thomas E. Woods Jr., "Great Depression: Ending," in *History in Dispute*, vol. 3, *American Social and Political Movements, 1900–1945: Pursuit of Progress*, ed. Robert J. Allison (Detroit: St. James Press, 2000), 66.

16. Best, *Pride, Prejudice, and Politics,* 63.

17. Ibid., 141.

18. Benjamin M. Anderson, *Economics and the Public Welfare: A Financial and Economic History of the United States, 1914–1946* (Indianapolis: Liberty Press, 1979 [1949]), 357.

19. Robert Higgs, "Regime Uncertainty: Why the Great Depression Lasted So Long and Why Prosperity Resumed After the War," *Independent Review* 1 (Spring 1997): 561–90; Woods, "Great Depression: Ending," 67–68.

20. Higgs, "Regime Uncertainty," 586.

21. Best, *Pride, Prejudice, and Politics,* 73.

22. Ibid., 72–73; Woods, "Great Depression: Ending," 68.

23. Best, *Pride, Prejudice, and Politics,* 106; Woods, "Great Depression: Ending," 68.

24. John Joseph Wallis and Daniel K. Benjamin, "Public Relief and Private Employment in the Great Depression," *Journal of Economic History* 41 (March 1981): 97; cited in Jim Powell, *FDR's Folly: How Roosevelt and His New Deal Prolonged the Great Depression* (New York: Crown Forum, 2003), 103.

25. Henry Hazlitt, *Economics in One Lesson* (New York: Crown, 1979 [1946]), 33. Thanks to Joe Salerno for reminding me of Hazlitt's chapter on make-work programs.

26. Ibid., 34.

27. Bresiger, "Revolution of 1935," 93.

QUESTION 25

1. Randy E. Barnett, "The Original Meaning of the Commerce Clause," *University of Chicago Law Review* 68 (Winter 2001), available online at http://www.bu.edu/rbarnett/Original.htm.

2. Ibid.
3. Ibid.
4. Raoul Berger, "Judicial Manipulation of the Commerce Clause," *Texas Law Review* 74 (March 1996): 704.
5. Thomas Jefferson, "Opinion Against the Constitutionality of a National Bank," in *The American Republic: Primary Sources,* ed. Bruce Frohnen (Indianapolis: Liberty Fund, 2002), 475.
6. Berger, "Judicial Manipulation of the Commerce Clause," 705.
7. Ibid., 707.
8. Barnett, "Original Meaning of the Commerce Clause."
9. Raoul Berger, commenting on *Lopez,* observed that the Founders "conceived of 'commerce' as 'trade,' the interchange of goods by one state with another. The ban on gun possession within one thousand feet of a school does not fit within that conception. It does not entail the shipment to or entry from of goods from one state to another." See Berger, "Judicial Manipulation of the Commerce Clause," 703.
10. The text of Justice Thomas's dissent is available online at http://www.law .cornell.edu/supct/html/03-1454.ZD1.html.
11. I owe this argument to author and legal scholar William Watkins.
12. Berger, "Judicial Manipulation of the Commerce Clause," 711.
13. On these and other forbidden questions, see Hans-Hermann Hoppe, *Democracy—the God That Failed: The Economics and Politics of Monarchy, Democracy, and Natural Order* (New Brunswick, N.J.: Transaction, 2001).

QUESTION 26

1. He maintained this position in his 1840 abridgment as well; see Joseph Story, *A Familiar Exposition of the Constitution of the United States* (New York: American Book Company, 1840), 101–4.
2. Robert G. Natelson, "The General Welfare Clause and the Public Trust: An Essay in Original Understanding," *University of Kansas Law Review* 52 (2003): 46.
3. Ibid.; emphasis in original.
4. This is the opinion of Robert Natelson in ibid., 47.
5. Kevin R. C. Gutzman, "Edmund Randolph and Virginia Constitutionalism," *Review of Politics* 66 (Summer 2004): 491.
6. Natelson, "General Welfare Clause and the Public Trust," 12–13.
7. Marshall L. DeRosa, *The Confederate Constitution of 1861: An Inquiry into American Constitutionalism* (Columbia: University of Missouri Press, 1991), 90–91.
8. *The Federalist Papers,* ed. Clinton Rossiter (New York: Penguin, 1961), 262, 263; emphasis added.
9. James Madison to James Robertson, April 20, 1831, in *Letters and Other Writings of James Madison, Fourth President of the United States,* ed. Philip R. Fendall (Philadelphia: Lippincott, 1865), 4:171–72.
10. John C. Eastman, "Restoring the 'General' to the General Welfare Clause," *Chapman Law Review* 4 (2001): 80.

11. James Madison, "Veto Message," March 3, 1817, in *The American Republic: Primary Sources,* ed. Bruce Frohnen (Indianapolis: Liberty Fund, 2002), 501.
12. Thomas Jefferson, "Opinion Against the Constitutionality of a National Bank," in ibid., 475.
13. Ibid.
14. Eastman, "Restoring the 'General' to the General Welfare Clause," 69.
15. Ibid., 69, 70.
16. Ibid., 72–87; Natelson, "General Welfare Clause and the Public Trust," 29–30, 47ff.
17. James Ronald Kennedy, *Reclaiming Liberty* (Gretna, La.: Pelican, 2005), 40.

QUESTION 27

1. Randy E. Barnett, *Restoring the Lost Constitution: The Presumption of Liberty* (Princeton: Princeton University Press, 2004), 155.
2. Ibid., 156; emphasis added.
3. *The Federalist Papers,* ed. Clinton Rossiter (New York: Penguin, 1961), 202; emphasis added.
4. Barnett, *Restoring the Lost Constitution,* 165.
5. Thomas Jefferson, "Opinion Against the Constitutionality of a National Bank," in *The American Republic: Primary Sources,* ed. Bruce Frohnen (Indianapolis: Liberty Fund, 2002), 475–76; emphasis in original.
6. St. George Tucker, *View of the Constitution of the United States with Selected Writings* (Indianapolis: Liberty Fund, 1999), 227.
7. Ibid., 228.
8. Gerald Gunther, ed., *John Marshall's Defense of McCulloch v. Maryland* (Stanford, Calif.: Stanford University Press, 1969), 33.
9. Ibid., 106.
10. Ibid., 124, 126.
11. John Taylor, *Construction Construed and Constitutions Vindicated* (Richmond, Va.: Shepherd & Pollard, 1820), 165, 166. Thanks to Kevin Gutzman for suggesting I consult Taylor.
12. Quoted in Barnett, *Restoring the Lost Constitution,* 183.

QUESTION 28

1. Vincent Buranelli, *The Trial of Peter Zenger* (New York: New York University Press, 1957), 56.
2. Clay S. Conrad, *Jury Nullification: The Evolution of a Doctrine* (Durham, N.C.: Carolina Academic Press, 1998), 34–35.
3. Ibid., 35.
4. Ibid., 46–47; emphasis added. The first American English dictionary (Noah Webster's 1828 volume) noted that at least in criminal cases a jury could "decide both the law and the fact." Ibid., 47.
5. Ibid., 46.

6. Ibid., 48.
7. *State v. Brialsford*, 3 Dall. 1, 4; quoted in James Ostrowski, "The Rise and Fall of Jury Nullification," *Journal of Libertarian Studies* 15 (Spring 2001): 98.
8. Thomas Jefferson, *Notes on the State of Virginia*, ed. David Waldstreicher (Boston: Bedford/St. Martin's, 2002), 168–69.
9. Conrad, *Jury Nullification*, 48.
10. Ibid., 49.
11. Ibid., 50.

QUESTION 29

1. Doug Bandow, "The First World's Misbegotten Economic Legacy to the Third World," in *The Revolution in Development Economics*, ed. James A. Dorn, Steve H. Hanke, and Alan A. Waters (Washington, D.C.: Cato Institute, 1998), 223.
2. James A. Dorn, "Economic Development and Freedom: The Legacy of Peter Bauer," *Cato Journal* 22 (Fall 2002): 360, 362.
3. Evan Osborne, "Rethinking Foreign Aid," *Cato Journal* 22 (Fall 2002): 309.
4. Alvaro Vargas Llosa, "Millennium Flop," Independent Institute Commentary, September 16, 2005.
5. Melinda Ammann, "Cry the Beloved Continent," *Reason*, July 2005.
6. Fredrik Erixon, *Aid and Development: Will It Work This Time?* (London: International Policy Network, 2005), 9–10.
7. Ian Vasquez, "The New Approach to Foreign Aid: Is the Enthusiasm Warranted?" Cato Institute Foreign Policy Briefing No. 79, September 17, 2003, 4.
8. World Bank, *Assessing Aid: What Works, What Doesn't and Why* (New York: Oxford University Press, 1998), 49; cited in ibid., 2.
9. Tom Bethell, *The Noblest Triumph: Property and Prosperity Through the Ages* (New York: St. Martin's, 1998), 190–91. On foreign aid as an emollient, see, for example, Alan Rufus Waters, "Economic Growth and the Property Rights Regime," in Dorn et al., eds., *Revolution in Development Economics*, 118.
10. Jim Peron, "The Sorry Record of Foreign Aid in Africa," *Freeman*, August 2001.
11. P. T. Bauer, *Equality, the Third World and Economic Delusion* (Cambridge, Mass.: Harvard University Press, 1981), 111.
12. Cited in Melvyn Krauss, *Development Without Aid: Growth, Poverty and Government* (New York: McGraw-Hill, 1983), 158–59.
13. Ibid., 159.
14. Alberto Alesina and Beatrice Weder, "Do Corrupt Governments Receive Less Foreign Aid?" *American Economic Review* 92 (September 2004): 1126–38.
15. Benjamin Powell and Matt Ryan, "U.S. Money Aids World's Worst Dictators," Independent Institute Commentary, online at http://www.independent .org/newsroom/article.asp?id=1671.

16. James Bovard, *The Bush Betrayal* (New York: Palgrave Macmillan, 2004), 110.
17. Ibid.
18. Peron, "Sorry Record of Foreign Aid in Africa."
19. Thomas E. Woods Jr., *The Politically Incorrect Guide to American History* (Washington, D.C.: Regnery, 2004), 189–92; Tyler Cowen, "The Marshall Plan: Myths and Realities," in *U.S. Aid to the Developing World,* ed. Doug Bandow (Washington, D.C.: Heritage Foundation, 1985), 61–74.
20. Ian Vásquez, "The False Promise of Aid to Africa," *Washington Times,* July 8, 2005.
21. Thomas J. DiLorenzo, "Ron Brown's Corporate Welfare Scam," *Free Market,* June 1996.
22. Peter Bauer, "Subsistence, Trade, and Exchange: Understanding Developing Economies," in Dorn et al., eds., *Revolution in Development Economics,* 279.
23. Bauer, *Equality, the Third World and Economic Delusion,* 104; George B. N. Ayittey, "The Failure of Development Planning in Africa," in *The Collapse of Development Planning,* ed. Peter J. Boettke (New York: New York University Press, 1993), 173.
24. Bauer, "Subsistence, Trade, and Exchange," 279; Peter T. Bauer, *From Subsistence to Exchange and Other Essays* (Princeton: Princeton University Press, 2000), 45.
25. Bauer, *Equality, the Third World and Economic Delusion,* 99; Waters, "Economic Growth and the Property Rights Regime," 109; Dorn, "Economic Development and Freedom" 361; Bandow, "First World's Misbegotten Economic Legacy to the Third World," 223.
26. Bauer, *Equality, the Third World and Economic Delusion,* 100.
27. Waters, "Economic Growth and the Property Rights Regime," 123. For a lengthier critique of foreign aid along these lines, see Thomas E. Woods Jr., *The Church and the Market* (Lanham, Md.: Lexington Books, 2005), ch. 4.
28. Tim Worstall, "Bill Easterly Is About to Spoil the Poverty Party," TechCentralStation.com, September 8, 2005.
29. Ibid.
30. Vásquez, "New Approach to Foreign Aid," 1. The literature in support of the so-called new economics of foreign aid includes Craig Burnside and David Dollar, "Aid, Policies, and Growth," *American Economic Review* 90 (September 2000): 847–68; Paul Collier and David Dollar, "Aid Allocation and Poverty Reduction," *European Economic Review* 46 (September 2002): 1475–1500; and Paul Collier and David Dollar, "Development Effectiveness: What Have We Learnt?" *Economic Journal* 114 (June 2004): F244–71. Contradicting these conclusions is William Easterly, Ross Levine, and David Roodman, "New Data, New Doubts: Revisiting 'Aid, Policies, and Growth,'" Center for Global Development Working Paper no. 26, March 2003.
31. Harold J. Brumm, "Aid, Policies and Growth: Bauer Was Right," *Cato Journal* 23 (2003): 167–74; William Easterly, Ross Levine, and David Rood-

man, "New Data, New Doubts: A Comment on Burnside and Dollar's 'Aid, Policies, and Growth,'" NBER Working Paper 9846 (Cambridge, Mass.: National Bureau of Economic Research, 2003).

32. Vásquez, "False Promise of Aid to Africa."
33. Alan Waters, "In Africa's Anguish, Foreign Aid Is a Culprit," *Heritage Foundation Backgrounder,* August 7, 1985; emphasis added.
34. Bovard, *Bush Betrayal,* 111.
35. William Easterly, "The Cartel of Good Intentions: The Problem of Bureaucracy in Foreign Aid," *Policy Reform* (2002): 235.
36. Bethell, *Noblest Triumph,* 201.
37. Vásquez, "New Approach to Foreign Aid," 6.

QUESTION 30

1. For a reliable account of the Homestead strike, see Charles W. Baird, "Labor Law Reform: Lessons from History," *Cato Journal* 10 (Spring/Summer 1990): 186–92; Baird, too, argues that it was the strikers who were violating people's rights.
2. Good overviews of this material include Charles W. Baird, "Freedom and American Labor Relations Law, 1946–1996," *Freeman,* May 1996, 299–309, and Richard A. Epstein, "A Common Law for Labor Relations: A Critique of the New Deal Labor Legislation," *Yale Law Review* 92 (July 1983): 1357–1408.
3. Charles W. Baird, "American Union Law: Sources of Conflict," *Journal of Labor Research* 11 (Summer 1990): 271.
4. In fact, yellow-dog contracts were sometimes supported as much by workers themselves as by employers. Some antiunion workers, who opposed the disruptive tactics of unions and the sacrificed wages that went along with them, favored such contracts. Morgan Reynolds, "An Economic Analysis of the Norris-LaGuardia Act, the Wagner Act, and the Labor Representation Industry," *Journal of Libertarian Studies* 6 (Summer/Fall 1982): 232, 233.
5. Ibid., 235.
6. Baird, "American Union Law," 277.
7. See Charles W. Baird, "Toward Equality and Justice in Labor Markets," *Journal of Social, Political and Economic Studies* 20 (Summer 1995): 183; Charles W. Baird, *Opportunity or Privilege: Labor Legislation in America* (New Brunswick, N.J.: Transaction, 1984), chs. 2–3.
8. Baird, "American Union Law," 283.
9. Ibid., 284.
10. Ibid., 284–85.
11. See Charles Baird, "On Strikers and Their Replacements," *Government Union Review* 12 (Summer 1991): 1–29.
12. Morgan O. Reynolds, *Power and Privilege: Labor Unions in America* (New York: Universe Books, 1984), 104.

13. Edward H. Chamberlin, *The Economic Analysis of Labor Union Power* (Washington, D.C.: American Enterprise Association, 1958), 41–42.
14. Friedrich A. Hayek, *The Constitution of Liberty* (Chicago: University of Chicago Press, 1960), 267.
15. Morgan O. Reynolds, "The Myth of Labor's Inequality of Bargaining Power," *Journal of Labor Research* 12 (Spring 1991): 169, 184.
16. Baird, "American Union Law," 278–79.

QUESTION 31

1. John Dean, "Ranking Presidents: Utter Nonsense or Useful Analysis?" FindLaw.com, May 11, 2001.
2. Woodrow Wilson, *Constitutional Government in the United States* (New York: Columbia University Press, 1908), 70.
3. Lew Rockwell, *Speaking of Liberty* (Auburn, Ala.: Ludwig von Mises Institute, 2003), 299.
4. Ibid., 301.
5. Robert Higgs, "No More 'Great Presidents,'" *Free Market,* March 1997.
6. John Toland, *Adolf Hitler: The Definitive Biography* (New York: Anchor, 1992 [1976]), 312.
7. Jeffrey Rogers Hummel, "Martin Van Buren: The American Gladstone," in *Reassessing the Presidency,* ed. John V. Denson (Auburn, Ala.: Ludwig von Mises Institute, 2001), 169–201.
8. Ibid., 186.
9. Ibid., 170, 176.
10. Higgs, "No More 'Great Presidents.'"

QUESTION 32

1. Elizabeth Wright, "S. B. Fuller: Master of Enterprise," *Issues & Views,* Winter 1989.
2. David Beito, "S. B. Fuller Centenary," available online at http://www.hnn.us/blogs/entries/12280.html.
3. Mary Fuller Casey, *S. B. Fuller: Pioneer in Black Economic Development* (Jamestown, N.C.: BridgeMaster Press, 2003), 106.
4. See ibid., 112.
5. Thomas Sowell, *Civil Rights: Rhetoric or Reality?* (New York: William Morrow, 1984), 32, 30.
6. Casey, *S. B. Fuller,* 111.
7. Ibid., 116.
8. Ibid., 99.
9. Wright, "S. B. Fuller: Master of Enterprise."
10. Casey, *S. B. Fuller,* 124.

11. Ibid., 119.
12. Wright, "S. B. Fuller: Master of Enterprise."
13. Beito, "S. B. Fuller Centenary."
14. Wright, "S. B. Fuller: Master of Enterprise."

QUESTION 33

1. Bill Clinton, *My Life* (New York: Random House Large Print, 2004), 1383.
2. "Clinton: Serbs Must Be Stopped Now," CNN.com, March 23, 1999.
3. Srdja Trifkovic, "Kosovo: Five Centuries of Strife and Ethnic Cleansing," *Chronicles,* March 23, 2004, available online at http://www.chroniclesmagazine .org/News/Trifkovic04/NewsST032304.html.
4. Michael Mandel, *How America Gets Away with Murder* (London: Pluto Press, 2004), 81.
5. Ibid.
6. James Bovard, *Feeling Your Pain: The Explosion and Abuse of Government Power in the Clinton-Gore Years* (New York: St. Martin's, 2000), 327.
7. Seth Ackerman and Jim Naureckas, "Following Washington's Script: The United States Media and Kosovo," in *Degraded Capability: The Media and the Kosovo Crisis,* ed. Philip Hammond and Edward S. Herman (London: Pluto Press, 2000), 103.
8. Srdja Trifkovic, "The Hague 'Tribunal': Bad Justice, Worse Politics," March 20, 2000, available online at http://www.chroniclesmagazine.org/News/ Trifkovic00/NewsST032000.html.
9. See, for example, Hammond and Herman, eds., *Degraded Capability,* 73, 139.
10. Edward S. Herman and David Peterson, "Milosevic's Death in the Propaganda System," *Z Magazine,* May 2006.
11. Mick Hume, "Nazifying the Serbs, from Bosnia to Kosovo," in Hammond and Herman, eds., *Degraded Capability,* 73–74.
12. Trifkovic, "Kosovo: Five Centuries of Strife and Ethnic Cleansing."
13. John Pilger, "Censorship by Omission," in Hammond and Herman, eds., *Degraded Capability,* 139.
14. Mandel, *America,* 62; emphasis omitted.
15. John Pilger, "Acts of Murder," *Guardian,* May 18, 1999.
16. Ackerman and Naureckas, "Following Washington's Script," 99–100.
17. Alexander Cockburn and Jeffrey St. Clair, *Imperial Crusades* (London: Verso, 2004), 42.
18. Raju G. C. Thomas, "India," in Hammond and Herman, eds., *Degraded Capability,* 192.
19. Cockburn and St. Clair, *Imperial Crusades,* 40.
20. Doug Bandow, "Remember Kosovo?" *American Conservative,* April 10, 2006, 23.

21. Sani Rifati, "The Roma and 'Humanitarian' Ethnic Cleansing in Kosovo," *CounterPunch,* October 15, 2002, available online at http://www.counterpunch .org/rifati1015.html.
22. "Institute Condemns Violence in Kosovo, Targeting of Religious Sites," Institute on Religion and Public Policy, March 18 2004, available online at http://www.religionandpolicy.org/show.php?p=1.1.1091.
23. Ibid.
24. Mandel, *America,* 63.
25. Bandow, "Remember Kosovo?" 23.
26. Ibid., 24.

CONCLUSION

1. H. L. Mencken, *A Mencken Chrestomathy* (New York: Knopf, 1949), 145–46.
2. On Christianity and its contributions to the West, see Thomas E. Woods Jr., *How the Catholic Church Built Western Civilization* (Washington, D.C.: Regnery, 2005); Rodney Stark, *The Victory of Reason: How Christianity Led to Freedom, Capitalism, and Western Success* (New York: Random House, 2005); Alvin J. Schmidt, *How Christianity Changed the World* (Grand Rapids, Mich.: Zondervan, 2004); and Robert Royal, *The God That Did Not Fail: How Religion Built and Sustains the West* (San Francisco: Encounter, 2006).
3. Murray N. Rothbard, "A Strategy for the Right," in *The Irrepressible Rothbard,* ed. Llewellyn H. Rockwell Jr. (Burlingame, Calif.: Center for Libertarian Studies, 2000), 9.

ACKNOWLEDGMENTS

I am exceptionally fortunate in being able to count so many knowledgeable scholars and fine human beings among my friends. For steering me in the right direction when I had a question about current scholarship, I am grateful to Ben Powell of Suffolk University, Robert Higgs of the Independent Institute, Shawn Ritenour of Grove City College, Christopher Westley of Jacksonville State University, Michael Mandel of Canada's Osgoode Hall Law School, and Pierre Desrochers of the University of Toronto. I have also benefited from the valuable insights of Jeff Herbener of Grove City College, Kevin Gutzman of Western Connecticut State University, and George Reisman of Pepperdine University's Graziadio School of Business. Thanks are also due Greg Perry, who suggested the topic of jury nullification, and to Srdja Trifkovic and Christopher Deliso for their helpful comments on Questions 5 and 33.

I would like to thank the Foundation for Economic Education, which has permitted me the use of portions of "The Myth of Wartime Prosperity" and "Why Wages Used to Be So Low," which originally appeared in a different form in their monthly publication, *The Freeman. The American Conservative,* for which I have been privileged to serve as a contributing editor, also permitted me the use of material from my articles "All the President's Power," "Fathers Knew Best," and "The Progressive Peacenik Myth." The Ludwig von Mises Institute has permitted me the use of portions of "Theodore Roosevelt and the Modern Presidency," the chapter I contributed to *Reassessing the Presidency,* edited by John V. Denson (Auburn, Ala.: Ludwig von Mises Institute, 2001).

I also wish to thank Fred De Caro III, who designed my website, ThomasEWoods.com, as a favor for an old college friend.

Crown Forum's Jed Donahue, who was a pleasure to work with, was a meticulous and conscientious editor whose labors definitely improved the clarity and readability of the text.

I am also indebted to Lew Rockwell, a great benefactor of mine, and to the Ludwig von Mises Institute, of which he is founder and president. I began as a resident scholar at the Institute as this project was drawing to a close, and I could not have asked for a more hospitable and intellectually stimulating environment for scholarly work.

My wife and I are deeply grateful to my sister-in-law Elizabeth Robinson, whose heroic assistance during another difficult pregnancy for my wife made the completion of this book possible and our lives much easier and happier. We have known few people as selfless as Beth.

Thanks also to my mother for all her help–given cheerfully and often–as we adapted to our lives with three children under age three. We'll repay her somehow.

Above all, I am thankful to Heather, my generous and loving wife, for her indispensable support throughout my professional endeavors. And thanks, finally, to our children–Regina, Veronica, and Amy–for their sweet dispositions and for greeting me every day with their smiling faces.

INDEX

Armor, David, 73
Army Foreign Military Studies
    Office, U.S., 40
Arthur, Chester, 139
Articles of Confederation, 64, 66
Asian Americans, 70–72, 143–46,
    148, 150
Atkinson, Edward, 54
Attarian, John, 113
Austrian School (economics), 174–76,
    178–79
auto industry, 170, 236, 241
Avery, Dennis, 224

B

Bacon, Augustus, 140
Baechler, Jean, 77
Baird, Charles, 239, 241
Baker, Russell, 136
Baker, Vincent, 249–51
Baldwin, Leland, 161
Balkans, 38–44, 59, 252–60
Bangladesh, 224–25
Barbary states, 88–89
Barnett, Randy, 199
Bastiat, Frédéric, 98
Bauer, Peter, 224, 226–28
Beadle, J. H., 48
Bedford, Gunning, 210, 211
Begala, Paul, 139
Beisner, Robert, 54
Beito, David, 247, 251
Benjamin, Daniel K., 196
Berger, Raoul, 200
Bethell, Tom, 224
Bicentennial Commission, U.S., 62
Binder, David, 41
Black Law Students Association, 149
Bond, Clifford, 43

Boone, Peter, 223
Bordewich, Fergus, 17
Bosnia, 38–44, 59, 94
Bourne, Randolph, 56
Bovard, James, 230–31
Boxer Rebellion, 91
Boyd, Charles G., 40–42
Breyer, Stephen, 202
Bringham, A. G., 131
Brookings Institution, 225
Brownback, Sam, 259
Brown v. Board of Education (1954), 68
Bryan, William Jennings, 53
Buchanan, James, 209
Buffett, Howard, 57
Bush, George H. W., 41, 59
Bush, George W., 134, 230–31, 259
business cycles theory, 174–75,
    178–79
Butler, Pierce, 85
Byler, Valentine, 110

C

Calhoun, John C., 138
California, 49–50, 202
Canasatego, 63, 64, 65
capitalism, 14–16, 167–68, 170,
    174–79, 262
Carnegie, Andrew, 54
Carnegie Steel Company, 233
cartels, 191
Carter, Jimmy, 57
Carver, George Washington, 114–19
Cassen Development Committee
    Task Force on Foreign Aid, 231
Catholic Church, 25
Ceci, Lynn, 130, 131–32
Chamberlin, Edward, 239–40
Chile, 224

Chinese Americans, 144, 248
Chomsky, Noam, 257
Chou En-lai, 60
CIA, 40, 256
Civil Rights Commission, U.S, 68–69
Civil War, U.S., 75–83, 136, 139
Clayton, John Middleton, 91
Cleveland, Grover, 54, 139, 246
Clinton, Bill, 52, 134, 139, 152, 209
  Balkans and, 38–44, 59, 252–60
  war powers and, 93–95
Clinton, Hillary, 51, 52, 59, 258
Cockburn, Alexander, 258
Cody, Buffalo Bill, 47
Cold War, 57–58
Cole, Harold L., 190, 191, 192
Coleman Report, 69
Colombia, 90
command economy, 103
commerce clause, 198, 200, 202
common law, 49
Confederate Constitution (1861), 206
Congress, U.S.
  commerce clause and, 198, 200,
    202
  foreign aid and, 231
  general welfare clause and, 204–5,
    207, 208
  necessary and proper clause and,
    210, 214
  presidential power expansion and,
    139, 140–41
  war powers and, 84–96
Congress of Racial Equality, 249
Connecticut, 30–31
Conrad, Clay, 219
conscription, 81
conservatives, 54–55, 134, 142, 222
  antiwar position and, 52, 58, 59
  on judicial activism, 121
  nullification principle and, 153

Constitution, U.S., 106, 138, 198–215,
    244, 262
  commerce clause, 198–203
  general welfare clause, 154, 204–9
  Iroquois Indians and, 62–67
  jury nullification and, 219
  as "living, breathing" document,
    120–28
  necessary and proper clause, 154,
    210–15
  states' rights and, 26–35, 154–57
  strict construction of, 54–55
  supremacy clause, 27–28, 211
  war powers and, 84–96
contract rights, 232, 234, 237
Corning, 146
corruption, 225–26, 229, 246
Corwin, Edward S., 92, 136
Cosby, Bill, 72
Croatia, 39–40
Croatian-Muslim Federation, 42
Croly, Herbert, 54
Cronon, William, 130
Cuba, 53, 76, 141
cult of personality, 136–38
Cutileiro, José, 41

D

Dayton accords (1995), 42
Dean, Howard, 52
Declaration of Independence, 64, 65
Defense Department, U.S., 255
Delancey, James, 217–18
democratic socialism, 13–14
Democrats, 52, 84, 95
Denevan, William, 17–18
Dennison, Henry S., 182
Denny's, 151–52
Dewey, John, 57

Frost, Robert, 59
Fugitive Slave Act (1850), 32–34, 76
Fuller, S. B., 247–51

Holmes, Oliver Wendell, 202–3
Homestead Strike, 233, 241
Hong Kong, 231
Hoover, Herbert, 179–88, 235, 240
Hummel, Jeff, 76, 245

I

Ignatieff, Michael, 255
Illinois Manufacturers' Association,
  194–95
immigration, 5–10
imperialism, 53–54
"imperial presidency," 134–42
income, 143–48, 165–73
infant mortality rates, 144
Information Agency, U.S, 254–55
injunctions, 235, 239
Inouye, Daniel, 62
interest rates, 175–78
International Crisis Group, 259
International Monetary Fund,
  229–30
interstate commerce, 198–203
Iraq war, 52, 59, 95–96
Iroquois League, 18, 62–67
Islam, 38–44, 259
Italy, 81, 191, 244
Izetbegovic, Alija, 39, 40, 41, 43

J

Jackson, Andrew, 137, 138
Jackson, Jesse, 251
Jackson, Stonewall, 76
James, William, 54
Jay, John, 9–10, 220
Jefferson, Thomas, 85, 122, 127, 164
  on commerce regulation, 199

general welfare clause and, 206,
  208, 209
immigration views of, 6–7
jury nullification and, 220
necessary and proper clause and,
  212, 213, 215
nullification theory and, 26–28,
  35, 153–54, 156, 157–58
peaceable coercion policy and,
  28
states' rights and, 25–28, 35, 36
war powers and, 88–90
Johansen, Bruce E., 63, 64, 65, 66
John Paul II, Pope, 257
Johnson, Andrew, 139
Johnson, Hugh, 111, 191
Johnson, Lyndon, 57, 58, 68
Johnstone, Diana, 43
judicial activism, 120–22
jury nullification, 216–21

K

Kaiser, Rudolf, 20
Kennan, George, 60
Kennedy, John F., 135, 231
Kentucky, 160, 161, 163, 164
Kentucky Fried Chicken, 146
Kentucky Resolutions (1798), 26,
  29, 34, 36, 157
King, Martin Luther, Jr., 11–16
King, Rufus, 9
Kissinger, Henry, 254
Korean War, 84, 92
Kosovo, 59, 95, 252–60
Kosovo Liberation Army, 253,
  255–58
Krech, Shepard, III, 18, 19
Krnjevic-Miskovic, Damjan de,
  259

L

labor unions, 138, 168, 172, 233–41, 262
Laden, Osama bin, 38, 43
LaFeber, Walter, 91
laissez-faire, 180–84, 186, 188
Law School Admissions Service, 149–50
League of Nations, 55
Lee, Robert E., 76, 80, 82
legal positivism, 123
lending practices, 150–51
Leuchtenburg, William, 53, 54–55, 192
Lewinsky, Monica, 38, 42
liberals, 52–61, 134, 257–58
libertarians, 82, 121, 245
Lincoln, Abraham, 86, 90, 115, 137, 242
    Civil War and, 75–77, 79, 82, 83, 136
Lippmann, Walter, 195
Lisbon peace agreement (1992), 41
Livingston, Donald, 77, 80, 81
Lloyd, William, 31
Locke, John, 78
Low, Denise, 21

M

Mackintosh, Barry, 116, 117, 118
Madison, James, 66, 83, 199, 205
    general welfare clause and, 206–7
    necessary and proper clause and, 211, 213, 214, 215
    states' rights and, 26, 157
    war powers and, 85, 89, 90
Magazine of Wall Street, 193
Maguire, Timothy, 149

Malaysia, 145
Mandel, Michael, 41
Mann, Charles, 132
Mao Zedong, 60
marijuana, medicinal, 202
Marks, Bruce, 150–51
Marshall, John, 200, 213, 215
Marshall Plan, 225–26
Marx, Karl, 60
Maryland, 63, 160
Massachusetts, 29, 30–32, 124
Massachusetts Institute of Technology, 149
McCulloch v. Maryland (1819), 213–15
McDougall, Walter, 58
McElvaine, Robert, 190
McGrath, Roger, 46–47
McHenry, James, 88
McKinley, William, 91, 139
McMaken, Ryan, 47–48
McMurry, Linda, 117–18
McWhorter, John, 72, 148–49
Mead Corporation, 146
Melman, Seymour, 101
Mencken, H. L., 1–3, 261, 262
Mexican War, 49, 90–91
Millennium Challenge Account, 231, 232
Milosevic, Slobodan, 256
minimum wage, 192
mining districts, 49–51
modern state, rise of, 76–82
Mohan, C. Raja, 257–58
Monroe, James, 141
Monroe Doctrine, 90, 139–40
Montenegro, 40, 254
Moore, John Bassett, 87
Moore, Kelly, 255
Morgenthau, Henry, 195
Morley, Felix, 55
Morris, Edmund, 137